Foundations of
Chumash Complexity

Perspectives in California Archaeology, Volume 7
Cotsen Institute of Archaeology
University of California, Los Angeles

Foundations of Chumash Complexity

Edited by Jeanne E. Arnold

Cotsen Institute of Archaeology
University of California, Los Angeles

THE COTSEN INSTITUTE OF ARCHAEOLOGY AT UCLA
Charles Stanish, Director
Julia L. J. Sanchez, Assistant Director and Director of Publications
Shauna Mecartea, Publications Assistant

Edited by Joe Abbott
Production by Leyba Associates
Index by Robert and Cynthia Swanson

Library of Congress Cataloging-in-Publication Data

Foundations of Chumash complexity / edited by Jeanne E. Arnold.
p. cm. — (Perspectives in California archaeology ; v. 7)
Papers presented at a symposium held in conjunction with the annual
Society for American Archaeology Meeting in Denver in 2002.
ISBN 1-931745-18-8 (alk. paper)
1. Chumash Indians—Antiquities. 2. Chumash Indians—Material culture. 3.
Hunting and gathering societies—California—Channel Islands. 4. Hunting
and gathering societies—California—Pacific Coast. 5. Channel Islands
(Calif.)—Antiquities. 6. Pacific Coast (Calif.)—Antiquities. I. Arnold,
Jeanne E. II. Cotsen Institute of Archaeology at UCLA. III. Society for
American Archaeology. Meeting (2002 : Denver, Colo.) IV. Series.
E99.C815F68 2004
979.4'91—dc22
                                                  2004022947

Contents

Figures

Tables

Contributors

Jeanne E. Arnold
Department of Anthropology
Cotsen Institute of Archaeology
University of California, Los Angeles

Julienne Bernard
Department of Anthropology
University of California, Los Angeles

Ray Corbett
Department of Anthropology
University of California, Los Angeles

Gary Coupland
Department of Anthropology
University of Toronto

Michael A. Glassow
Department of Anthropology
University of California, Santa Barbara

Anthony P. Graesch
Department of Anthropology
University of California, Los Angeles

Sandra E. Hollimon
Anthropological Studies Center
Sonoma State University

Jennifer E. Perry
Department of Anthropology
Pomona College

Scott Pletka
LSA Associates, Inc.
San Luis Obispo

Torben C. Rick
Department of Anthropology
Southern Methodist University

Preface

This volume originated in discussions on several campuses and at annual meetings with a number of archaeologists and ethnographers in southern California. We shared the view that in just the last few years so much new research on later Chumash prehistory and early history was underway, and so many new ideas had emerged about why and how complex institutions came to develop among the coastal Chumash, that it seemed time for a "state-of-the-art" session at the annual Society for American Archaeology conference in Denver in 2002. I co-organized and co-chaired that symposium with Anthony P. Graesch, and this volume is the outcome.

Our goal was to bring current research on the foundations of sociopolitical complexity in coastal California to a national and international audience. As we explore in chapter 1, archaeologists' awareness of complex hunter-gatherers is often limited to the celebrated cultures of the Northwest Coast: the Tlingit, the Kwakwaka'wakw (Kwakiutl), the Haida, the Nuu-chah-nulth (Nootka), and other nearby groups. The cultures of California are quite poorly understood outside of the Pacific Coast region. Few scholarly articles and even fewer archaeology textbooks refer at all to California groups in discussions on complex hunter-gatherers, chiefly leadership, strong maritime subsistence foci, intensive trade systems, or specialized craft production activities, yet Chumash sites provide some of the most robust data on these subjects available in the Americas.

We hope to draw some further attention to these discoveries.

Moreover, many important new advances in our understanding of these cultural developments derive from several major research projects concluded during the past three to four years. These results are published here for the first time. Diverse perspectives on the constitution of complexity and diverse approaches to archaeological and ethnographic data are well represented in these chapters. All but two symposium contributors were able to convert their presentations into chapters for this volume. Anthony Graesch adds an important invited chapter on households and bead making. Gary Coupland, bringing a wealth of insight from his work on complex hunter-gatherers of the Northwest Coast, served as symposium discussant and succinctly compares the two regions in the final chapter of this volume.

We jointly thank three anonymous reviewers who provided detailed and constructive suggestions that greatly improved these chapters. I also acknowledge the support and assistance of the Publications Office at the UCLA Cotsen Institute of Archaeology, particularly Julia Sanchez, Director of Publications, freelance editor Joe Abbott, and production designer Carol Leyba.

Jeanne E. Arnold
University of California, Los Angeles
June 2004

1

The Later Evolution of the Island Chumash

Jeanne E. Arnold and Anthony P. Graesch

The populous maritime societies of coastal southern California, particularly the groups known collectively as the Chumash (Figure 1.1), have gone largely unrecognized as prototypical complex hunter-gatherers, only recently beginning to emerge from an obscure position in scholarly analyses of sociopolitical complexity. Their counterparts on the Northwest Coast of North America, who are renowned for such complex institutions as ceremonial potlatches, slavery, cedar-plank-house villages, and rich artistic traditions, are always touted as the rare, exceptional, cultural zenith of hunter-gatherers on the world stage, and they have been widely discussed and acknowledged as "complex" for decades.

The respective ethnographic histories may shed light on this uneven portrayal of the two regions. Certainly the much earlier arrival of prominent Northwest Coast ethnographers in the region and their far greater scholarly productivity contributed in a significant way to this pattern. The leading figure, Franz Boas, began his long period of research on the northern Pacific Coast in 1886, and many of his students and associates followed thereafter, including the well-published Edward Sapir, Frederica De Laguna, Wayne Suttles, and Philip Drucker, to note just a few. Their growing list of monographs, theses, and papers drew the further scholarly attention of distinguished academics Claude Lévi-Strauss, George P. Murdock, Ruth Benedict, Kalervo Oberg, and others (Suttles and Jonaitis 1990). By the last one-third of the twentieth century, hundreds of empirical and analytical works on Northwest Coast cultures, including the Makah, Kwakwaka'wakw (Kwakiutl), Nuu-chah-nulth (Nootka), Tsimshian, Coast Salish, Tlingit, and many others, were available for broader anthropological scrutiny.

On the other hand, the principal ethnographer of California's Chumash (and several other North American groups, mostly in California), John Peabody Harrington, toiled for some 60 years in virtual academic obscurity.[1] Having produced only a handful of very short reports on the Chumash to the Smithsonian Institution, one archaeological monograph on a site in the Santa Barbara area for the Bureau of American Ethnology, and one published ethnographic trait list of the Chumash (Harrington 1942) before he died (but well over 200,000 pages of unpublished notes), the gifted but eccentric ethnographer-linguist unwittingly relegated the people he greatly admired to a much smaller role in anthropological annals than they deserved. Harrington was driven by the urgency of his fieldwork among rapidly thinning ranks of knowledgeable Chumash informants, with whom he worked principally between 1912 and about 1930 (Blackburn 1975:6). Moreover, he was reportedly so utterly disinterested in scholarly recognition and in sharing his observations with a broader audience that he simply did not stop to organize, synthesize his data, or write.

More than a century ago, archaeologists began to excavate large, impressive village sites and to record elaborate rock art, ornamental worked shell, large stone vessels, and the like at sites in Chumash territory, and although anthropologists in California remained aware of the rich material culture of the Chumash in the ensuing decades, it has been largely during the past 25 years that new generations of ethnographers, archaeologists, and other scholars have steadily directed a great deal of effort toward expanding

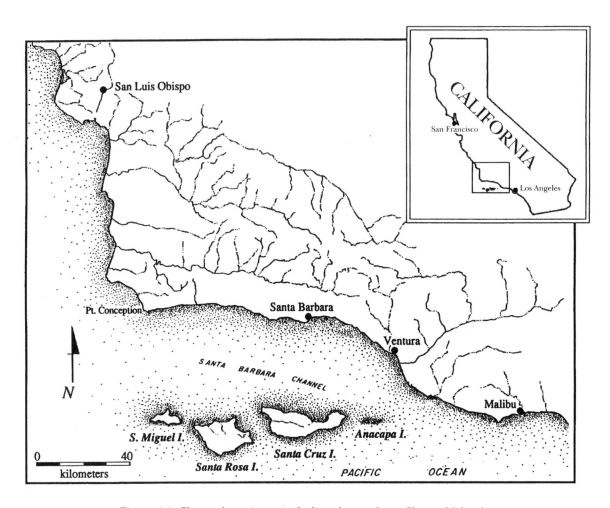

Figure 1.1. Chumash territory, including the northern Channel Islands.

our understanding of the organizational features of the coastal and Island Chumash. Most recently, important new understandings of Chumash linguistic history, social organization, and genealogy have emerged from current research by scholars using an array of historic documents (e.g., mission registers) and undertaking analyses of Harrington's extensive notes at the National Anthropological Archives of the Smithsonian (e.g., Johnson 2001; Klar 2000; McLendon and Johnson 1999). Exciting discoveries have emerged from archaeological field research, ranging from evidence for pre-12,000–13,000 BP occupation of ancient Santa Rosae Island (the terminal Pleistocene landform encompassing Santa Cruz, Santa Rosa, San Miguel, and Anacapa islands during the period when sea levels were much lower; Connolly et al. 1995; Johnson et al. 2000; Rick et al. 2001) to evidence for unex-

pectedly vibrant early Historic period villages on Santa Cruz Island (Arnold 2001a; Arnold et al. 1997; Graesch 2001, this volume). Other new field data have been reported from hundreds of important Santa Barbara Channel area sites of all ages, including information on changing conditions of health, warfare, paleoclimate, and more (see the major compendium by Holmes and Johnson [1998] and selected chapters in Erlandson and Jones 2002).

Contributors to the present volume focus on recent findings that further illuminate the foundations of the complex sociopolitical organization and dynamic later cultural evolution of the Chumash of the coastal zones and northern Channel Islands. These chapters present fresh new directions in archaeological and ethnographic research, all completed within the past few years. Authors explore anthropologically significant problems regarding status-seeking behaviors, the role of ceremonialism in political evolution, occupational specializations, processes of cultural transmission, household-level economic strategies, technological innovations, coordinated acquisition of oceanic animals, and more—all the while focusing on these populous groups who were clearly among North America's most politically and economically complex hunter-gatherers.

Evidence for the overall cultural complexity of the coastal Chumash in later prehistory has been presented by a number of scholars. Arnold (1993, 1996a, 2000) has defined complexity in primarily sociopolitical terms, equating complexity—for purposes of rigorous cross-cultural comparison—with the concept of the "simple chiefdom" and focusing on ascribed status and elite leaders' control of nonkin labor. Arnold and others have examined cases worldwide in these terms and place the Chumash and Northwest Coast groups among the most complex of hunter-gatherers (Arnold 1996a, 1996b, 2001a, 2004; Hayden 1995, 1996; Keeley 1988; Matson and Coupland 1995; Prentiss and Kuijt 2004). Substantial empirical evidence of sociopolitical and economic complexity in the Santa Barbara Channel region has been collected by many scholars, including, but by no means limited to, Kennett (1998), King (1990), and contributors to the Erlandson and Jones volume (2002).

Here we review several stimulating interpretations derived from the region's most recent fieldwork and archival work and endeavor to place Chumash cultural evolution in perspective. (For discussions of new data from more northerly and southerly areas of California see Arnold et al. 2004 and Erlandson and Jones 2002). We have two principal goals. First, we provide an overview of research results from recent archaeological field investigations on the northern Channel Islands by teams from the University of California, Los Angeles (UCLA); we refer to this research as the Santa Cruz Island Project. These investigations ultimately involved several of the volume's authors in the field, the laboratory, or both, and they build on and owe a great deal to several other scholars, including archaeologists Michael Glassow and Albert Spaulding, who undertook a significant Santa Cruz

Island survey and excavation program in the 1970s and refined local cultural histories, and ethnographers Travis Hudson and Thomas Blackburn (1987; Hudson et al. 1978), who pieced together Chumash lifeways and material culture through extensive analysis of narratives from the J. P. Harrington notes.

Second, we interweave this discussion with comments that establish the context for other chapters in this volume. Contributors present cutting-edge analyses and comparatively explore their new data within the broader Chumash region. Some chapters focus on newly synthesized data from the Santa Cruz Island Project. Other contributions represent independent field projects on the northern Channel Islands mounted by several investigators. Still others represent new archival and collections-based studies drawing on materials and data from a range of sources. A final chapter by Gary Coupland, a leading Northwest Coast specialist, places the maritime Chumash in the broader context of New World complex hunter-gatherers.

THE EMERGENCE AND OPERATION OF A SIMPLE CHIEFDOM

The Chumash were vigorous maritime traders, moving people and impressive quantities of foods and manufactured goods across the Santa Barbara Channel, among the northern Channel Islands, and into neighboring territories (Glassow 1980; King 1976). They were highly specialized occupationally, and the villagers living on the northern Channel Islands made stone microdrills and shell beads by the millions (Arnold 1987; Arnold and Graesch 2001; Arnold and Munns 1994; Arnold et al. 2001). High-ranking craft guild members made sophisticated plank canoes on the offshore islands and along several sections of the mainland coasts, and prominent individuals were involved in well-defined curing, religious, and political occupations, among others (Arnold 1995; Arnold, ed. 2001; Blackburn 1975; Johnson 2001; Walker and Hudson 1993; see also Corbett, this volume; Hollimon, this volume). Hereditary chiefly families held sway over multiple communities (Johnson 2001) and could manipulate the specialized labor of both kin and nonkin (Arnold 2000; Arnold, ed. 2001). These and other important cultural characteristics are explored at greater length throughout this volume.

Chumash mean community sizes and population densities were among the highest recorded for hunter-gatherers worldwide. Village populations were generally nucleated into permanent communities of 125 to 250 people (and up to 1,000) near productive constellations of resources and were deeply engaged in complex social, ceremonial, ritual, and political networks. Data marshaled by Arnold (2001b, 2001c), Glassow (1980), Johnson (1982), and McLendon and Johnson (1999) suggest that the larger and more ecologically diverse of the northern Channel Islands may have supported as many as 4.5 to 6.5 persons per square kilometer. For example, Santa Cruz Island's 10 Historic period villages consisted of about 1,500 to 1,700 people across 256 km^2, or roughly 6.5 persons per square kilometer (Arnold 2001b:31).

The mainland coast likely supported even higher population densities, but these are not as well documented (Glassow 1980). Keeley (1988) and Kelly (1995:223) use secondary data to suggest that there were more than eight persons per square kilometer in Chumash territory as a whole, although this number would drop slightly if newer data and more sparsely populated inland areas were taken fully into consideration. Given community sizes and other records from Santa Cruz Island sites, we have confidence in the figure of about 6.0 to 6.5 persons per square kilometer. Many Northwest Coast groups and other complex and affluent hunter-gatherers typically had population densities in the 0.5 to 2.0 persons-per-square-kilometer range. In contrast, most foragers in tundra, forest, desert, and tropical areas had population densities well under 0.1 to 0.2 persons per square kilometer (Kelly 1995:221–226). The relatively high population figures in southern California and among complex hunter-gatherers in the Northwest Coast and elsewhere clearly had an effect, although certainly not a simple or unilateral one, on the development of sociopolitical complexity in these respective regions. The impacts of population pressure, paleoclimatic change, and large household and community size (among related issues) on com-

plex social formations are adequately examined elsewhere and are not a focus of further discussion here (see Ames 1995; Arnold 2001a; Erlandson and Rick 2002; Hayden 1995; Keeley 1988).

The chronology for the region, based on King (1990) and Arnold (1992), is provided in Table 1.1. Previous investigations, including King's (1976, 1990) studies of trade and burial assemblages, Glassow's (1980) examinations of subsistence and settlement change, and Arnold's (1987) analysis of the microlithic industry, addressed various segments of the Early period (5500–600 BC), Middle period (600 BC–AD 1150), and/or later (post-AD 1150) regional record. These (and other) studies seemed to bracket the late Middle period and early Late period as the span within which certain significant social, political, and economic transformations started to take place in the region. This phase was later dubbed the Transitional period (AD 1150–1300; Arnold 1992), and we now know that it was marked by a series of notable changes, several of which directly underpinned the greater complexity of the Late and Historic periods. To explore basic questions regarding when, why, and how the Island Chumash came to function politically as a simple chiefdom—a polity that was thriving when the coastal Santa Barbara Channel populations were first encountered by European explorers in 1542—field investigations were thus initiated at several well-preserved Middle and Late period communities on Santa Cruz Island (Arnold 1992, 1995, 2001a, 2001b; Arnold, ed. 2001).

Clearly, we needed data to observe important developmental stages preceding this Transitional period as well as to elucidate the

Table 1.1. Chronology of the Santa Barbara Channel Region

Period	Dates
Early period	5500–600 BC
Middle period	600 BC–AD 1150
Transitional period	AD 1150–1300
Late period	AD 1300–1782
Historic period	AD 1782–

Sources: Arnold (1992), King (1990).

dynamics of the periods that followed. The selected archaeological deposits at sites on northern and western Santa Cruz Island span 1,500 years and encompass several centuries of Middle period cultural foundations, the emergence of new sociopolitical forms during the Transitional period, and the subsequent operation of new organizational systems (total span: AD 400 through the Mission era). For a more complete discussion of the research design and rationale see discussions by Arnold (2001a, 2001b).

Middle period villages, as the research of several scholars has recently revealed (see Erlandson and Rick 2002; Kennett and Conlee 2002), appear to have been year-round homes for coastal-based Chumash people. Most villages had good-sized populations living in dome-shaped pole-and-thatch houses about 6 to 8 m in diameter, a residential style still in use by the Chumash during the 1540s through the 1820s. We know less about Middle period villages than Late and Historic ones, but there seems to be little doubt that coastal Chumash folk were fairly sedentary during the Middle period and possibly long before that (see chapters in this volume by Glassow, Rick). Some scholars have taken evidence for settled villages to mean that therefore the Chumash were politically complex by (or before) the Middle period, but extensive cross-cultural research has refuted the notion that sedentism occurs in lockstep with complexity.

On this point we must bear in mind that many residentially sedentary groups around the world, both hunter-gatherer and horticultural, were "tribal" in organization rather than led by formal, hereditary chiefs, and many of the most complex groups in places such as the Northwest Coast were not actually sedentary, moving their large villages (and all of their moveable possessions, including cedar-plank-house boards) at least twice per year to follow their most productive resources (Ames and Maschner 1999:148; Arnold 1996a; Matson and Coupland 1995). It is essential to decouple good evidence for sedentism—seemingly established at relatively early dates among the Chumash—from unsubstantiated presumptions about local cultural complexity at the same time.

Although Middle period villages on the northern Channel Islands may well have supported good-sized, year-round populations, we must also note that they have not produced evidence for the specialized craft production, strong labor interrelationships, and hierarchical leadership that clearly developed during the following periods (Transitional and Late). Rick's chapter (this volume) shows that his recently tested sites on San Miguel Island follow this broad pattern. His data yield no hint of Early period specialization. He identifies moderate late Middle period production of ground-stone tools (unique to San Miguel Island) and an increase in shell bead production, as also seen elsewhere on the islands, but the intensive and systematic production of beads heralding the emergence of formal craft specialization dates to later periods. Excavation work by UCLA archaeologists at five villages spanning parts of the Middle, Transitional, and Late periods on Santa Cruz Island has revealed—after comprehensive analyses of faunal, lithic, and shell materials by a large team of colleagues and students—that quite a notable array of economic and technological changes began to unfold as, and just after, the Middle period came to an end (ca. AD 1150; Arnold 2001a). Taken together, these developments significantly changed the way that the Island Chumash lived their everyday lives, organized their labor, and governed themselves (Arnold 2001a; Arnold, ed. 2001). We see these changes knitting together formerly autonomous villages and marking the emergence of simple chiefdom-level leadership.

At roughly this same juncture, or perhaps slightly earlier, an important, broad-based religious association, known historically as the 'antap, may have been developing in Chumash territory, if the first appearances of key instruments such as deer tibia whistles are reliable indicators of their activity. Ray Corbett (this volume) makes a good case—citing the appearance and evolution of precontact ritual gear—that the 'antap emerged and then exerted a growing influence on Chumash society by about the terminus of the Middle period. Sandra Hollimon (this volume) also employs data pertaining to prehistoric ritual activities and suggests that shamans and 'aqi, or third-gender undertakers, may have been among the first occupational specialists in Chumash prehistory, chronologically antedating other forms of specialized ritual leadership. Later, the emergence of the 'antap marked the rise of more formal ceremonial integration across much of Chumash territory. Its broad membership likely had regional-level impacts on cultural organization. These changes may have contributed in important ways to the emerging political clout of rising elites, perhaps when secular and religious leaders formed alliances or co-opted ancillary sources of knowledge or power.

Starting with the onset of the Transitional period, mortuary data and data from residential contexts on the Channel Islands provide numerous indications of strongly interdependent economic relationships, political (or politico-religious) developments on a regional level, and well-defined hereditary inequality. Nothing in the archaeological record prior to the Transitional period provides any reliable sign of chiefdomlike organization, complex socioeconomic relationships, or hereditary wealth and leadership on the Channel Islands (Arnold and Green 2002). We discuss lines of evidence that support these assertions briefly in turn, focusing on three topics highlighted in this volume: specialized craft production, advanced boating technology, and intensive trade systems and subsistence.

Specialized Craft Production

The Chumash on the northern Channel Islands began at about AD 1150 to invest substantial labor in the manufacturing of chert microliths and shell beads. During the preceding Middle period, people throughout the Chumash region made modest numbers of shell beads, using nonstone perforators, simple flake drills, and, late in the period, the first formal microdrills (Arnold 1987; Arnold and Graesch 2001; Arnold et al. 2001; see also Perry, this volume). The earliest microblade type was rather gracile, generally trapezoidal in cross section, and relatively thin, and it was used to drill *Olivella biplicata* (purple olive) shell wall disk beads, among others. Both microblade making and bead making were spatially quite widely distributed across the territory of the mainland and Island Chumash, and these production activities were not at all inten-

sive by later standards. Even in this terminal phase of the Middle period (ca. AD 900–1150), when relatively more *Olivella* detritus (bead-making waste) is found compared to preceding centuries (as noted by Kennett 1998; Kennett and Conlee 2002; see also Rick, this volume), the nature and intensity of production remained small-scale and orders of magnitude lower than the volume of production that was shortly to emerge. No practitioners in these activities would qualify as *specialists* using the term the way most archaeologists have employed it since the 1980s (Arnold 1987; Arnold and Munns 1994; Brumfiel and Earle 1987; Clark and Parry 1990; Costin 1991).

The following Transitional period was an era of punctuated economic and technological developments that extended from ca. AD 1150 to 1300. Several interrelated changes in labor organization and the place of specialized activities in Chumash lifeways occurred during this interval (Arnold 2001c; Arnold, ed. 2001). First, microblade making and bead making contracted spatially to the three permanently occupied northern Channel Islands: Santa Cruz, Santa Rosa, and San Miguel. The mainland coastal Chumash, for all practical purposes, dropped out of the microlith-making and bead-making game (Arnold 1987, 2001a). Second, microlith manufacturers began to make primarily thick, triangular, and dorsally retouched (TDR) microblades. Simultaneously, bead makers began to make the first *Olivella* cupped and lipped beads from the extremely tough and thick "callus" (upper columella) part of the shell. Third, the intensity of production was stepped up dramatically compared with previous periods. Millions of microblades and beads began to be made at about 10 highly specialized villages on Santa Cruz Island. And fourth, with the exception of the elite village of *Xaxas*, on northeastern Santa Cruz Island, and perhaps one other community, Santa Cruz Islanders engaged predominantly in either microlithic *or* bead-making specializations, not both. Village-level specializations emerged largely as a function of proximity to key chert or shell raw materials.

Since the primary chert sources for the entire northern Channel Islands chain were concentrated in a series of quarries on eastern Santa Cruz Island

(Arnold 1987; Arnold et al. 2001; Perry, this volume), all of the microblade-focused production villages were on the eastern one-third of that island. Perry (this volume) presents a range of data from the Early through Late periods to show how sharply the blossoming of the microblade specialization affected settlement patterns across eastern Santa Cruz Island. In addition, several other coastal villages at favorable locations on Santa Rosa and San Miguel islands (along with those already mentioned on Santa Cruz) began to make large numbers of shell beads, employing microblades imported from eastern Santa Cruz Island.

Equally significant, *Olivella* callus beads came to be used as a currency governing exchange. This important symbolic transformation occurred either during the Transitional or early Late period. The Island Chumash, who had become the sole manufacturers of the region's chert microdrills, became the operators of a "mint" for the Chumash region (and some of these beads were traded into other areas of California and beyond; see Bennyhoff and Hughes 1987; Hudson and Blackburn 1987; King 1976). These multiple, labor-intensive, and very socially and economically charged changes did not happen without substantial coordination and leadership (Arnold 2001c). Indeed, the Island Chumash of that era practiced two of the largest scale, most sustained, and most specialized craft-manufacturing activities in North America, rivaling or even exceeding the production of the Hohokam stone and shell workers of the southern Southwest and significantly exceeding the production of Mississippian lithic drill makers and shell workers at centers like Cahokia.

We have accumulated a reasonably good record of the places on the coastal Chumash landscape where these developments took place, the nature and scale of manufacturing at various villages, and even the ebb and flow of changing craft production emphases (lithic and shell artifact types) from the mid-Middle period to the time that Spaniards began to settle on the mainland coast during the late 1700s (for details see Arnold 2001a, 2001b; Graesch 2000, 2001; Kennett 1998; Kennett and Conlee 2002; Munns and Arnold 2002; see also chapters by Perry, Rick, and Graesch, this volume). It is widely assumed that the shift in the dominant *Olivella* bead type from the wall disk to thicker callus disk bead forms (cupped and lipped beads) during the Transitional period—and their enduring popularity through the Late period—is related to several physical/material characteristics.

These include (1) the durability of the callus material, which likely made callus beads better suited (than fragile shells or shell parts) to the regular handling that would attend their use as standards of value in transactions; (2) the difficulty of drilling through the thick, tough callus portion of the *Olivella* (Moh's hardness of 5.0 to 5.5; see Arnold and Rachal 2002:193), which would have meant that more skill and/or experience (and/or effort) was required of producers (along with the superior new triangular microblade tools) to make callus beads; and (3) the more limited number of callus beads (essentially, one per shell from the tiny callus area) that could be made from a given population of *Olivella* shell specimens, making it a potentially more valued and inherently rarer type than the wall bead. Each of these attributes of the callus bead type likely contributed to its perceived worth. Islanders took control of its production and participated in a central way in creating its role as a standard of value for transactions throughout the region.

Scott Pletka's chapter in this volume takes the study of Chumash material culture and its evolution in a new direction through an innovative approach to explaining the appearance of *Olivella* callus bead types. He poses questions such as by what cultural evolutionary means did the emergence and eventual dominance of callus bead types occur, and how rapidly did this happen? He identifies three mechanisms of cultural transmission that are appropriate to evaluate in this case—indirect bias, conformist transmission, and drift—and runs a series of simulations to address these questions. Simulation rules and population and sample sizes vary, but to summarize, conformist transmission assumes that bead makers, in deciding what types to make, responded (conformed) to what most other producers were doing. Drift assumes that random processes govern decision making. Indirect bias assumes that bead makers responded to the differential *success* and/or *status* of the various producers they observed, meaning that they more often imitated the types made by successful bead makers than those made by lower-status or less successful bead makers. Pletka's discussion and results provide fresh insights into the possible social and communicative processes that create short- and long-term change in the artifactual assemblages of people living in villages of up to a few hundred people.

Advanced Boating Technology

Another key occupational specialization—one very highly regarded among the coastal Chumash—was the construction of the swift and valued plank canoe, or *tomol*. Travis Hudson and others have detailed the sophistication and engineering of the renowned tomol (Hudson et al. 1978), basing their discussion largely on J. P. Harrington's extensive unpublished notes on the subject. These watercraft required huge investments of labor, and only members of a hereditary craft guild known as the Brotherhood of the Tomol could make them. It is clear that only wealthy Chumash elites could marshal the resources to commission a tomol by the brotherhood. Recent archaeological collections research by Julienne Bernard (this volume) sheds new light on the invention of this important form of transportation. Her results support earlier suggestions that the tomol was first being developed by the Chumash at about AD 500, and it took several centuries before it was sufficiently refined and reliable to become a symbol of elite status and a major tool for social manipulation, control over cross-channel trade, and acquisition of powerful and dangerous marine species (Arnold 1995; Hudson et al. 1978). These important social, political, and economic ramifications started to be felt at roughly the end of the Middle period.

The tomol was very important in the constitution of coastal Chumash hereditary elite standing. This role for the tomol, both we and Bernard would argue, did not unfold until early in the second millennium AD, perhaps because such broad and far-reaching social changes first necessitated the full refinement of the size, form, and safe operation of the plank boats. Certain other

social and ecological changes may have also been momentous in elevating the importance of the plank canoe over a period of several centuries. Bernard analyzes the tomol and its specific relationship to increasingly systematic open-ocean fishing of several large-bodied species that were significant from both a subsistence and symbolic standpoint, including swordfish and certain tuna species. She uses carefully selected, robust faunal data sets to provide a meticulous and creative solution to the long vexing problem of the timing of the origin of the plank canoe in this region. This line of analysis is completely independent of some of the extant studies of limited, ambiguous, and often badly curated and poorly recorded mortuary assemblages from the later first millennium AD that include small plank fragments or tenuous indicators of boats or boat making. By drawing on substantial, well-dated zooarchaeological collections from a broad spectrum of sites, Bernard is able to bring rigor to this interesting discussion.

Intensive Trade Systems and Subsistence

A topic closely allied to the emergence of the plank canoe as a reliable technology is the expansion of the locally intensive trade systems between the northern Channel Islands and the mainland coastal areas east of Point Conception. Before the plank canoe was available as a reasonably safe means of cross-channel travel, goods and bulk foods could not have moved regularly across the Santa Barbara Channel in any appreciable volume. Simple tule (reed) boats and rafts certainly could move people and small loads across the 25 to 40 km of the channel (Arnold 1995, 2001a), and they (or some similar craft) were undoubtedly in use very early in local prehistory (Fagan 2004; see also Glassow, this volume), but the waters of the channel could be quite rough and unpredictable on a daily and seasonal basis, and boaters would not have routinely risked life and limb by engaging in frequent, heavy cross-channel trade. The two-ton capacity of the tomol in the early Historic era (Hudson et al. 1978)—and its probable development into a watercraft of this size no later than the early second millennium AD, as discussed above—changed all that. As populations grew and pressure on local resources mounted, people on both sides of the channel likely began to specialize in generating surpluses of locally abundant resources and trading the foods and manufactured products for which there was some demand elsewhere.

Cross-channel exchange relationships may have blossomed, particularly as certain ecological stresses arose. The Channel Islands populations were quite vulnerable to droughts because of the narrower range of plant species found there, compared to the mainland, and the limited number of preferred residential locales consistently watered by reliable springs. They would also have been quite affected by oceanic fluctuations that periodically diminished nearshore marine resources. When climatic conditions on several fronts worsened for a number of decades from ca. AD 1150 to 1250 (see summary of current paleoclimatic and oceanographic evidence in Arnold 2001b:26–31), islanders appear to have worked in concert with emerging leadership by significantly ratcheting up the intensity of their microblade and shell bead manufacturing. They also exercised some form of control over their chert sources. After this date distinctive Santa Cruz Island chert was no longer moving freely through the economy. Virtually all chert that was quarried came to be used in microlith manufacturing on eastern Santa Cruz Island (Arnold et al. 2001; Perry, this volume).

Great quantities of *Olivella* shell disk beads (well into the millions over a few centuries; see Arnold 2001a; Arnold and Graesch 2001) and several other important bead types (e.g., red abalone beads) came to be made almost exclusively on the northern Channel Islands. These intensive island-based shellworking industries (a term used advisedly) constituted essentially the sole bead-making enterprises in Chumash territory during the Transitional and Late periods. The beads were exported to mainland communities for mainland-produced foods and goods. The tomol, as a bearer of burdens and as an expensive technology owned by the few and emergent elites, was crucial in the execution of this large-scale trade, which continued through the early Historic period.

HISTORIC-ERA HOUSEHOLDS

The Santa Cruz Island Project also focuses on the internal organization of northern Channel Islands communities during the early Historic period. Islanders were able to maintain many of their traditional lifeways for about two generations following the beginning of Spanish colonization on the mainland in 1782. The absence of colonial activity on the islands was key to the basic maintenance of traditions. This span of about 40 years is preserved in a relatively pristine archaeological record at several island village sites and affords the opportunity to examine the inner workings of a simple chiefdom from a bottom-up perspective. Our particular interest is in the organization of the political economy as it may be reconstructed from household and village activities. Household-by-household data can be used because many Late and Historic Santa Cruz Island villages are intact, with deep, circular house depressions in well-defined middens (see Arnold 2001b:46–47). Surface cultural materials have been trampled over the years, and several sites have been damaged by modern earth-moving activities, but in most villages there are few significant signs of disturbance other than sea cliff erosion because of the virtual absence of modern development along the perimeter of the island.[2]

Field investigations, including experimental remote sensing (Arnold et al. 1997), targeted surface and subsurface deposits in about 35 of these house depressions distributed across five Historic Santa Cruz Island coastal communities, corresponding to the villages of *Xaxas*, *L'akayamu*, *Ch'oloshush*, *Shawa* (Graesch 2000, this volume), and *Lu'upsh* (Dietler 2003). Populations at these villages ranged between about 125 and 250 people. They were composed of up to 18 contemporaneous households apiece. Project goals included testing for differences among targeted households in how (and how intensively) they participated in specialized craft production, differences in their access to prestige goods and local and exotic animal products, and houses' overall size and placement on the sociopolitical landscape. These households were core units of production on which higher levels of social and economic integration were established. We suggest that many dimensions of economic inequality, hierarchical relations, and specialized craft production can be inferred based on detailed examination of these kinds of households.

Recent analyses of the organization of intensive bead making at the household level by Graesch (2000, this volume) and ongoing analyses of significant samples of the large, well-preserved faunal assemblages from these field investigations (well over 500,000 vertebrate elements recovered) by Anna Noah (UCLA) are providing valuable glimpses into interhousehold variability. Noah (2003) is documenting differential acquisition of many species of marine mammals, large-bodied pelagic fish species, and nearshore fishes, birds, and shellfish by household and by village.

Graesch (this volume) employs large samples of surface and subsurface artifactual data to analyze how ownership of prestige goods and degree of intensity of specialized shellworking varied across 31 households at four of the Santa Cruz Island villages (*Xaxas*, *L'akayamu*, *Ch'oloshush*, and *Shawa*). Several insights into the internal organization of Historic-era Island Chumash communities emerge from these data. For instance, both surface and subsurface data indicate that *all* Historic period households in these four villages were allocating some labor to the production of shell beads, but with some significant variations. Relative investments of time and energy in bead-making activities were probably linked to each household's calculations of its overall needs and appetites for acquiring foods and nonlocal goods through regional trade networks. Households appear to have been able to diversify their diets and raise their standing by allocating labor to the production of shell beads for exchange.

Santa Cruz Island Historic households were engaged in shellworking tasks at varying levels of intensity, and each adopted its own distinctive yet overlapping array of shell valuables to produce. Correspondence analyses demonstrate these distinctions in production strategies across households within and among communities (Graesch, this volume). These data, together with other observations from the floral and faunal assemblages and artifact assemblages, sug-

gest that there was considerable variability in the economic strategies that could be employed by households during the Historic period.

However, such data should not be interpreted in an overly simplistic way. Graesch's results suggest that if prestige goods can be used to gauge a household's role in the political economy and, in turn, its socioeconomic status, then early Historic household status was to some degree independent of its shellworking activities. The overall picture of household and village organization during this period would seem to suggest that neither the intensity with which households were engaging in the production of shell beads nor the types of beads that were being produced can be used as a singular measure of household status. Inhabitants of the house yielding the highest density of prestige goods in the project sample of 31 (a redwood pole house at the historically documented elite village of *Xaxas*, on the north shore of Santa Cruz Island) were allocating much less labor to bead-making activities than households in the other three villages.

In fact, this should not be particularly surprising, given that hierarchical structures of the late 1700s were directly rooted in precontact developments in the political economy. The basis for the wealth and status of such a high-ranking Historic household (see Arnold 2001b:48–52) may have been tomol ownership, hereditary high status, and/or lucrative trade partnerships dating back many generations rather than their efforts expended on bead manufacturing from the 1780s to the 1810s. Moreover, other routes to elevated status in these villages would certainly have included tomol making and perhaps such activities as acquiring open-ocean fish and hosting feasts. In short, some families, likely including those who lived in the redwood pole house at *Xaxas*, gained their wealth and social standing through means other than—or in addition to—their participation in specialized craft activities.

Still, beyond the highest status households, there does seem to have been a modest positive correlation between bead production and socioeconomic status. All households produced varying quantities of shell goods, and among households that do not appear to have been of the highest rank (perhaps nonelites), the data suggest that those who produced the most beads acquired relatively greater amounts of prestige goods and other items through regional trade networks. Hard workers (good producers) may have been differentially rewarded by canoe-owning elites who regularly brokered exchange between mainland and island communities.

Thus far, Historic-era islander households have not generated any evidence to suggest that elites rigidly controlled the specialized production of microliths or shell beads in the sense of a patron-client, "attached" specialist relationship. Considerable microblade or bead production occurred at a number of villages across the three largest northern islands. Field documentation of distributions of bead-making by-products at house after house in samples from these villages reveals that much of this activity took place in and around peoples' homes rather than in formal workshops or directly under the gaze of, or on-site supervision by, elites (project data housed at UCLA Channel Islands Laboratory). A number of years ago Arnold and Munns (1994) explored this issue in the abstract (household data were not available at the time), proposing that Island Chumash craft specialists were *neither* classic "attached" specialists operating under direct elite supervision nor "independent" specialists working at their own pace, responding to general demand, or delivering their wares directly to consumers. Rather, specialized Channel Islands bead makers probably responded to the requests or orders of elites, conducted their production work in and around their own homes, and supplied their products to tomol-owning elites who could in turn (and after taking a cut) deliver them to waiting consumers across the channel. The specialists themselves could not be independent because they did not command the means of regular and reliable distribution of their valued goods (across the channel), but much of their daily work may well have been (or seemed) "independent" of supervision (Arnold and Munns 1994). Graesch's recent analysis (this volume) of Historic households indicates that this is still an apt characterization of the organization of microlith making and bead making on the islands.

Such an organizational structure suggests to us that the labor relations between Late and His-

toric period elites and producers may be usefully represented as *interdependent* although not necessarily balanced. Higher-ranking traders and chiefs required adequate production from various island specialists to maintain a sufficient volume of goods (especially beads) for exchange with communities of producers and other traders on the mainland. Their livelihood and economic standing depended on a good, reliable supply of worked shell products, and they would have lost important trade partnerships if they failed to deliver. (Traders would have been equally dependent on producers of foods or goods on the mainland.) Channel Islands bead-producing households benefited by receiving important plant and animal foods and prized manufactured goods and tools from the outside. They maintained good standing with tomol-owning traders of higher status, who likely rewarded dependable producers with the more desirable imported goods. Elite boat owners no doubt got the better of such relationships, but cooperation and goodwill may have played more of a role than coercion and directives.

Finally, project data also provide good evidence of community-level shellworking foci. The proximity of a given village to spatially localized (patchy), manipulable shell resources such as large Pismo clams (found in expansive sandy beaches) or red abalones (found subtidally in very cool waters) was clearly an important factor in the evolution of some of these localized shellworking emphases (Arnold and Graesch 2001; Graesch, this volume). Comparative advantage in village location with respect to specific, patchy shell resources meant that all households in certain communities could in principle develop emphases in the production of those shell bead types, some of which were highly valued forms (e.g., Pismo clam beads; see Arnold and Rachal 2002).

Further studies are underway on these household data, including examinations of the role of animals in the Historic political economy. Such research will help to elucidate whether certain procurement activities constituted specialized occupations (e.g., possibly open-ocean harpoon fishing or marine mammal hunting) and will allow us to assess the extent to which such activities were important for status differentiation and political evolution (Bernard, this volume; Noah 2003). Findings should provide insights into how the activities of individual Chumash households articulated with the complex regional economy observed by early Europeans.

CONCLUSION

Archaeological investigations in the territory of the Chumash continue to generate valuable data for addressing issues of broad anthropological significance, including but not limited to how sociopolitical complexity developed and could be sustained without agriculture. Five to ten years from now, researchers will likely be both building on this work and focusing on other, as yet unexamined, topics. Future studies that will be of particular utility, in our view, include the following.

(1) Reconstructing the earliest stages of sedentism among mainland and island populations (perhaps during the later Early period).

(2) Investigating the several known subgroups of Chumash speakers and the potential links between subgroup language distinctions and the boundaries of Late-to-Historic period polities (perhaps chiefdom boundaries?). The purported uniqueness of Chumash languages in relation to other North American language groups (Chumashan is no longer considered a Hokan language) also has possible implications for their local longevity.

(3) Carrying out further household-level archaeology, which remains underdeveloped and significantly lags other regions, especially the Northwest Coast (see Ames 1995; Arnold 2004) and Northwest Plateau of North America (Prentiss and Kuijt 2004).

(4) Studying ancient DNA in Chumash populations, which may become salient in a wide range of investigations regarding population longevity in the region, genealogies of leadership, and social networks.

(5) Investigating in much greater depth the details of economic organization and village life during the Middle period.

(6) Exploring the shifting nature of intercultural connections between the Chumash and their northern (Salinan), eastern (Yokuts), and southern (Gabrielino/Tongva) neighbors throughout prehistory. Many Late and Historic period Chumash elites seem to have built (or sustained) their wealth by means of middle-distance trading within the Chumash sphere (e.g., moving beads and foods across the Santa Barbara Channel), but it is not clear what role long-distance trade with these non-Chumash neighbors played (if any) in the constitution of elite standing. Long-distance trade of goods such as obsidian peaked more than 1,000 years ago in many areas of California (during the Early and/or Middle periods) and was greatly diminished during the late phases of prehistory (Arnold et al. 2004). These and other issues will be important in furthering our understanding of the foundations of Chumash complexity in the coming years.

Acknowledgments. Arnold acknowledges the National Science Foundation (BNS 88-12184 and SBR 95-11576) for many years of generous support, the UCLA Academic Senate for several faculty research grants pertaining to this project (1989–1999), and the UCLA Department of Anthropology and the Cotsen Institute of Archaeology for their logistical support for a series of UCLA Field Schools and NSF field seasons on Santa Cruz Island. The UCLA Summer Sessions office and UCLA Office of Instructional Development also supported the Field School programs in many important ways. This fieldwork was performed (in part) at the University of California Natural Reserve System's Santa Cruz Island Reserve, on property owned and managed by The Nature Conservancy. We are grateful to the UC-NRS and TNC staffs for facilitating our fieldwork.

NOTES

1. H. W. Henshaw and Lorenzo Yates, among others, sporadically gathered archaeological and/or linguistic data, but very limited ethnographic data, on the Chumash during the late nineteenth century (Blackburn 1975:5).

2. In the mid-1990s, feral pigs started to root heavily in some Santa Cruz Island archaeological sites, creating the worst damage the sites have sustained in more than 200 years.

REFERENCES CITED

Ames, K. M.
1995   Chiefly Power and Household Production on the Northwest Coast. In *Foundations of Social Inequality*, edited by T. D. Price and G. M. Feinman, pp. 155–187. Plenum, New York.

Ames, K. M., and H. D. G. Maschner
1999   *Peoples of the Northwest Coast: Their Archaeology and Prehistory.* Thames and Hudson, London.

Arnold, J. E.
1987   *Craft Specialization in the Prehistoric Channel Islands, California.* University of California Press, Berkeley.
1992   Complex Hunter-Gatherer-Fishers of Prehistoric California: Chiefs, Specialists, and Maritime Adaptations of the Channel Islands. *American Antiquity* 57:60–84.
1993   Labor and the Rise of Complex Hunter-Gatherers. *Journal of Anthropological Archaeology* 12:75–119.
1995   Transportation Innovation and Social Complexity among Maritime Hunter-Gatherer Societies. *American Anthropologist* 97:733–747.
1996a   The Archaeology of Complex Hunter-Gatherers. *Journal of Archaeological Method and Theory* 3:77–126.
1996b   Organizational Transformations: Power and Labor among Complex Hunter-Gatherers and Other Intermediate Societies. In *Emergent Complexity: The Evolution of Intermediate Societies*, edited by J. E. Arnold, pp. 59–73. International Monographs in Prehistory, Ann Arbor, Michigan.
2000   Revisiting Power, Labor Rights, and Kinship: Archaeology and Social Theory. In *Social Theory in Archaeology*, edited by M. B. Schiffer, pp. 14–30. University of Utah Press, Salt Lake City.
2001a   The Chumash in World and Regional Perspectives. In *The Origins of a Pacific Coast Chiefdom: The Chumash of the Channel Islands*, edited by J. E. Arnold, pp. 1–19. University of Utah Press, Salt Lake City.
2001b   The Channel Islands Project: History, Objectives, and Methods. In *The Origins of a Pacific Coast Chiefdom: The Chumash of the Channel Islands*, edited by J. E. Arnold, pp. 21–52. University of Utah Press, Salt Lake City.
2001c   Social Evolution and the Political Economy in the Northern Channel Islands. In *The Origins of a Pacific Coast Chiefdom: The Chumash of the Channel Islands*, edited by J. E. Arnold, pp. 287–296. University of Utah Press, Salt Lake City.
2004   Households on the Pacific Coast: The Northwest Coast and California in Comparative Perspective. In *Household Archaeology on the Northwest Coast*, edited by E. A. Sobel, D. A. Trieu, and K. M. Ames. International Monographs in Prehistory, Ann Arbor, Michigan. In press.

Arnold, J. E. (editor)
2001   *The Origins of a Pacific Coast Chiefdom: The Chumash of the Channel Islands.* University of Utah Press, Salt Lake City.

Arnold, J. E., E. L. Ambos, and D. Larson
1997   Geophysical Surveys of Stratigraphically Complex Island California Sites: New Implications for Household Archaeology. *Antiquity* 71:157–168.

Arnold, J. E., and A. P. Graesch
2001   The Evolution of Specialized Shellworking among the Island Chumash. In *The Origins of a Pacific Coast Chiefdom: The Chumash of the Channel Islands*, edited by J. E. Arnold, pp. 71–112. University of Utah Press, Salt Lake City.

Arnold, J. E., and T. M. Green
2002   Mortuary Ambiguity: The Ventureño Chumash Case. *American Antiquity* 67:760–771.

Arnold, J. E., and A. Munns
1994   Independent or Attached Specialization: The Organization of Shell Bead Production in California. *Journal of Field Archaeology* 21:473–489.

Arnold, J. E., A. M. Preziosi, and P. Shattuck
2001   Flaked Stone Craft Production and Exchange in Island Chumash Territory. In *The Origins of a Pacific Coast Chiefdom: The Chumash of the Channel Islands*, edited by J. E. Arnold, pp. 113–131. University of Utah Press, Salt Lake City.

Arnold, J. E., and D. Rachal
2002 The Value of Pismo Clam Tube Beads in California: Experiments in Drilling. *North American Archaeologist* 23(3):187–207.

Arnold, J. E., M. R. Walsh, and S. E. Hollimon
2004 The Archaeology of California. *Journal of Archaeological Research* 12:1–73.

Bennyhoff, J. A., and R. E. Hughes
1987 Shell Bead and Ornament Exchange Networks between California and the Western Great Basin. *Anthropological Papers of the American Museum of Natural History* 64(2):79–175. New York.

Blackburn, T. C.
1975 *December's Child: A Book of Chumash Oral Narratives.* University of California Press, Berkeley.

Brumfiel, E. M., and T. K. Earle
1987 Specialization, Exchange, and Complex Societies: An Introduction. In *Specialization, Exchange, and Complex Societies,* edited by E. M. Brumfiel and T. K. Earle, pp. 1–9. Cambridge University Press, Cambridge, UK.

Clark, J. E., and W. J. Parry
1990 Craft Specialization and Cultural Complexity. *Research in Economic Anthropology* 12:289–346. JAI Press, Greenwich, Connecticut.

Connolly, T. J., J. M. Erlandson, and S. E. Norris
1995 Early Holocene Basketry and Cordage from Daisy Cave, San Miguel Island, California. *American Antiquity* 60:309–318.

Costin, C. L.
1991 Craft Specialization: Issues in Defining, Documenting, and Explaining the Organization of Production. In *Archaeological Method and Theory,* vol. 3, edited by M. B. Schiffer, pp. 1–56. University of Arizona Press, Tucson.

Dietler, J. E.
2003 The Specialist Next Door: Microblade Production and Status in Island Chumash Households. Unpublished Master's thesis, Department of Anthropology, University of California, Los Angeles.

Erlandson, J. M., and T. L. Jones (editors)
2002 *Catalysts to Complexity: Late Holocene Societies of the California Coast.* Cotsen Institute of Archaeology, University of California, Los Angeles.

Erlandson, J. M., and T. C. Rick
2002 Late Holocene Cultural Developments along the Santa Barbara Coast. In *Catalysts to Complexity: Late Holocene Societies of the California Coast,* edited by J. M. Erlandson and T. L. Jones, pp. 166–182. Cotsen Institute of Archaeology, University of California, Los Angeles.

Fagan, B.
2004 The House of the Sea: An Essay on the Antiquity of Planked Canoes in Southern California. *American Antiquity* 69:7–16.

Glassow, M. A.
1980 Recent Developments in the Archaeology of the Channel Islands. In *The California Islands: Proceedings of a Multidisciplinary Symposium,* edited by D. M. Power, pp. 79–99. Santa Barbara Museum of Natural History, Santa Barbara, California.

Graesch, A. P.
2000 Chumash Houses, Households, and Economy: Post-Contact Production and Exchange on Santa Cruz Island. Unpublished Master's thesis, Department of Anthropology, University of California, Los Angeles.
2001 Culture Contact on the Channel Islands: Historic-Era Production and Exchange Systems. In *The Origins of a Pacific Coast Chiefdom: The Chumash of the Channel Islands,* edited by J. E. Arnold, pp. 261–285. University of Utah Press, Salt Lake City.

Harrington, J. P.
1942 Culture Element Distributions: XIX. Central California Coast. *Anthropological Records* 7:1. University of California, Berkeley.

Hayden, B.
1995 Pathways to Power: Principles for Creating Socioeconomic Inequalities. In *Foundations of Social Inequality,* edited by T. D. Price and G. M. Feinman, pp. 15–86. Plenum, New York.
1996 Thresholds of Power in Emergent Complex Societies. In *Emergent Complexity: The Evolution of Intermediate Societies,* edited by J. E. Arnold, pp. 50–58. International Monographs in Prehistory, Ann Arbor, Michigan.

Holmes, M. S., and J. R. Johnson
1998 *The Chumash and Their Predecessors: An Annotated Bibliography.* Contributions in Anthropology 1, Santa Barbara Museum of Natural History, Santa Barbara, California.

Hudson, T., and T. C. Blackburn
1987   *The Material Culture of the Chumash Interaction Sphere.* Vol. V: *Manufacturing Processes, Metrology, and Trade.* Ballena Press Anthropological Papers No. 31. Ballena Press/ Santa Barbara Museum of Natural History Cooperative Publication, Menlo Park and Santa Barbara, California.

Hudson, T., J. Timbrook, and M. Rempe (editors)
1978   *Tomol: Chumash Watercraft as Described in the Ethnographic Notes of John P. Harrington.* Anthropological Papers No. 9. Ballena Press, Socorro, New Mexico.

Johnson, J. R.
1982   An Ethnohistoric Study of the Island Chumash. Unpublished Master's thesis, Department of Anthropology, University of California, Santa Barbara.

2001   Ethnohistoric Reflections of Cruzeño Chumash Society. In *The Origins of a Pacific Coast Chiefdom: The Chumash of the Channel Islands*, edited by J. E. Arnold, pp. 53–70. University of Utah Press, Salt Lake City.

Johnson, J. R., T. W. Stafford Jr., H. O. Ajie, and D. P. Morris
2000   Arlington Springs Revisited. In *Proceedings of the Fifth California Islands Symposium*, edited by D. R. Browne, K. L. Mitchell, and H. W. Chaney, pp. 541–545. U.S. Department of the Interior, Minerals Management Service, Washington, DC.

Keeley, L. H.
1988   Hunter-Gatherer Economic Complexity and "Population Pressure": A Cross-Cultural Analysis. *Journal of Anthropological Archaeology* 7:373–411.

Kelly, R. L.
1995   *The Foraging Spectrum: Diversity in Hunter-Gatherer Lifeways.* Smithsonian Institution Press, Washington, DC.

Kennett, D. J.
1998   Behavioral Ecology and the Evolution of Hunter-Gatherer Societies on the Northern Channel Islands, California. Unpublished Ph.D. dissertation, Department of Anthropology, University of California, Santa Barbara.

Kennett, D. J., and C. A. Conlee
2002   Emergence of Late Holocene Sociopolitical Complexity on Santa Rosa and San Miguel Islands. In *Catalysts to Complexity: Late Holocene Societies of the California Coast*, edited by J. M. Erlandson and T. L. Jones, pp. 147– 165. Cotsen Institute of Archaeology, University of California, Los Angeles.

King, C. D.
1976   Chumash Inter-Village Economic Exchange. In *Native Californians: A Theoretical Retrospective*, edited by L. J. Bean and T. C. Blackburn, pp. 288–318. Ballena Press, Socorro, New Mexico.

1990   *Evolution of Chumash Society: A Comparative Study of Artifacts Used for Social System Maintenance in the Santa Barbara Channel Region before A.D. 1804.* Garland, New York.

Klar, K. A.
2000   The Island Chumash Language: Implications for Interdisciplinary Work. In *Proceedings of the Fifth California Islands Symposium*, edited by D. R. Browne, K. L. Mitchell, and H. W. Chaney, pp. 654–658. U.S. Department of the Interior, Minerals Management Service, Washington, DC.

Matson, R. G., and G. Coupland
1995   *The Prehistory of the Northwest Coast.* Academic Press, San Diego.

McLendon, S., and J. R. Johnson (editors)
1999   *Cultural Affiliation and Lineal Descent of Chumash Peoples in the Channel Islands and the Santa Monica Mountains.* Report prepared for the National Park Service, Washington, DC.

Munns, A. M., and J. E. Arnold
2002   Late Holocene Santa Cruz Island: Patterns of Continuity and Change. In *Catalysts to Complexity: Late Holocene Societies of the California Coast*, edited by J. M. Erlandson and T. L. Jones, pp. 127–146. Cotsen Institute of Archaeology, University of California, Los Angeles.

Noah, A. C.
2003   Status and Fish Consumption: Inter-Household Variability in a Simple Chiefdom Society on the California Coast. In *Presencia de la Arqueoictiología en México*, edited by A. F. Guzmán, Ó. J. Polaco, and F. J. Aguilar, pp. 125–134. Libro de Memorias de la 12ª Reunión del Grupo de Trabajo en Restos de Peces del Consejo Internacional para la Arqueozoología. Instituto Nacional de

Antropología e Historia e Museo de Paleontología de Guadalajara "Federico A.
Solórzano Barreto," México.

Prentiss, W. C., and I. Kuijt (editors)
2004   *Complex Hunter-Gatherers: Evolution and Organization of Prehistoric Communities on the
Plateau of Northwestern North America.* University of Utah Press, Salt Lake City.

Rick, T. C., J. M. Erlandson, and R. L. Vellanoweth
2001   Paleocoastal Marine Fishing on the Pacific
Coast of the Americas: Perspectives from
Daisy Cave. *American Antiquity* 66:595–613.

Suttles, W., and A. Jonaitis
1990   History of Research in Ethnology. In *Northwest Coast.* Vol. 7, *Handbook of North American Indians,* edited by W. Suttles, pp. 73–87.
Smithsonian Institution, Washington, DC.

Walker, P. L., and T. Hudson
1993   *Chumash Healing: Changing Health and Medical Practices in an American Indian Society.*
Malki Museum Press, Banning, California.

2

Identifying Complexity during the Early Prehistory of Santa Cruz Island, California

Michael A. Glassow

At the time of contact with Euro-American colonists, the Chumash of the Santa Barbara Channel had a complex social and political organization characterized by hereditary leadership, some amount of regional political organization, social status ranking, and a sophisticated economic system based on shell bead money and concentration of wealth among a social elite (Arnold 1992a; King 1990:56–60; King 1982; and many others). Arnold (1991, 1992b, 1995, 2001:287–296) makes a good case for these various aspects of complexity coming together as an integrated system sometime between AD 1150 and 1300, when environmental perturbations disrupted many aspects of subsistence and economic organization.

Although archaeologists working in California have devoted considerable attention to this period of cultural development in recent years (e.g., Arnold 2001; Colten and Stewart 1996; Jones et al. 1999; Kennett and Kennett 2000; Raab and Larson 1997), most have not considered earlier periods of prehistory during which relatively rapid sociopolitical and economic development also may have occurred. King (1990) is among the few who have given explicit attention to these earlier phases of sociopolitical development in the Santa Barbara Channel region, and his proposals deserve more attention than they have been given to date. Before presenting my analysis, however, I think it necessary to make a distinction between *complex* and *complexity*. Arnold (2001:4) has formally defined the term *complex* as referring to societies in which "leadership and social status are traditionally strictly inherited *and* leaders have substantial,

renewable control over labor of numerous non-kin" (see also Arnold 1993:77). *Complexity*, on the other hand, may have a more general and flexible meaning; that is, it may be used to refer to relative conditions, such as a social organization that exhibits greater or lesser complexity than another. It is important, of course, to have terms such as this that refer to relative conditions for addressing the evolution of sociopolitical and economic systems over the long term.

In this chapter I consider a period of Santa Barbara Channel prehistory when an initial step toward social complexity may have been made, that is, a period between 6500 and 5000 BP. The data for my analysis come from a series of sites dating within this interval located on the southern and western coasts of Santa Cruz Island, one of the four Channel Islands forming the southern margin of the Santa Barbara Channel (Figure 2.1). My research over the last couple of decades has resulted in identification of a dozen sites known to date to this period (Glassow 1993; ongoing research). Most of these sites appear to be 50 m or less in diameter and to have deposits less than 40 cm thick, most do not contain earlier or later deposits, and none has shown evidence of residential structures (Glassow 1993). Nearly all are buried under alluvial or windblown deposits and are visible only along sea cliffs and banks of watercourses. A distinctive characteristic of these sites compared to those dating earlier or later is the prevalence of complete or nearly complete red abalone shells mixed with mussel shell fragments and shells of smaller abalone species. Because of the prevalence of red abalone shells, I have referred to these sites as red abalone middens.

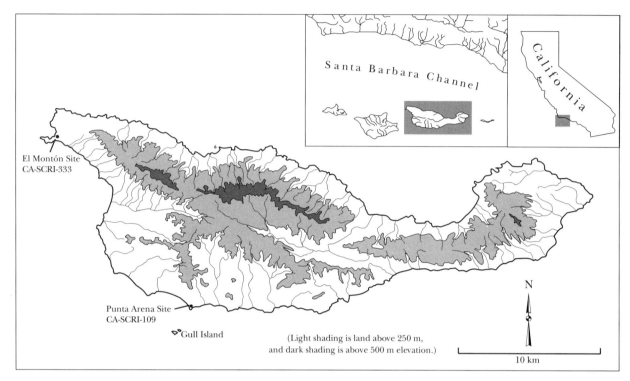

Figure 2.1. Santa Cruz Island, showing the locations of the Punta Arena Site and the El Montón Site.
Map by David Lawson.

The Punta Arena site (SCRI-109), located on the south coast of the island (Figure 2.1), is an exception. This site has a red abalone midden up to 1.5 m thick dating between 6300 and 5300 BP, it is substantially larger in area, and for the most part it is not buried under alluvial or aeolian deposits (Glassow 2000). As well, the deposits are unique in that they contain quantities of dolphin bone as well as a greater concentration of fish bone than is present at other sites of the 6500–5000 BP time interval. The uniqueness of the Punta Arena site compared to others of this time interval undoubtedly is due to its location adjacent to an extensive offshore shallow reef and a submarine canyon. Both provide conditions for high productivity of fish and other marine fauna.

Another site located near the western extreme of Santa Cruz Island, the El Montón site (SCRI-333), also is anomalous, in this case because it is the only site pertaining to the 6500–5000 BP time interval known to be associated with a cemetery. All or a major segment of this cemetery (and another dating later in time) was

excavated in 1927 (Hoover 1971:69–93; King 1990:269–275; Olson 1930). Another cemetery at this site that Van Valkenburgh excavated in 1932, which may simply have been part of the one excavated in 1927, also may have had burials pertaining to this time interval (Van Valkenburgh 1933). Although King (1990:31) places the burials excavated by Van Valkenburgh into a succeeding phase (phase Eyb), burial-associated artifacts imply that the 1932 collection may date to both earlier and later time intervals. Because of this possibility, and because records do not exist regarding which artifacts pertain to particular burials, the 1932 data will not be considered further.

Test excavation at this site carried out by Wilcoxon in the 1980s resulted in the discovery of a red abalone midden buried under wind-blown sand and extensive overlying archaeological deposits dating later than 4500 BP (Wilcoxon 1993). Auger testing by the author in 2003 established that this lowermost stratum is approximately a meter thick in parts of the site and that it is extensive in area, probably in the order of 75 m in diameter. Two radiocarbon dates pertain to the red abalone midden at the site: 5025 and 5727 BP[1] (Breschini et al. 1996:70). The cemetery has been assigned to the 6500–5000 BP time interval based primarily on seriation of diagnostic forms of beads and ornaments interred with the dead. King (1990:30–31) used the artifacts from this cemetery to define a phase he designates as Eya (i.e., the earlier part of phase "y" of the Early period).

The mortuary goods and other aspects of burial treatment revealed in the cemetery at the El Montón site are the most direct source of data available for investigating the degree of social complexity between 6500 and 5000 BP. Considering that the data are from only one cemetery dating to this time interval and from only 41 burials at this cemetery, I use two very simple relative measures of social and economic complexity: average number of beads associated with a burial and diversity of bead types in the mortuary collection. The quantity of beads typically associated with a burial gives some indication of the amount of time and effort invested in manufacture of items used as status markers and/or in economic exchange relationships. The more beads (and other kinds of ornaments) used for such purposes should correlate roughly with complexity of social organization and may also give some indication of the intensity of economic exchange. King (1990:5–16) argues that such characteristics of beads and ornaments as location of use, color, size, and shape are important in denoting social differences. I would add that quantity also is important, because the larger the quantity of strung beads worn by a person, the more display value they have. Diversity of bead types as a measure of social complexity is based on the observation that the most complex form of sociopolitical organization in Santa Barbara Channel prehistory—which existed after ca. AD 1300—correlates with the greatest diversity of shell bead types (King

1990:105). Of course, the relationship between these two measures and social and economic complexity is only approximate. However, if values associated with one cemetery are substantially different from those associated with another cemetery, an argument may be made that differences in social and/or economic complexity indeed may exist.

In his 1971 dissertation Hoover (1971) compiled data from Santa Cruz Island mortuary collections obtained by Olson, and in 1981 King (1981, 1990) presented an analysis of the evolution of prehistoric social organization of the Santa Barbara Channel region in which he used Hoover's compilation of data (along with observation of mortuary collections in museums). For purposes of this analysis I compare the Eya cemetery at the El Montón site with the only two earlier cemeteries for which data exist. One of these cemeteries is at SRI-3, located on the northwestern coast of Santa Rosa Island (Orr 1968:115–129) and dating from approximately 7900 to 7600 BP, and the other is at SBA-142, located near the former margin of the Goleta Slough, along the mainland coast, and dating from approximately 7900 to 7500 BP (Erlandson et al. 1988:239; Owen et al. 1964). It should be pointed out, however, that at least three burials at the SRI-3 cemetery probably pertain to a much later period (Erlandson 1994:188–189). All data in Table 2.1 are derived from King (1990:285)

The data presented in Table 2.1 reveal a significant increase in the quantity and diversity of beads by the time the phase Eya cemetery at the El Montón site (SCRI-333) was in use. Based on King's (1990:270–275) summary of mortuary goods associated with individual burials in this cemetery, all but two of the 41 burials were associated with beads or other decorative objects. By far the most common beads in the collection of mortuary goods were various types made by removing the spire from a purple olive shell (*Olivella*

Table 2.1. Quantity and Diversity of Beads at Early Period Sites

Site	Time Interval (BP)	No. of Burials	Average No. of Beads per Burial	No. of Bead Types
SCRI-333	6500–5000	41	93.2	14
SRI-3	7900–7600	79	3.8	7
SBA-142	7900–7500	8	11.6	6

biplicata) and grinding off its base. Five burials were associated with between 200 and 400 beads of these types, 21 burials were associated with between one and 200 beads, and 15 were associated with no beads. Most burials also were associated with other types of beads and a variety of ornaments made of shell of seven other taxa. Of special interest are several beads made of serpentine and hairpins made of lengthwise segments of deer metapodials. The serpentine and deer bone are from the mainland, and if these items were in common use, which the cemetery data imply, there must have been relatively regular contact with mainland populations.

The abundance and diversity of beads (and ornaments), the significant labor investment involved in making some types of these, and the presence of objects of imported materials imply at least a minimal degree of complexity in the social organization of the people who lived at the El Montón site prior to 5000 BP, even though the nature of this complexity cannot be ascertained. Moreover, when compared to the two cemeteries dating approximately 2,000 years earlier, the significantly larger quantity and greater diversity of beads buried with the dead at the El Montón site implies a greater degree of complexity than was the case earlier.

On the basis of the distribution of mortuary goods among the burials in this cemetery, C. D. King proposes that society at this time was one "in which artifacts used in the maintenance of power were attained by ability or age" (King 1990:95) and that "political, economic and religious institutions were not as clearly differentiated from each other" as came to be the case later (King 1990:117). He posits that during phase Eya times the El Montón site may have been a larger settlement whose population "probably controlled the most important ceremonies, and membership [in a community of this size] was probably necessary to acquire the most important positions" (King 1990:117). Although C. D. King recognizes some degree of social complexity during this interval, he argues that clearly evident social ranking did not develop until about 2,000 years later. Considering the small sample of burials from only one cemetery, C. D. King's interpretations must be treated as a hypothesis in need of substantially more

support. Indeed, the degree of social complexity still must have been relatively minimal. This is indicated by the nature and distribution of sites with red abalone middens, aside from the El Montón site, which imply relatively high mobility of a population probably living in much lower density on the island than was the case after about 4000 BP.

It is well to keep in mind that chronological information for the El Montón site is not ideal. Although the two dates from a test unit at the site give some indication of the date of the red abalone midden, it seems likely that a larger suite of dates would provide a somewhat different picture of the time interval during which the midden accumulated. It is also well to keep in mind that the phase Eya cemetery may have been used during a time interval not represented by the two radiocarbon dates; specifically, it may be somewhat earlier, as are some of the red abalone middens elsewhere on the island.

What might account for the evidence of the beginning of social complexity reflected in the nature of mortuary goods from the phase Eya cemetery at the El Montón site? Data from the Punta Arena site may hold some important clues. As mentioned above, the deposits dating between 6300 and 5300 BP at this site contain abundant bones of dolphins. However, underlying deposits dating between 8800 and 7500 BP do not. Assuming that the dolphins were hunted from boats, most likely about 1.5 km offshore over the steep slope of a submarine canyon (Glassow, in press), the origin of dolphin hunting may be related to the regular use of watercraft. Prior to 6300 BP watercraft may not have been of a type appropriate for dolphin hunting, or they may not have been regularly made and used. This inference is supported by changes in fishing practices. Prior to 6300 BP the dominant fish species caught was sheephead, most likely from shore along the rocky headland of Punta Arena. After 6300 a much greater diversity of fishes was caught, including jack mackerel and other fish taxa that inhabit nearshore waters adjacent to kelp beds—in other words, fishes that would have been caught from boats (Glassow, in preparation).

In discussing the social implications of the much later development of the Chumash plank canoe in the Santa Barbara Channel region, Jeanne Arnold (1995:732) notes that "where large-capacity, reliable watercraft were developed that enhanced food-getting, ritual, trade, and communication systems, *and* where the opportunities to own or operate such watercraft were limited, advanced boat technology helped to stimulate new levels of sociopolitical complexity." I propose that the more intensive use of an existing form of watercraft, or possibly the development of more sophisticated watercraft than existed before, also may lie behind the beginnings of social complexity between 6500 and 5000 BP on Santa Cruz Island. Undoubtedly, the kind of watercraft of this early time was much less elaborate than the plank canoe of the late prehistoric period, but it may nonetheless have entailed a significant investment of time and effort to manufacture and may also have entailed use of scarce raw materials.

Porcasi and her colleagues (Porcasi et al. 2000:215–216) proposed that more intensive use of watercraft began sometime around 6500 BP, in connection with evidence of dolphin hunting at two sites on Santa Catalina and San Clemente islands, which are analogous in many respects to the Punta Arena site. However, they do not explicitly relate the relatively abrupt expansion of dolphin hunting to changes in the nature of watercraft design.

The watercraft in question may have been as simple as a tule balsa, the use of which was widespread in western North America at the beginning of Euro-American colonization, both along the Pacific coast and on inland lakes. Arnold's proposal that the tule balsa "probably could not have been constructed regularly or in any quantity on the islands" (1995:738) may not be justified. Canyon mouth and canyon bottom habitats that may have supported stands of tules (or bulrush, *Scirpus californicus*) have been severely disrupted by erosion and alluvial deposition resulting from historic livestock grazing (Junak et al. 1995:37). Laguna Canyon, a large watershed approximately 1.5 km east of Punta Arena, may have contained tule marshlands that supplied the inhabitants of the Punta Arena site with the materials necessary for tule balsa construction. Nonetheless, even if tules were more abundant in aboriginal times than they are now,

they still may have been scarce enough to have induced some degree of territorial protection and enhanced the value of a tule balsa.

A tule balsa, although a relatively simple watercraft to construct, may have been elaborated around 6500 BP to make it more seaworthy and perhaps larger. For instance, Harrington (Hudson et al. 1978:31) mentions that the Chumash "also built a more complicated seagoing boat, using the tule bundles as if they were boards. They did this when boards were difficult to get and expensive. They would work the bundles like they worked the boards in putting them on the hull of the canoe-to-be. Cracks between the bundles were then tarred with *woqo* [asphaltum]." Consequently, a well-made and relatively elaborate tule balsa may have represented a significantly greater concentration of labor and materials than was the case with simpler, more conventional tule balsas documented ethnographically. Interestingly, Fagan (2004:13) proposed that the Chumash plank canoe may have evolved from the more elaborate form of tule balsa. However, a more seaworthy watercraft, if one indeed was developed around 6500 BP, may instead have entailed some sort of wood construction that was a predecessor to the Chumash plank canoe. At this point no clues exist to indicate the type of watercraft in use during the period beginning at 6500 BP; certainly no artifacts from the Punta Arena site can be related unequivocally to boat manufacture.

Whatever its nature, a more elaborate watercraft may have been owned by a kin group with a leader who supervised its construction and use. In other words, leadership, based perhaps on personal abilities, may have arisen when watercraft began to become more elaborate and more important to subsistence activities. These leaders may have distinguished themselves from the rest of the population by acquiring larger numbers of shell beads and ornaments than were used by the rest of the population. It is also worth noting that more seaworthy watercraft likely would have fostered more frequent contact between island and mainland populations and more exchange of goods. As a result, islanders may have had greater access to mainland raw materials and artifacts, such as the deer metapodial hairpins and serpentine beads mentioned previously. Thus, the processes of socioeconomic change that Arnold (1995) argues were the result of the use of the Chumash plank canoe may have begun on a much smaller scale as early as 6500 BP.

Relating the increased social complexity apparent after 6500 BP to the development of a more sophisticated watercraft is just one hypothesis among others that can be proposed. Implied earlier is the possibility that watercraft were not more elaborate than before and instead simply were made more frequently, perhaps with materials that were difficult to acquire. Another possibility is that dolphin hunting while populations occupied the Punta Arena site entailed an organized effort coordinated by a leader. Yet another possibility is that the apparent population growth reflected in the increased frequencies of sites dating after 6500 BP may have led to increased intergroup competition and warfare. Higher status may have been accorded to the more successful warriors or to those who became effective war leaders.

I am obliged to conclude this chapter by emphasizing how little we yet know about the earlier periods of prehistory on Santa Cruz Island and in the Santa Barbara Channel region generally. Very few excavated sites pertain to periods prior to 5000 BP, and they are not always adequately dated. Moreover, collections from these sites are small and are not likely to be representative of the larger region during the periods to which they pertain. Although there is some evidence that social complexity increased sometime around 6500 BP, available data do not give a clear indication of its nature, nor are they sufficient for more than rudimentary evaluation of hypotheses concerning its evolution. The kinds of data needed to evaluate the hypotheses proposed here are fairly obvious. Data concerning mortuary practices from a larger number of cemeteries dating prior to 5000 BP are needed to confirm the contrast drawn between the cemetery at the El Montón site and earlier cemeteries and to reveal more details about the nature of social organization during these periods. Larger samples of artifacts from such sites as the Punta Arena site, where offshore use of boats is fairly obvious, may reveal the nature of toolkits associated with boat manufacture and therefore give

some indication of the kind of boat manufactured. Finally, the distribution of sites on Santa Cruz Island dating to the period between 6500 and 5000 BP, as well as information regarding their contents, would provide a basis for identifying the size and territories of social units, which would allow inferences to be drawn regarding intergroup competition and intergroup differences in social complexity of the sort proposed by C. D. King.

I also wish to emphasize in concluding this study the importance of the axiom that any advance in sociopolitical and economic complexity rests on a foundation of what came before. In other words, changes of the sort occurring sometime between AD 1150 and 1300 are to a large extent modifications of earlier conditions and indeed may be said to be constrained to some extent by these conditions. A deeper understanding of change, therefore, will be gained by understanding the nature of sociopolitical and economic systems that existed just prior to the change. Furthermore, it is likely that some of the determinants of culture change have been in operation for many millennia and should be a focus of research in attempting to broaden the scale of inquiry to more general evolutionary processes. The prehistory of the Santa Barbara Channel is an ideal setting for investigation of evolutionary processes related to complexity, not only because of its long prehistory spanning at least 10 millennia but also because some degree of complexity may be discerned as early as 6500 BP.

NOTE

1. These two radiocarbon dates are reported in Breschini et al. 1996:70 in uncorrected and uncalibrated form. An estimated $^{13}C/^{12}C$ isotopic correction of 410 years and a reservoir effect of 225 ± 35 years were used to correct the dates. Calib 4.3 software was used to calibrate the dates, the results being 3288 (3075) 2910 cal BC and 3948 (3777) 3690 cal BC, with 1 sigma intervals. The sample consisted of abalone shells collected from the 220–230 cm level of Wilcoxon's Unit 6A. All other dates mentioned in this paper are derived from calibrated radiocarbon dates.

REFERENCES CITED

Arnold, J. E.
1991   Transformation of a Regional Economy: Sociopolitical Evolution and the Production of Valuables in Southern California. *Antiquity* 65:953–962.
1992a   Complex Hunter-Gatherer-Fishers of Prehistoric California: Chiefs, Specialists, and Maritime Adaptations of the Channel Islands. *American Antiquity* 57:60–84.
1992b   Cultural Disruption and the Political Economy in Channel Islands Prehistory. In *Essays on the Prehistory of Maritime California*, edited by T. L. Jones, pp. 129–144. Center for Archaeological Research Publication 10, University of California, Davis.
1993   Labor and the Rise of Complex Hunter-Gatherers. *Journal of Anthropological Archaeology* 12:75–119.
1995   Transportation Innovation and Social Complexity among Maritime Hunter-Gatherer Societies. *American Anthropologist* 97:733–747.
2001   The Chumash in World and Regional Perspectives. In *The Origins of a Pacific Coast Chiefdom: The Chumash of the Channel Islands*, edited by J. E. Arnold, pp. 1–19. University of Utah Press, Salt Lake City.

Breschini, G. S., T. Haversat, and J. Erlandson (compilers)
1996   *California Radiocarbon Dates*. 8th ed. Coyote Press, Salinas, California.

Colten, R. H., and A. Stewart
1996   An Adaptationist Model of Emergent Complexity among Hunter-Gatherers in the Santa Barbara, California, Region. *Research in Economic Anthropology* 17:227–250.

Erlandson, J. M.
1994   *Early Hunter-Gatherers of the California Coast*. Plenum, New York.

Erlandson, J. M., R. H. Colten, and M. A. Glassow
1988   Reassessing Owen's "Early Horizon" of the Southern California Coast: New Data on the Chronology of the Glen Annie Canyon Site (CA-SBA-142). *Journal of California and Great Basin Anthropology* 10:237–245.

Fagan, B. M.
2004   The House of the Sea: An Essay on the Antiquity of Planked Canoes in Southern California. *American Antiquity* 69:7–16.

Glassow, M. A.
In prep. Cultural Development during the Early and Middle Holocene on Santa Cruz Island, California. Ms. In preparation.
In press Dolphin Hunting on Santa Cruz Island, California. In *The Exploitation and Cultural Importance of Sea Mammals*, edited by G. Monks. Oxbow Press, Hatfield, Massachusetts.
1993   The Occurrence of Red Abalone Shells in Northern Channel Island Archaeological Middens. In *Third California Islands Symposium: Recent Advances in Research on the California Islands*, edited by F. G. Hochberg, pp. 567–576. Santa Barbara Museum of Natural History, Santa Barbara, California.
2000   Prehistoric Chronology and Environmental Change at the Punta Arena Site, Santa Cruz Island, California. In *Proceedings of the Fifth California Islands Symposium*, edited by D. R. Brown, K. L. Mitchell, and H. W. Chaney, pp. 555–562. U.S. Department of Interior, Minerals Management Service, Washington, DC.

Hoover, R. L.
1971   Some Aspects of Santa Barbara Channel Prehistory. Unpublished Ph.D. dissertation, Department of Anthropology, University of California, Berkeley.

Hudson, D. T., J. Timbrook, and M. Rempe (editors)
1978   *Tomol: Chumash Watercraft as Described in the Ethnographic Notes of John P. Harrington*. Anthropological Papers No. 9. Ballena Press, Socorro, New Mexico.

Jones, T. L., G. M. Brown, L. M. Raab, J. L. McVickar, W. G. Spaulding, D. J. Kennett, A. York, and P. L. Walker
1999   Environmental Imperatives Reconsidered: Demographic Crisis in Western North America during the Medieval Climatic Anomaly. *Current Anthropology* 40:137–140.

Junak, S., T. Ayres, R. Scott, D. Wilken, and D. Young
1995   *A Flora of Santa Cruz Island.* Santa Barbara Botanic Garden, Santa Barbara, California.

Kennett, D. J., and J. P. Kennett
2000   Competitive and Cooperative Responses to Climatic Instability in Coastal Southern California. *American Antiquity* 65:379–395.

King, C. D.
1981   The Evolution of Chumash Society: A Comparative Study of Artifacts Used in Social System Maintenance in the Santa Barbara Channel Region before A.D. 1804. Unpublished Ph.D. dissertation, Department of Anthropology, University of California, Davis.
1990   *Evolution of Chumash Society: A Comparative Study of Artifacts Used for Social System Maintenance in the Santa Barbara Channel Region before A.D. 1804.* Garland, New York.

King, L. B.
1982   Medea Creek Cemetery: Late Inland Chumash Patterns of Social Organization, Exchange, and Warfare. Unpublished Ph.D. dissertation, Department of Anthropology, University of California, Los Angeles.

Olson, R. L.
1930   Chumash Prehistory. *University of California Publications in American Archaeology and Ethnology* 28(1):1–21.

Orr, P. C.
1968   *Prehistory of Santa Rosa Island.* Santa Barbara Museum of Natural History, Santa Barbara, California.

Owen, R. C., F. Curtis, and D. S. Miller
1964   The Glen Annie Canyon Site, SBA-142: An Early Horizon Coastal Site of Santa Barbara County. *UCLA Archaeological Survey Annual Report* 6:431–520.

Porcasi, J. F., T. L. Jones, and L. M. Raab
2000   Trans-Holocene Marine Mammal Exploitation on San Clemente Island, California: A Tragedy of the Commons Revisited. *Journal of Anthropological Archaeology* 19:200–220.

Raab, L. M., and D. O. Larson
1997   Medieval Climatic Anomaly and Punctuated Cultural Evolution in Coastal Southern California. *American Antiquity* 62:319–336.

Van Valkenburgh, R. F.
1933   Archaeological Excavations on Frazier Point, Santa Cruz Island, California. Unpublished report on file at the Santa Barbara Museum of Natural History, Santa Barbara, California.

Wilcoxon, L. R.
1993   Subsistence and Site Structure: An Approach for Deriving Cultural Information from Coastal Shell Middens. In *Archaeology on the Northern Channel Islands of California: Studies of Subsistence, Economics, and Social Organization,* edited by M. A. Glassow, pp. 137–151. Archives of California Prehistory 34. Coyote Press, Salinas, California.

3

Status and the Swordfish

The Origins of Large-Species Fishing among the Chumash

Julienne Bernard

The plank canoe (or *tomol*) is widely acknowledged for its key role in the development of complexity in Chumash culture. Ownership of these expensive, sophisticated vessels allowed individuals to engage in and control cross-channel transportation, social contacts, and trade and to have privileged access to information about the region's social, economic, and political climates. Importantly, its invention also expanded the range of exploitable fish to include large-bodied, powerful, open-ocean species. In addition to the dietary importance of access to such high-meat-yield species, ethnographic and archaeological sources reveal that a number of open-ocean species had important symbolic and ritual value in Chumash culture. Further, some were status foods whose consumption and perhaps acquisition may have been limited to elite individuals. The exploration of the origins of acquisition of such status fish may shed light on the earliest foundations of complexity in Chumash culture, as individuals distinguished themselves by creating and employing a new, extraordinary technology and acquiring large, rare, dangerous, and novel food sources.

A brilliant innovation, the plank canoe represented degrees of time and labor investment and technological complexity far above that required for tule boats, dugout canoes, and perhaps any other watercraft used by native North Americans (Arnold 2001a). Plank canoes were made of drift redwood (from trees growing hundreds of kilometers to the north) collected along Santa Barbara Channel beaches. The wood was split and worked with shell or stone into planks,

drilled and sewn together with milkweed fibers, and caulked and sealed with a mixture of asphaltum and pine pitch (Arnold 2001a; Hudson et al. 1978). Because the dimensions of the vessel were not constrained by the size of the raw materials, it was possible to construct large, flat-bottomed watercraft that were far superior to all known previous designs in terms of speed, stability, safety, and carrying capacity.

Plank canoe construction involved a significant amount of highly skilled labor. At the time of historic contact this labor was restricted to a craft guild called the Brotherhood of the Tomol, whose members guarded knowledge about the process of tomol construction and labored up to six months on a single canoe (Arnold 1995; Hudson et al. 1978). As a result of the substantial time required for construction, as well as the Brotherhood's monopoly over skilled labor, only wealthy individuals could afford to commission and operate plank canoes (Arnold 1995). Thus, since tomols played an important role in facilitating transport and trade, by historic times they provided a means of enhancing the wealth and status of *already* wealthy and perhaps high-status individuals.

However, the invention of the tomol in its earliest form cannot be explained in reference to the transition to simple chiefdom complexity and the development of wealth through control of trade, since diverse archaeological evidence indicates that it was invented several centuries earlier, sometime between AD 1 and AD 900 (Arnold 1995; Hudson et al. 1978; King 1990). The initial phases of experimentation, which were likely to involve intensive and costly labor (Arnold 1995), certainly must have been pursued under different cultural and environmental circumstances and with vastly different goals in mind. Earlier models of the watercraft would not have entailed the same degree of highly organized labor investment and clearly would not have performed the same roles as in Late and Historic period Chumash culture.

The possibility I explore here is that the desire to pursue new fish species in part stimulated the creation of the plank canoe. Early investment in the development of new watercraft forms may have been a response to climatic changes that affected the productivity of nearshore marine habitats and necessitated expansion into open-ocean habitats. Alternatively, or additionally, experimentation with advanced watercraft technology may have been a product of social ambition as individuals attempted to expand the quantity and type of prestige species they could acquire and share publicly. The fact that several specific fish species were indeed accorded prestige value by the Historic Chumash lends significant support to this idea.

PRESTIGE FISH SPECIES ACQUIRED BY THE CHUMASH

Of the marine species identified as desirable status foods, including marlin, tuna, and dolphin (Arnold 1995:739), swordfish were accorded the most social and symbolic value in Chumash culture. In Chumash oral narratives swordfish were considered the marine counterpart of people (Blackburn 1975). These narratives indicate that swordfish lived at the bottom of the sea and hunted and killed the whales that drifted ashore. Because these whales provided such an abundance of meat, swordfish were venerated in Chumash culture and ritual (Blackburn 1975; Davenport et al. 1993). Ethnographic and archaeological evidence supports the symbolic importance of this species, including several rock art representations of swordfish in the Chumash region, portable effigies, a ceremony in which a "swordfish dancer" was the key performer, and a unique burial near Santa Barbara of a presumed swordfish dancer wearing an elaborate headdress made of a swordfish cranium and

spear (Davenport et al. 1993). Furthermore, household-based archaeological work on Santa Cruz Island has shown positive correlations between swordfish remains and elite households, which suggests that there may have been sumptuary rules related to the acquisition and/or consumption of this venerated animal (Noah n.d.).

Because of the swordfish's enormous size, fierce temperament, and open-ocean habitat, its capture requires the use of strong, stable, swift watercraft. Other watercraft used by the Chumash, such as tule balsas, would not have afforded the leverage and carrying capacity needed to safely pursue, land, and transport such a large animal. While some have used swordfish remains at specific sites to infer the use of the plank canoe, there has been no systematic and regional-level examination of the earliest appearance of swordfish or other large pelagic fish. This line of investigation provides the opportunity to address a number of questions regarding Chumash culture and the role of swordfish acquisition in emergent social complexity, including the timing of the invention of the tomol, subsequent improvements in its technological sophistication, and the social and environmental correlates of its invention.

In addition to broadbill swordfish (*Xiphias gladius*) remains, I considered the remains of six other fish species, including albacore (*Thunnus alalunga*), yellowfin tuna (*Thunnus albacares*), bluefin tuna (*Thunnus thynnus*), blue shark (*Prionace glauca*), shortfin mako (*Isurus oxyrinchus*), and striped marlin (*Tetrapturus audax*). The capture of each of these species likely necessitated the use of the tomol because of their size, ferocity, and largely open-ocean habitat. I term the seven selected species, collectively, "tomol-acquired species." In the following analysis the three tuna species (*Thunnus* spp.) are considered together, as are broadbill swordfish and striped marlin (family Xiphiidae). Although some species, such as dolphins and porpoises, also meet some or all of these criteria, they were excluded because of the fact that they may be easily captured without the use of sophisticated ocean-going watercraft (Porcasi and Fujita 2000). Similarly, several members of the tuna family (Scombridae), such as bonito (*Sarda chiliensis*) and skipjack tuna (*Katsuwonus pelamis*), were not considered, as they often come close to shore and do not regularly attain weights that would necessitate larger, stable watercraft for capture.

COLLECTIONS ANALYSIS

By assessing the timing and frequency of the acquisition of species whose capture was most likely limited to plank canoe technology, we gain a broad picture of the technological development of the tomol and changes in the exploitation of open-ocean habitats. I considered two forms of data: those drawn from published site reports and completed faunal analyses from throughout the Chumash region and those I gathered from previously unanalyzed museum collections and their records at the Fowler Museum of Cultural History (UCLA) and the Repository for Archaeological and Ethnographic Collections at UCSB.

Published Reports and Analyses

I consulted 90 completed analyses of fish remains in the Chumash region spanning the Early Holocene through the Historic period (see Bernard 2001 for complete bibliography). Of these, tomol-acquired species were present at a total of 67 sites. Several of the 23 analyses in

which no tomol-acquired species were identified provide important negative evidence that helps to illustrate changes in fishing practices through time. Data from 11 well-dated collections lacking tomol-acquired species (Table 3.1) will be included in various parts of the following analysis.

The 67 sites that contain tomol-acquired species are relatively evenly distributed among the northern Channel Islands and along the mainland coast between Malibu and Gaviota (30 miles west of Santa Barbara), with scattered locations inland and an isolated occurrence near San Luis Obispo. The homogeneity of this distribution reflects that regardless of proximity to the coast or to nearshore submarine canyons, many Chumash villages at some point gained limited access to tomol-acquired species, either through direct acquisition or by trade.

Of these 67 sites, only 15 were found to have fish remains that were acquired in a systematic, quantifiable way and were presented by analysts with some degree of stratigraphic and/or temporal provenience (Table 3.2). I refer to the data from these collections as the "high-resolution data." Definitive conclusions regarding the timing, frequency, and density of faunal remains through time necessitate data of this caliber. I also considered, at a broader level, less temporally

Table 3.1. Collections with Completed Analyses of Well-Dated Fish Bones but No Tomol-Acquired Species

Site	Date of Occupation	Reference
SBA-931	7200–6020 BC	Glassow 1991
SBA-1203[a]	ca. AD 500	Moore 1984
SBA-1541[a]	AD 650–1250	Moore et al. 1988
SBA-1807	6850–6350 BC	Erlandson 1991
SBA-2057	6340 BC	Erlandson 1991
SBA-2061	6350–5850 BC	Erlandson 1991
SCRI-330[a]	AD 1300–1810	Pletka 2001; data on file, Channel Islands Lab, UCLA
SCRI-474[a]	AD 700–1150	Pletka 2001; data on file, Channel Islands Lab, UCLA
SMI-261	8550–6550 BC	Rick et al. 2001
SMI-504[a]	1050 BC–AD 1200	Bowser 1993
SMI-525[a]	1050 BC–AD 1200	Bowser 1993

[a]Available data include quantitative information and provenience.

Table 3.2. The High-Resolution Data: Collections Containing Well-Dated, Quantifiable Tomol-Acquired Species

Site	Time of Occupation[a]	Species	Element	NISP	References
LAN-52 Arroyo Sequit	ca. AD 500–1500	albacore	vertebrae	17	Curtis 1963; Follett 1963b
		bluefin tuna	vertebrae	3	Curtis 1963; Follett 1963b
		shortfin mako	teeth	4	Curtis 1963; Follett 1963b
		swordfish	unmodified remains	n/a	Davenport et al. 1993
LAN-227 Century Ranch	AD 500–1300	albacore	vertebrae	44	Follett 1963a; King et al. 1968
		blue shark	vertebrae	1	Follett 1963a; King et al. 1968
		shortfin mako	teeth, vertebrae	4	Follett 1963a; King et al. 1968
LAN-229 *Talepop*	AD 1100–1830	albacore	vertebrae	12	Follett 1963a, 1968
		shortfin mako	teeth	2	Follett 1963a, 1968
		blue shark	vertebrae	n/a	Johnson 1982
		shortfin mako	tooth	1	Johnson 1982
		albacore	vertebrae	n/a	Johnson 1982
		blue shark	tooth	1	Gobalet 1990
		shortfin mako	teeth, centra	3	Gobalet 1990
		albacore	gill raker	1	Gobalet 1990
SBA-27 *Amolomol*	AD 1070–1470	albacore	vertebrae	18	Salls 1992
		blue shark	vertebrae, tooth	2	Salls 1992
		swordfish	cup	n/a	Davenport et al. 1993
SBA-72 N Tecolote 1	AD 400–600	shortfin mako	tooth	1	Johnson 1980
SBA-72 S Tecolote 1	AD 900–1150	blue shark	tooth	1	Johnson 1980
		swordfish	vertebrae	>2	Johnson 1980
SBA-1731	AD 1150–1550	albacore	n/a	2	Bowser 1993
		tuna sp.	n/a	22	Bowser 1993
		yellowfin tuna	n/a	1	Bowser 1993
	AD 850–1150	blue shark	vertebrae, teeth	8	Moss 1983
		shortfin mako	teeth	4	Moss 1983
SCRI-191 Christy Beach	ca. AD 700–1560	shortfin mako	n/a	2	Arnold 2001b; Colten 2001; Pletka 2001
SCRI-192 Morse Point	AD 1300–1810	blue shark	centrum	1	Johnson 1993
		swordfish		167	Data on file, UCLA Channel Islands Lab; Pletka, personal communication 2001
		tuna sp.	vertebra	5	Data on file, UCLA Channel Islands Lab; Pletka, personal communication 2001
		shortfin mako		5	Data on file, UCLA Channel Islands Lab; Pletka, personal communication 2001

Table 3.2. The High-Resolution Data: Collections Containing Well-Dated, Quantifiable Tomol-Acquired Species (continued)

Site	Time of Occupation[a]	Species	Element	NISP	References
SCRI-236 Christy Beach	AD 1782–1810	swordfish		37	Data on file, UCLA Channel Islands Lab
		tuna sp.		1	Data on file, UCLA Channel Islands Lab
SCRI-240 Prisoners Harbor	AD 1700–1820	shortfin mako		21	Data on file, UCLA Channel Islands Lab; Arnold 2001c:292; Pletka 2001:243
		swordfish		212	Data on file, UCLA Channel Islands Lab; Arnold 2001c:292; Pletka 2001:243
		tuna sp.		8	Data on file, UCLA Channel Islands Lab; Arnold 2001c:292; Pletka 2001:243
SMI-481 Otter Point	AD 730–800	swordfish		4	T. Rick, personal communication 2001
VEN-11 *Muwu*	ca. AD 1500–1700	marlin	vertebrae	5	Love 1980
		shortfin mako	teeth	3	Love 1980
		swordfish	vertebrae, sword	6	Love 1980
		tuna sp.	vertebrae, hypural fans	21	Love 1980
VEN-69 Conejo Rockshelter	AD 1000–1600	shortfin mako	teeth	11	Follett 1965; Glasgow 1965
VEN-87 Mission San Buenaventura	1600 BC–400 BC, AD 1782–1834	shortfin mako	teeth	8	Roeder 1976
VEN-110 Point Mugu	AD 750–1650	albacore		74	Greenwood et al. 1986; Roeder 1987
		blue shark		5	Greenwood et al. 1986; Roeder 1987
		shortfin mako		1	Greenwood et al. 1986; Roeder 1987
		tuna sp.		14	Greenwood et al. 1986; Roeder 1987

[a] Time of occupation is that spanned by the particular high-resolution collection from a site. The site may have a longer occupation reflected in additional collections.

precise data: those from 15 additional collections that originate from quantifiable excavations and are dated to discrete periods of time but lack crucial information regarding quantification and provenience (i.e., NISP and/or accurate volume estimates and/or stratigraphic provenience of specific faunal remains) (Table 3.3). I refer to these data as the "low-resolution data." Although the least informative or reliable results of this analysis come from this set of data, their inclu-

sion is necessary to mitigate the bias that results when a limited range of sites is selected for more detailed consideration. The general trends that emerge in the low-resolution analysis will be supplemented and refined by the analysis of the more definitive, more reliable high-resolution data and the new faunal data from previously unanalyzed museum collections. Thus, our confidence in the results will increase progressively with each data set.

Table 3.3. The Low-Resolution Data: Dated Collections Producing Tomol-Acquired Species

Site	Time of Occupation	Species	NISP	Problems with Presented Data	References
LAN-114 Dume Canyon	ca. 500 BC–AD 500	blue shark	n/a	No NISP; no stratigraphic provenience	Bradford 1996
		shortfin mako	n/a		
		albacore	n/a		
LAN-311 Corral Canyon	ca. AD 1000–1800	shortfin mako	2	No stratigraphic provenience	Dillon 1987; Salls 1987, 1988
		albacore	1		
LAN-243 Medea Creek	AD 1500–1785	swordfish	1	Isolated find; no systematic faunal analysis	King 1982
SBA-1 Rincon Point	4000 BC–AD 1800	blue shark	1	No stratigraphic provenience; analysis not yet complete	Huddleston and Barker 1978; J. Johnson, personal communication 2001; Peterson 1984
		shortfin mako	4		
		swordfish	7		
SBA-46 Helo', Mescalitan Island	1830 BC–AD 400, AD 1100–1650	swordfish	n/a	No stratigraphic provenience; some materials from mixed deposits	Davenport et al. 1993; Gamble 1990; Glenn 1990; Huddleston 1985; McKenna 1985
		blue shark	1		
		shortfin mako	6		
		albacore	39		
SBA-53 Aerophysics	3660–3300 BC	swordfish	6	No stratigraphic provenience	Harrison and Harrison 1966
SBA-143	4670–1010 BC	shortfin mako	2	No stratigraphic provenience	Colten 1987
SBA-1900 Arroyo Quemado	ca. 1550 BC	blue shark	2	No stratigraphic volumetric data available	Salls 1993; Santoro et al. 1993
		shortfin mako	4		
SCRI-306 China Harbor	AD 1300–1785	swordfish	n/a	Ichthyological analysis not yet completed	Arnold 1987; Davenport et al. 1993
		blue shark	n/a		
VEN-3 Shisholop	AD 1000–1500	swordfish	1	No stratigraphic provenience	Fitch 1969; Greenwood and Browne 1969
		shortfin mako	5		
VEN-7 Deer Creek	AD 180–1400	shortfin mako	n/a	No NISP; no stratigraphic provenience	Tartaglia 1976
		albacore	n/a		
VEN-27 Pitas Point	AD 1000–1500	swordfish	n/a	No NISP; no stratigraphic provenience	Wake 2001
VEN-122 Oak Park	AD 1250–1700	shortfin mako	n/a	No NISP; no stratigraphic provenience	Roeder 1979

Table 3.3. The Low-Resolution Data: Dated Collections Producing Tomol-Acquired Species (continued)

Site	Time of Occupation	Species	NISP	Problems with Presented Data	References
VEN-168	AD 630–1120	shortfin mako	n/a	No stratigraphic provenience; missing NISP	Fitch 1975; Romani et al. 1987
		blue shark	20		
		albacore	1		
VEN-261 Running Springs	AD 1300–1600	shortfin mako	2	No stratigraphic provenience	Roeder 1979; Whitley et al. 1979

Note: Fish assemblages in this table were presented by report authors without specific provenience or data recovery information.

Low-resolution data came from a total of 30 collections from sites occupied between 4670 BC and AD 1834 (Table 3.3). These include the 15 collections from which only low-resolution analysis was possible, as well as the 15 high-resolution collections that were analyzed in this phase at a broader level. The number of sites represented per period is generally reflective of the total number of sites occupied in the Santa Barbara Channel region, as inferred from the quantity of radiocarbon dates for given periods of time (Figure 3.1) (Breschini and Haversat 1990). Therefore, we may consider this sample of sites to be reasonably representative of the total assemblage of sites in the region. Because many of these collections lack sufficiently detailed provenience information (units, depths, levels, etc.), they cannot be used to precisely assess the distribution of tomol-acquired species through time. Instead, the most productive use of these data is to assess the maximum possible numbers of tomol-acquired species for each period, based on the 30 collections considered, in order to gain a broad picture of changes in tomol-acquired species acquisition through time. The meaning of "maximum possible" is clarified below.

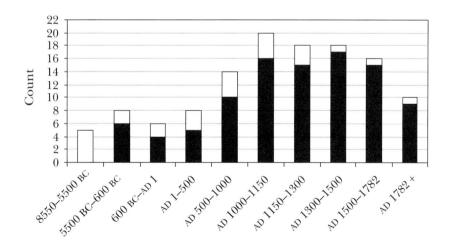

Figure 3.1. Number of low-resolution collections containing tomol-acquired species arranged by period. Unshaded areas represent the number of well-dated collections at which no tomol-acquired species were identified.

Figures 3.2 and 3.3 show, respectively, the maximum possible NISP and taxonomic group NISP of tomol-acquired species from sites occupied during each period. Because detailed provenience data are not available for this set of sites (or if they are available, they are not considered for this stage of analysis), these figures do not reflect the *actual* number of specimens taken during each period but instead assign *all* known specimens to *each* period during which a particular site was occupied. As a result, this analysis can only be expected to produce broad patterns, which I will later test with more refined data sets (see below).

Several important results are gained from the analysis of this low-resolution data set. To begin with, none of the species under consideration here are found in the sites with Early Holocene (8550–5500 BC) components (Figure 3.1). The absence of tomol-acquired species in these contexts helps validate the assumptions made about the role of advanced watercraft in their capture. Surprisingly, tomol-acquired species do occur in a few sites dating to the Early period (5500–600 BC), which predates the commonly hypothesized timing of the tomol's invention. Although six sites with components dating to the Early period contain tomol-acquired species, only three (SBA-53, SBA-143, and SBA-1900) do not have later components from which the re-

mains may have come (Table 3.3). Nonetheless, comparison with later site contexts (in both maximum possible NISP data and density of remains per excavated volume) suggests that there was no distinctive change in the ability of the local populations to acquire large, open-ocean fish from the Early period well into the Middle period (through ca. AD 500) (Bernard 2001).

A clear change in the maximum possible NISP of tomol-acquired species occurs at AD 500–1000 (Figures 3.2 and 3.3). This substantial increase occurs for all species, particularly tuna and blue shark. Although tuna constitute the largest portion of the total maximum possible NISP between AD 500 and 1500, xiphiids dominate from AD 1500 to 1782+. These results are supported by calculations of the density of tomol-acquired species at these sites (Bernard 2001). The data reflect a further notable increase in tomol-acquired species from AD 1300 to 1500, particularly swordfish.

The significance of these broad findings is difficult to ascertain, given that the incomparability of the data sets and a lack of temporal specificity heavily bias the above results. However, there does seem to be strong support from many data sets for intensified tomol-acquired species capture beginning at about AD 500–1000, increasing at AD 1300–1500, and continuing through the Historic period. The taking of these

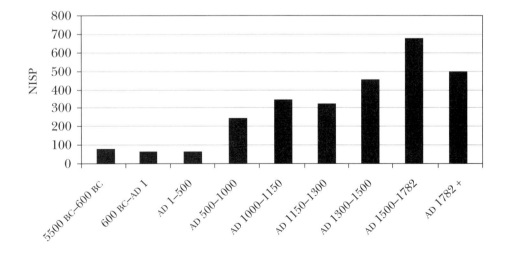

Figure 3.2. Maximum possible NISP of tomol acquired species per period, based on low-resolution data. The full NISP total for a particular site is included in all periods during which the site was occupied.

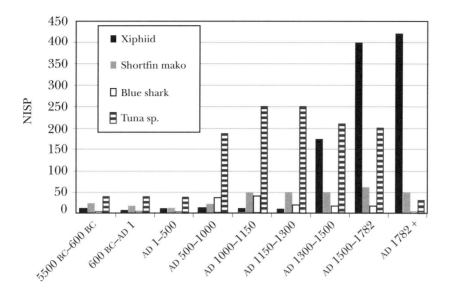

Figure 3.3. Maximum possible NISP, by taxon, per period, based on low-resolution data. The NISP total for a particular site is included in all periods during which that site was occupied.

species did, however, occur to some degree prior to this time. For this reason a better understanding of their earliest acquisition and the implications for the invention of the tomol require further analysis using the higher caliber "high-resolution" data.

As noted earlier, I identified 15 sites containing tomol-acquired species with fish remains that were acquired in a systematic, quantifiable way and were presented with some degree of stratigraphic and/or temporal provenience (Table 3.2). As the above discussion makes readily apparent, this caliber of data is extremely important if any more definitive statements are to be made regarding the timing of the earliest regular acquisition of large fish species and the invention of the tomol. The fish specimens from these sites range from 1600 BC to AD 1834, although as demonstrated below, tomol-acquired species do not appear throughout this entire span of time. Figure 3.4 shows the number of high-resolution collections that contain tomol-acquired species, shown per chronological period over the last 10,000 years. The number of collections containing tomol-acquired species rises sharply at AD 500–1000 and remains relatively high through

the Historic period. Considering the same data at 100-year increments, a more refined picture of changing exploitation through time is available (Figure 3.5). Both modes of analysis reveal that there are very few sites with components dating earlier than AD 500 that contain well-dated and provenienced tomol-acquired species. As demonstrated by the analysis of low-resolution data, tomol-acquired species exploitation was minimal prior to AD 500.

Although these observations offer a broad picture of the number of communities that were engaged in large fish acquisition through time, they are not an accurate measure of the *degree* to which swordfish and other large, open-ocean species were actually being acquired through time. More definitive inferences come from an assessment of the NISP of tomol-acquired species through time. By correlating stratigraphic units with radiocarbon or temporally diagnostic artifact dates, I was able to estimate the number of tomol-acquired species taken per 100-year period. Tomol-acquired species first emerge at ca. AD 500, and NISP values are extremely small (Figure 3.6). There were notable increases at both AD 700–800 and AD 1200–1300. The largest NISP

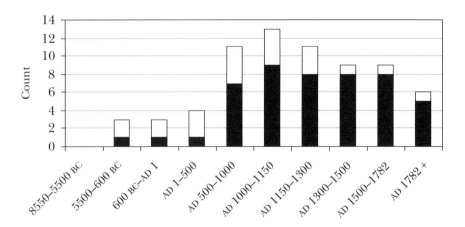

Figure 3.4. Number of high-resolution collections containing tomol-acquired species arranged by period. Unshaded areas represent well-dated, high-resolution collections at which no tomol-acquired species were identified.

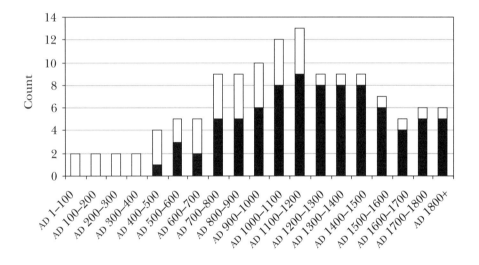

Figure 3.5. Number of high-resolution collections containing tomol-acquired species arranged by 100-year period after AD 1. Unshaded areas represent well-dated, high-resolution collections at which no tomol-acquired species were identified.

values appear at AD 1700–1800 and remain high through the Historic period.

Separating NISP values per 100-year period by species (or species group) reveals different patterns for each taxon (Figures 3.7 and 3.8). Tuna specimens appear to be heavily guiding the total NISP for the period between AD 700 and 1400, whereas swordfish (xiphiids) dominate NISP totals after AD 1400 (with the notable exception of AD 1600–1700). These results may

have important implications for interpretations regarding diachronic change in the targeting of particular species or groups of species.

Although tracking NISP gives a good general measure of the distribution of tomol-acquired species through time, these data must be further standardized because different volumes of site deposit were excavated at each site. Calculations of density, the NISP per cubic meter of analyzed excavated material, provide a way to

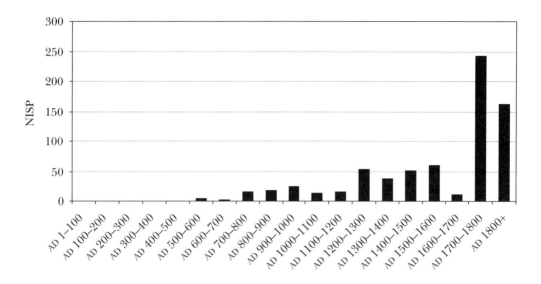

Figure 3.6. NISP of tomol-acquired species per 100-year period (based on stratigraphic provenience) from all high-resolution collections.

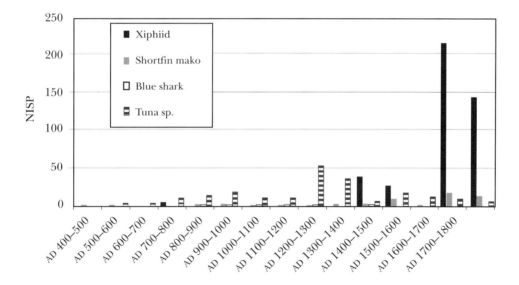

Figure 3.7. NISP of tomol-acquired species, by taxon, per 100-year period (based on stratigraphic provenience) from all high-resolution collections.

make diverse data fully comparable. My analysis of the density of tomol-acquired species remains per stratigraphic level, correlated with 100-year periods, reinforces the above results (Figure 3.9). The three tunas dominated much of the span between AD 500 and 1400, gradually increasing and peaking from AD 1300 to 1400, followed by a sudden and significant decline (Figure 3.10). Densities remained low for tuna after AD 1400, despite

their presence in every temporal period. Swordfish density was relatively low until AD 1400 to 1500, when it increased dramatically (Figure 3.11). Again, all of these patterns corroborate those found in the analysis of low-resolution data (Bernard 2001).

As discussed above, swordfish are known ethnographically to have been the most symbolically important fish in early Historic-era Chumash

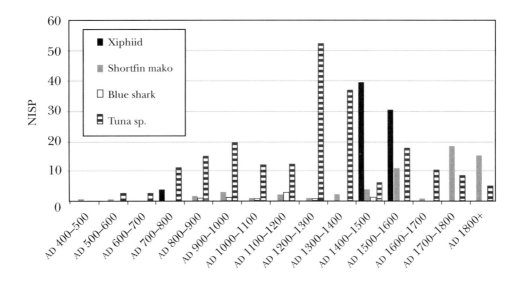

Figure 3.8. NISP of tomol-acquired species, by taxon, per 100-year period (based on stratigraphic provenience) from all high-resolution collections, without xiphiids, after AD 1700.

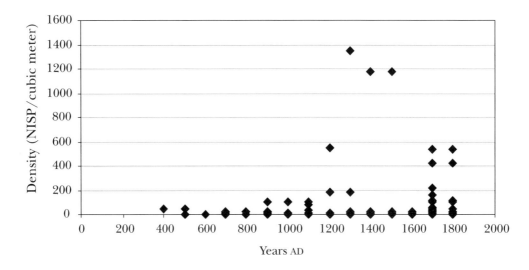

Figure 3.9. Densities of all tomol-acquired taxa per 100-year period (based on stratigraphic provenience) from all high-resolution collections. Each point represents the density of tomol-acquired species at a particular site.

culture. They are also undeniably the most challenging fish to land of all the tomol-acquired species. Thus, it is not surprising that their initial numbers and densities in archaeological assemblages were relatively low. Truly significant quantities of swordfish remains did not occur until AD 1400–1500, ultimately peaking several centuries after tuna were being exploited in their highest numbers and proportions. While it is

possible that the capture of swordfish and other billfish required enough knowledge and technological sophistication to delay their regular acquisition by hundreds of years, it also seems clear that these results are affected strongly by the fact that swordfish remains from high caliber data sets are associated with only four collections, three of which date after AD 1300.

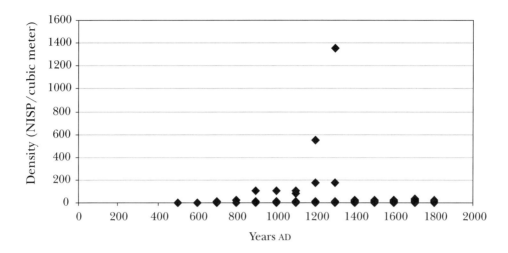

Figure 3.10. Densities of tuna remains per 100-year period (based on stratigraphic provenience) from all high-resolution collections. Each point represents the density of tuna remains at a particular site.

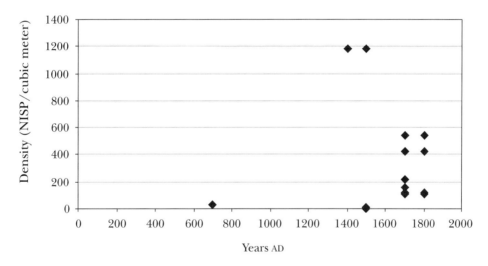

Figure 3.11. Densities of xiphiid remains per 100-year period (based on stratigraphic provenience) from all high-resolution collections. Each point represents the density of xiphiid remains at a particular site.

Previously Unanalyzed Collections

To derive a more balanced and comprehensive picture of swordfish/marlin acquisition over time, I selected six additional, previously unanalyzed faunal collections for further investigation (Table 3.4). All of these collections were known to have swordfish or marlin remains (Davenport et al. 1993), all were relatively well dated and quantifiable, and each represented long spans of time between 2500 BC and AD 1820. My analysis was the first to quantify the xiphiid remains for these

collections. The sites selected are fairly evenly distributed along the mainland coast and on Santa Cruz Island, representing varying proximity to nearshore submarine canyons or other factors that may have particularly fostered swordfish acquisition. One site is located more than 16 kilometers inland and thus provides the opportunity to evaluate swordfish acquisition through trade. The sites selected are Malibu (LAN-264), Arroyo Sequit (LAN-52), *Simo'mo* (VEN-24), Winchester Canyon (SBA-71), Soule

Table 3.4. Collections Used to Assemble New Xiphiid Data

Site	Date of Occupation	Excavators	Location of Collection
LAN-52 Arroyo Sequit	AD 500–1800	Meighan	Fowler Museum, UCLA
LAN-264 Malibu	800 BC–AD 1805	Meighan, Ruby, King, Glassow, and Romoli	Fowler Museum, UCLA
SBA-71 Winchester Canyon	AD 1–400	Warren	Repository for Archaeological and Ethnographic Collections, UCSB
SCRI-240 Prisoners Harbor	2480 BC–AD 1820	Spaulding, Glassow	Repository for Archaeological and Ethnographic Collections, UCSB
VEN-24 *Simo'mo*	AD 220–1050	Meighan	Fowler Museum, UCLA
VEN-61 Soule Park	AD 1–1500	Susia	Fowler Museum, UCLA

Park (VEN-61), and Prisoners Harbor (SCRI-240) (Table 3.4). I examined all faunal remains from these sites and counted, weighed, and recorded the provenience of those I identified as swordfish or marlin. These collections are discussed in greater detail elsewhere (Bernard 2001).

LAN-264: Malibu. The village of *Humaliwu* (Malibu) represents the southeasternmost extent of the Chumash region. It is situated on the coast at the mouth of Malibu Creek and dates from 800 BC to the Historic period (AD 1805) (Gamble et al. 2001; Green 1999). The components represented by the collections I examined date from 800 to 560 BC (uncorrected), AD 300 to 700, AD 900 to 1150, and AD 1325 to 1451. The Malibu swordfish assemblage is extremely small, composed of nine swordfish elements from over 255 m³ of midden, a density of 0.035/m³. Over half of the swordfish assemblage postdates a level with a corrected radiocarbon date of AD 1325–1451; the density of these elements is approximately 0.22/ m³. The three remaining datable swordfish elements came from a locus dated from AD 300 to 700 (based on bead types). Because of their shallow stratigraphic location, these may reflect later deposition as well. The density of swordfish remains from the AD 300–700 component is no higher than 0.06/m³, less than one-third the density for the later period. Despite the fact that faunal remains from over 116 m³ of midden and cemetery dating from AD 900 to 1150 (based on bead types) were examined, no swordfish ele-

ments were found. Additionally, no swordfish elements could be conclusively attributed to the 800–560 BC (uncorrected) component of the site. Thus, swordfish acquisition at Malibu appears to have begun during or possibly later than AD 300–700, was low or nonexistent at AD 900–1150, and perhaps resumed at modest intensity during or after AD 1325. The sample of recovered specimens is extremely small, but the volume of excavated soil from which they were derived is substantial, lending some weight to these observations. Overall, the patterns are very reminiscent of those presented by the high-resolution data and thus might be significant regardless of the low NISP values.

LAN-52: Arroyo Sequit. Arroyo Sequit is situated in Leo Carrillo State Beach, on the coast just west of Point Dume and about 24 km west of Malibu. Although this site is included in my analysis of high- and low-resolution data sets, that sample consists of the materials from a 1961 excavation by Freddie Curtis. Here I analyze additional materials collected by Clement Meighan and a UCLA field school in 1954. Christenson (1987) partially analyzed the faunal materials from the Meighan collection, but she did not address the provenience data and only quantified swordfish vertebrae. Because Arroyo Sequit spans considerable time and contains a fairly large number of swordfish remains (*n* = 111), this site presents an ideal opportunity to assess diachronic changes in swordfish acquisition. Unfortunately, Meighan did not collect radiocarbon samples during his excavations at LAN-52 and excavated in thick (12″) levels. As a result, the picture gained from an analysis of this site's faunal remains is somewhat hazy. Based on comparison to the uncorrected radiocarbon dates obtained through Curtis's excavation and the presence of historic artifacts in the Meighan collection, this data set is likely to span the period of AD 500–1800 (see Bernard 2001 for further discussion).

Meighan's excavations at Arroyo Sequit yielded an NISP of 111 swordfish bones. For the site as a whole, this represents a density of 2.12 swordfish elements per cubic meter of midden

(including burials) excavated, the second-highest density of all the sites from which the new xiphiid data were collected. Swordfish remains were found in all levels of the site (Figure 3.12). The earliest levels contain few swordfish remains in very low densities (0.39–0.71/m³) (Figure 3.13). The swordfish gradually increase until the 12–24″ (below surface) level, when counts and densities spike dramatically (4.5/ m³). Assuming roughly steady site deposition rates, if time is divided evenly over levels, the 12–24″ level can be estimated to date to approximately AD 1280–1540. Following this level, swordfish NISP and density decline substantially

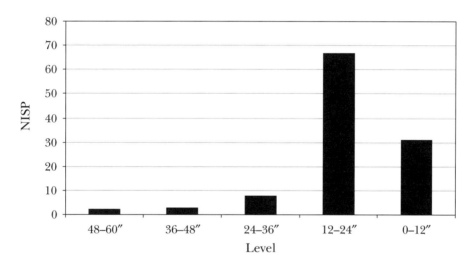

Figure 3.12. NISP of xiphiid remains per level at LAN-52, Arroyo Sequit.

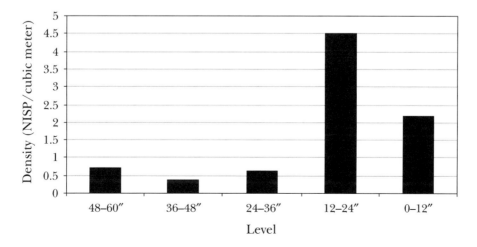

Figure 3.13. Density of xiphiid remains per level at LAN-52, Arroyo Sequit.

but remain relatively high compared to their earlier representation in the site. Thus, data from Arroyo Sequit suggest infrequent and sporadic early swordfish acquisition, perhaps as early as AD 500, which remained largely unchanged until roughly AD 1280–1540, when swordfish NISP and density rose notably. Greater insights into shorter-term fluctuations in the capture of swordfish are not possible because of the coarse excavation levels (12″) and the paucity of radiocarbon dates and temporally diagnostic artifacts. More extensive research on collections from this site could help to resolve the aforementioned dating issues and may yield valuable results regarding changes in fishing practices through time.

VEN-24: Simo'mo. The Chumash village of *Simo'mo* is located upstream from Mugu Lagoon, near the city of Camarillo. Excavations were conducted by Meighan and a UCLA field class in 1955, and the complete collections are housed at the UCLA Fowler Museum. Uncorrected radiocarbon dates from the site suggest an occupation from approximately AD 220 to AD 1050, with a possible Historic period occupation (Breschini et al. 1990; Greenwood et al. 1986).

Swordfish remains from *Simo'mo* are relatively sparse, although they are more numerous and dense than at Malibu. Fifteen swordfish bones were found in 38.2 m³ across seven levels, reflecting a total density of approximately 0.39/m³. Figure 3.14 presents the NISP of swordfish bones found per level for all the pits combined. One NISP value has been halved because its provenience was given as a 12″ (rather than 6″) level. The earliest swordfish remains at *Simo'mo* are found at AD 615 ± 150, despite several levels of occupation as early as AD 220 ± 120. Swordfish remains are most abundant at the 12–18″ (below surface) level, which would date sometime after AD 950. There is also a small peak at the 36–42″ level, which probably dates to about AD 700–785. Because each level reflects an equal volume of excavated soils, these patterns are exactly the same when density is considered. Overall, it appears that swordfish acquisition at *Simo'mo* began around AD 615, rose during the AD 700–785 period and again after AD 950, and declined shortly afterward.

SBA-71: Winchester Canyon. Winchester Canyon is a site well known for a specific set of swordfish remains. It was here in 1926 that David Banks Rogers discovered the famous swordfish dancer burial. One of the abalone ornaments on this individual's cape was radiocarbon dated to ca. 2000 BP (corrected), leading Davenport et al. (1993:261, 265) to suggest that the capacity to acquire swordfish and the invention of the tomol had occurred by about AD 1. Aside from Rogers's explorations the site was also excavated by Claude Warren in 1971 and by Pandora Snethkamp in 1979 (Serena 1980). SBA-71 dates to ca. AD 1–400 (based on bead types) and is located

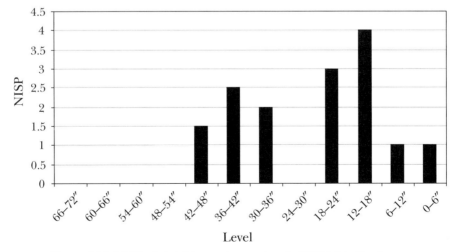

Figure 3.14. NISP of xiphiid remains per level at VEN-24, *Simo'mo.*

near Tecolote Canyon, west of Santa Barbara (DuBarton 1991; Erlandson 1994; Serena 1980).

Analysis of the ichthyological remains from the Snethkamp excavations revealed no swordfish (or other tomol-acquired species) remains, possibly because of the relatively small amount of midden excavated (1.05 m^3) (Johnson 1980; Serena 1980). Because this site was used by both Davenport et al. and DuBarton to demonstrate a relatively early invention of the tomol, it seemed imperative to investigate whether swordfish remains appeared when a sufficiently large volume of material was available for analysis. Thus, I also examined the 1971 Warren collection. The collection, housed at the Repository for Archaeological and Ethnographic Collections at UCSB, contains faunal remains from more than 70 units and trenches of varying dimensions placed throughout the site, reflecting an absolute minimum of 65 excavated cubic meters (although the collection is more likely to represent several hundred excavated cubic meters) (Serena 1980). My assessment of the entire faunal collection produced zero swordfish specimens. Thus, for at least this site, there appears to have been no swordfish acquisition from AD 1–400, except for the one used in the swordfish dancer's headdress.

VEN-61: Soule Park. Living approximately 19 km inland, near Ojai, people inhabiting the site of Soule Park most likely would have acquired swordfish remains only through trade with coastal, seafaring neighbors. Davenport et al. (1993) noted the presence of an unknown number of swordfish swords at VEN-61 based on the collections made by Orr in the 1940s (these excavations were unsystematic and unquantifiable). Systematic excavations were conducted by Susia (1962) in 1960, and a total of 38.4 m^3 of midden representing a long span of time (AD 1–1500) was excavated to sterile soil. My examination of the faunal materials from these excavations yielded no swordfish remains. Consequently, the specimen or specimens found by Orr appear to have been unique at the Soule Park site. The absence of swordfish in dated contexts here suggests that the trade of swordfish to the inland may have been a very limited and late phenomenon (perhaps after the AD 1500 estimated abandonment date of this site).

SCRI-240: Prisoners Harbor. By far the densest collection of swordfish remains evaluated here, and perhaps in the entire Chumash region, comes from Prisoners Harbor, the Early to Historic period village of *Xaxas*, located on Santa Cruz Island. At the time of contact this village was home to high-ranking families and plank canoe owners, and it was a major departure point for cross-channel travel (Arnold 2001b:48; Johnson 1993). Because of the long span of its occupation, ca. 2480 BC–AD 1820 (McLendon and Johnson 1999; Spaulding and Glassow n.d.), and the high density of swordfish remains found archaeologically (as demonstrated through the high-resolution data), SCRI-240 provides an exceptional opportunity to evaluate the development of swordfish acquisition through time.

Research by Arnold (2001c) and Pletka (2001) reveals the high frequency and density of swordfish remains at *Xaxas* from household contexts of the Late and Historic periods. In the Historic period deposits, for example, densities are over 200/m^3 (Pletka 2001; see below). Further data from much earlier periods of occupation at SCRI-240 are available from excavations directed by Albert Spaulding in 1973 and 1974 and Michael Glassow in 1976 (Arnold 1987; Spaulding and Glassow n.d.; Zimmer n.d.). Spaulding excavated two long trenches (termed Trench 1 and Trench 2) at Prisoners Harbor, comprising approximately 114.5 m^3 of midden. Later, Glassow excavated a pit (designated "M") in Trench 2 in an effort to reach sterile deposits; the earliest date of the site is derived from that excavation. Data from the Spaulding and Glassow excavations of Trenches 1 and 2 are analyzed here. All dates presented for these collections are uncorrected radiocarbon dates (Arnold 1987; Spaulding and Glassow n.d.).

Trench 1 contained a total of 311 swordfish specimens. Figure 3.15 shows the total NISP of swordfish remains from all strata of all sections in Trench 1. I correlated arbitrary strata from the eastern and western sections with cultural stratigraphic levels of the central section (according to depth), and I present the totals from each of these strata collectively. The correlations between arbitrary and stratigraphic levels should provide a relative measure of age but are not expected to be precise because the site is a mound with numerous sloping strata. The only radio-carbon date from Trench 1 is from one of the lowest strata (Cut 27) and dates to AD 895 (Spaulding and Glassow n.d.). As Figures 3.15 and 3.16 demonstrate, swordfish remains appear in the level below this but only in very small numbers and low densities. Swordfish remains appear to substantially increase in quantity and density after this time, peaking at Cuts 7 and 8. Although radiocarbon dates are not available for these later strata, my examination of the strata and dates from Trench 2 suggests that this peak

occurred sometime after AD 1425. Additional ev-idence from adequately dated site collections is needed to further assess the timing of these changes in swordfish acquisition through time.

Although both NISP and density values in Trench 1 would seem to indicate no swordfish ac-quisition prior to ca. AD 895, this of course cannot be stated as a beginning date for regular sword-fish acquisition at this village because earlier lev-els were not excavated at that locus. Trench 2, however, was excavated into much older site strata, and despite its significantly lower fre-

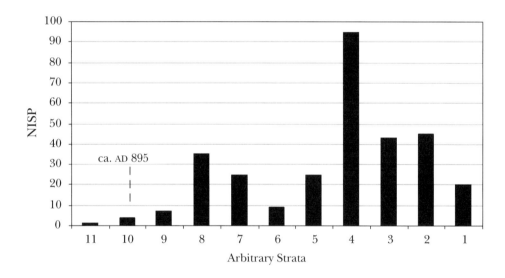

Figure 3.15. NISP of xiphiid remains per level, Trench 1, SCRI-240, arranged earliest to latest, beginning at left.

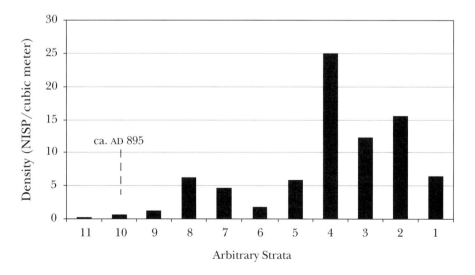

Figure 3.16. Density of xiphiid remains per level, Trench 1, SCRI-240, arranged earliest to latest, beginning at left.

quencies and densities of swordfish remains, it provides a better opportunity to substantiate the earliest time of swordfish acquisition. Trench 2 yielded 30 swordfish bones, 18 of which were found in the portion of the trench excavated with the most controlled methods, the central section. Figures 3.17 and 3.18 show the NISP and density per stratigraphic level, arranged from oldest to most recent, for swordfish remains from the central portion of Trench 2. No swordfish remains appear in test pit M, indicating a long span from at least 625 BC to 190 BC and probably much later. Swordfish remains first appear at Cut (stratum) 20, just below Cut 19, for which there is a date of AD 710 (Spaulding and Glassow n.d.). Swordfish

density is relatively low after this initial occurrence and then zero until Cut 12, which dates sometime after AD 1425, the date for Cut 10 (Arnold 1987; Spaulding and Glassow n.d.). At Cut 12 it begins to rise again, dramatically increasing in density at Cut 6. Thus, this collection reveals very limited swordfish acquisition just prior to AD 710, a notable absence of swordfish remains between approximately AD 900 and AD 1425, and a significant increase (but sporadic occurrences) after AD 1425.

Taken together, Trenches 1 and 2 at SCRI-240 reveal that swordfish remains appeared shortly before ca. AD 710 and were found in relatively low to moderate densities until sometime after

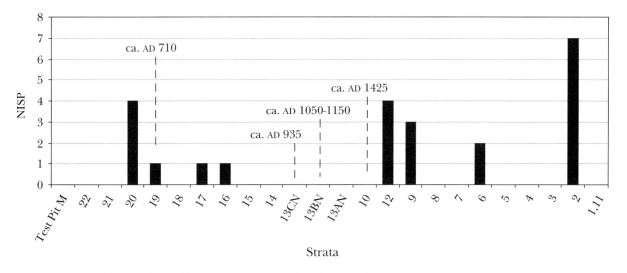

Figure 3.17. NISP of xiphiid remains per level, Trench 2, Central portion, SCRI-240, arranged earliest to latest, beginning at left.

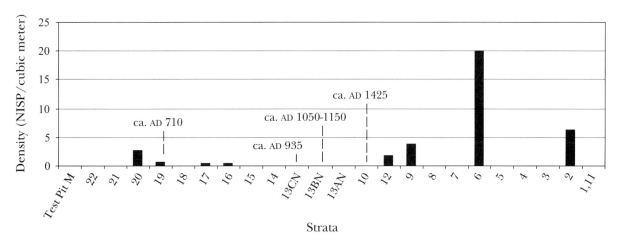

Figure 3.18. Density of xiphiid remains per level, Trench 2, Central portion, SCRI-240, arranged earliest to latest, beginning at left.

AD 1425, when quantities and densities increased significantly in both trenches. The Late period Prisoners Harbor data analyzed by Pletka (2001) support these patterns, showing a great density of swordfish remains after AD 1700. The extraordinarily high density of swordfish remains found in the Historic deposits from Arnold's excavations at SCRI-240 (245/m³; Pletka 2001:243) was not duplicated in the upper levels of the Spaulding collections, suggesting some notable spatial variability in site use and depositional practices. Some of this variability may be attributed to the distribution of house locations at the site (J. Arnold, personal communication 2001).

DISCUSSION

Overall, the data from these six sites reveal that small numbers of swordfish bones appear between AD 615 and 710, with comparably early occurrences at both mainland and island sites. The density and frequency of swordfish remains after this time is variable among sites, although there does seem to be a general decline between AD 950 and 1100 at Malibu, *Simo'mo*, and Trench 2 of Prisoners Harbor. Evidence from Arroyo Sequit (LAN-52), Malibu (LAN-264), and Prisoners Harbor (SCRI-240) suggests a dramatic increase in swordfish acquisition sometime after AD 1425. The absence of swordfish in the extensive collection from Winchester Canyon (SBA-71), occupied from AD 1 to 400, supports the inference that regular xiphiid acquisition did not occur prior to ca. AD 500.

Collectively, the low-resolution data, high-resolution data, and new xiphiid data reveal a long history of large-species acquisition in the Santa Barbara Channel region. Swordfish and other tomol-acquired species do occur archaeologically prior to AD 500 (SBA-71, SBA-143, and SBA-1900), in some cases as early as 3300 BC (SBA-53) (Colten 1987; Davenport et al. 1993; Harrison and Harrison 1966; Salls 1993; Santoro et al. 1993). However, these remains occur in extremely low numbers and frequencies, often as single specimens, and the small samples are separated from each other in time by as many as 2,000 years. Viewed in comparison to the region-wide picture of large fish acquisition developed

here, they undoubtedly represent isolated occurrences such as fortuitous acquisition via washed up carcasses (or perhaps rare fishing successes) in the more distant past. The high-resolution data and new xiphiid data demonstrate that tomol-acquired species appear in very low numbers and densities beginning ca. AD 500, increase substantially around AD 700–800 and again at AD 1200–1300 and after AD 1700. All scales and modes of analysis for both the high-resolution data and the new xiphiid data yield similar patterns. Although these patterns occur fairly consistently from data set to data set, our understanding of the origins of large fish species acquisition will benefit immensely from further research and analysis of representative samples from additional sites occupied throughout the Middle period.

CONCLUSIONS

Multiple lines of faunal evidence strongly support separate studies placing the invention of the Chumash plank canoe at about AD 500, confirming estimates made by reference to canoe construction materials, such as asphaltum plugs, drills, and caulking (Arnold and Bernard 2005; Gamble 2002; Hudson et al. 1978; King 1990). While the species selected for this analysis were indeed found in very small numbers in temporal contexts before this time, they appear to be isolated occurrences, sometimes separated by thousands of years. Since there is a possibility that the occasional dead or injured individual of these species may have been found on the beach or taken opportunistically by Chumash people without tomols, in order to infer the use of a tomol in their capture we must find evidence that is consistent with regular acquisition. There is no temporal continuity or increase in frequency of the occurrence of tomol-acquired species until after ca. AD 500, thus suggesting that the use of plank canoe technology for large, pelagic fish acquisition prior to this time is highly unlikely.

The acquisition of tomol-acquired species appears to have been minimal, however, until the eighth and ninth centuries AD, when multiple lines of evidence suggest a moderate increase in their frequency and density. This seems to resonate with the suggestion that the tomol was being improved and refined from its inception through the AD 800–1000 era (Arnold 1995, 2001a). The fact that swordfish exploitation is rare prior to ca. AD 700 also supports this claim. Further investigation must be conducted to better clarify the progressive development of the tomol through time.

Now having an idea of the timing of the tomol's development, how might we explain the motivations behind its invention? Complicated and often contradictory paleoclimatic evidence precludes definitive conclusions regarding the development of the tomol as a response to environmental fluctuations. With reference to Kennett and Kennett's (2000) paleoclimatic data, it is possible that tomols were developed ca. AD 500 as a response to unpredictability in terrestrial climatic conditions and the desire to take advantage of suddenly abundant, high-meat-yield, warm-water species. However, the fact that such warm-water species as swordfish and tuna never constituted a large proportion of the Chumash diet calls such an interpretation into question.

While it remains probable that the tomol was created to facilitate transport to and perhaps trade with neighboring communities who might aid in times of duress, several lines of evidence suggest that the ability to acquire tuna and swordfish may have been a means of status enhancement during the Middle period and therefore a social, biological, and ideological impetus to experiment with watercraft (see also Hildebrandt and McGuire 2002). First, the symbolic importance of swordfish appears to have been in place as long as 2,000 years ago, as evidenced by the possibly high status "swordfish dancer" burial. This individual was distinguished by his elaborate headdress, the large quantity of grave goods with which he was interred, and his placement near the center of the cemetery (Davenport et al. 1993; King 1980). Whether or not this individual attained some degree of status from acquiring the swordfish bones, this burial elucidates the swordfish's symbolic importance and demonstrates a connection between differential burial treatment and swordfish remains. Thus, it seems that since some degree of symbolic significance of swordfish was in place many hundreds of years before

the tomol was fully developed, the desire to acquire symbolically important status fish, such as swordfish, may be posited as one of possibly several stimuli in the invention of the tomol.

If this were true, however, how might we account for the fact that swordfish numbers and frequencies remain so low until the Late period, after AD 1300? Figures 3.7, 3.8, 3.10, and 3.11 reveal an interesting pattern with regard to the acquisition of species determined to be status-enhancing fish. Tuna remains were present and abundant in earlier levels, gradually increasing from AD 500 until AD 1400–1500, when swordfish numbers and densities suddenly increased dramatically and tuna quantities declined. Therefore, since these species exhibit similar habitat preferences, it appears that swordfish were preferred over tuna, indicating that people were not merely taking as many large fish as possible but were directing their efforts toward the capture of specific species. This would have been most significant during the Late period, when, as diverse archaeological data indicate, elites would have been faced with the task of maintaining and likely expanding their social, economic, and political status. One way of achieving that may have been through the organization and sponsorship of feasts, which are frequently built around large, rare, or labor-intensive animal species (Hayden 2001), of which swordfish are a perfect example.

Tuna also are likely to have been important in the creation and maintenance of status, as seen by the gradual increase in quantity and density of these fish after AD 500 and, more significantly, by the substantial increase in tuna NISP at AD 1200–1300, during the Transitional period. Nonetheless, they seem to have possessed less ideological and symbolic significance in Chumash culture than swordfish. Perhaps tuna would have been the most "optimal" status fish until climatic and sociocultural conditions favored an emphasis on the more ideologically significant and more difficult-to-acquire swordfish. Additional data are needed to further substantiate these conclusions and to better understand changing fishing practices during the underexplored Middle period. Such information is crucial if we are to understand the total picture of emergent complexity among the Chumash.

In summary, it appears that status in the Chumash world was achieved at least in part as a result of individuals' unique ownership of a labor-intensive and highly useful technology, the tomol, and the ability (and willingness) to pursue and obtain desirable, rare, dangerous, and/or difficult-to-acquire resources, including (but not limited to) large, pelagic fish. It is likely that there was an extended period characterized by achieved status distinctions prior to the more formal social, political, and economic complexity that seems to have emerged later in prehistory. While the acquisition of large fish was certainly not the only factor contributing to status differences, it is likely that such activities played an important role in the emergence of social differentiation in Chumash culture, thereby contributing to broader processes of sociopolitical complexity.

Acknowledgments. I am grateful to the many people who provided various forms of assistance and support throughout the course of this research. Wendy Teeter and Peter Paige facilitated access to collections at the Fowler Museum (UCLA) and at the Repository for Archaeological and Ethnographic Collections (UCSB), respectively. Jeanne Arnold, John Johnson, Scott Pletka, and Torrey Rick generously allowed access to and use of their data. Tom Wake (Zooarchaeology Lab at the Cotsen Institute of Archaeology) and Rick Feeney (Los Angeles County Museum of Natural History) provided access to comparative specimens. Thanks also to my committee members, Daniel Fessler and Richard Lesure, and the other individuals who reviewed early drafts of the master's thesis on which this chapter is based, particularly Jeanne Arnold, whose guidance and insight have been invaluable. This research was supported by a National Science Foundation Graduate Fellowship. Any errors or omissions are my own.

REFERENCES CITED

Arnold, J. E.
1987   *Craft Specialization in the Prehistoric Channel Islands, California.* University of California Press, Berkeley.
1995   Transportation Innovation and Social Complexity among Maritime Hunter-Gatherer Societies. *American Anthropologist* 97(4):733–747.
2001a   The Chumash in World and Regional Perspectives. In *The Origins of a Pacific Coast Chiefdom: The Chumash of the Channel Islands*, edited by J. E. Arnold, pp. 1–19. University of Utah Press, Salt Lake City.
2001b   The Channel Islands Project: History, Objectives, and Methods. In *The Origins of a Pacific Coast Chiefdom: The Chumash of the Channel Islands*, edited by J. E. Arnold, pp. 21–52. University of Utah Press, Salt Lake City.
2001c   Social Evolution and the Political Economy in the Northern Channel Islands. In *The Origins of a Pacific Coast Chiefdom: The Chumash of the Channel Islands*, edited by J. E. Arnold, pp. 287–296. University of Utah Press, Salt Lake City.

Arnold, J. E., and J. Bernard
2005   Negotiating the Coasts: Status and the Evolution of Boat Technology in California. In press. *World Archaeology.*

Bernard, J.
2001   The Origins of Open-Ocean and Large Species Fishing in the Chumash Region of Southern California. Unpublished Master's thesis, Department of Anthropology, University of California, Los Angeles.

Blackburn, T. C.
1975   *December's Child: A Book of Chumash Oral Narratives.* University of California Press, Berkeley.

Bowser, B.
1993   Fish Remains. In *Archaeological Investigations at CA-SBA-1731: A Transitional Middle-to-Late Period Site on the Santa Barbara Channel*, edited by J. L. Gerber, pp. 141–170. Report prepared by Dames and Moore, Santa Barbara, California, for Exxon Company, Goleta, California.

Bradford, K.
1996   Influence of Submarine Canyons on Fish Species Found in Coastal Archaeological Sites. *Pacific Coast Archaeological Society Quarterly* 32(1):37–49.

Breschini, G., and T. Haversat
1990   Analysis of California Radiocarbon Dates. In *California Radiocarbon Dates*, edited by G. Breschini, T. Haversat, and J. Erlandson, pp. 87–114. Coyote Press, Salinas, California.

Breschini, G., T. Haversat, and J. Erlandson (compilers)
1990   *California Radiocarbon Dates*. Coyote Press, Salinas, California.

Christenson, L.
1987   Faunal Analysis Results, LAn-52, Arroyo Sequit. Report on file, California Department of Parks and Recreation, San Diego, California, and Fowler Museum, UCLA, Accession 112.

Colten, R. H.
1987   Intrasite Variability in Early and Middle Period Subsistence Remains from CA-SBA-143, Goleta, Santa Barbara County, California. Archives of California Prehistory 13. Coyote Press, Salinas, California.

2001   Ecological and Economic Analysis of Faunal Remains from Santa Cruz Island. In *The Origins of a Pacific Coast Chiefdom: The Chumash of the Channel Islands*, edited by J. E. Arnold, pp. 199–219. University of Utah Press, Salt Lake City.

Curtis, F.
1963   *Arroyo Sequit—LAn-52: Archaeological Investigations in Leo Carrillo Beach State Park, Los Angeles County, California*. Archaeological Report No. 9. California Department of Parks and Recreation, Sacramento, California.

Davenport, D., J. R. Johnson, and J. Timbrook
1993   The Chumash and the Swordfish. *Antiquity* 67:257–272.

Dillon, B.
1987   Preliminary Summary of Archaeological Boundary Test Investigations on the Malibu Coast: CA-LAN-19, 210, 226, 264, 311, and 1298, Los Angeles County, California. Manuscript on file at South Central Coast Information Center, California State University, Fullerton.

DuBarton, A.
1991   From Hunters to Fishermen? Developing Marine Resource Specialization on the Santa Barbara Channel. Analysis of the Artifacts and Midden Constituents from CA-SBa-71. Unpublished Master's thesis, Department of Anthropology, University of Nevada, Las Vegas.

Erlandson, J. M.
1991   Shellfish and Seeds as Optimal Resources: Early Holocene Subsistence on the Santa Barbara Coast. In *Hunter-Gatherers of Early Holocene Coastal California*, edited by J. M. Erlandson and R. H. Colten, pp. 89–100. Institute of Archaeology, University of California, Los Angeles.

1994   *Early Hunter-Gatherers of the California Coast*. Plenum, New York.

Fitch, J. E.
1969   Fish Remains, Primarily Otoliths, from a Ventura, California, Chumash Village Site (Ven-3). In *A Coastal Chumash Village: Excavation of Shisholop, Ventura, California*, edited by R. Greenwood and R. Browne, pp. 56–71, Memoir No. 8, Southern California Academy of Sciences, Los Angeles.

1975   Fish Remains from a Chumash Village Site (Ven-87) at Ventura, California. In *3500 Years on One City Block, Ventura Mission Plaza Archaeological Project 1974*, edited by R. S. Greenwood, pp. 435–469. Report prepared for the Redevelopment Agency, City of San Buenaventura, Ventura, California.

Follett, W. I.
1963a   Fish Remains from the Century Ranch Site (LAn-227), Los Angeles County, California. *UCLA Archaeological Survey Annual Report* 5:299–314.

1963b   Fish Remains from Arroyo Sequit Shellmound (LAn-52), Los Angeles County, California. In *Arroyo Sequit—LAn-52: Archaeological Investigations in Leo Carrillo Beach State Park, Los Angeles County, California*, edited by F. Curtis, pp 113–121. Archaeological Report No. 9. California Department of Parks and Recreation, Sacramento, California.

1965   Appendix: Fish Remains from the Conejo Rock Shelter. *UCLA Archaeological Survey Annual Report* 7:81–90.

1968   Appendix IV: Fish Remains from Century Ranch Site LAn-229, Los Angeles County, California. *UCLA Archaeological Survey Annual Report* 10:132–140.

Gamble, L. (editor)

1990   Archaeological Investigations at *Helo'* on Mescalitan Island. Manuscript on file, Central Coast Information Center, Department of Anthropology, University of California, Santa Barbara.

2002   Archaeological Evidence for the Origin of the Plank Canoe in North America. *American Antiquity* 67(2):301–315.

Gamble, L., P. Walker, and G. Russell

2001   An Integrative Approach to Mortuary Analysis: Social and Symbolic Dimensions of Chumash Burial Practices. *American Antiquity* 66:185–212.

Glassow, M. A.

1965   The Conejo Rock Shelter: An Inland Chumash Site in Ventura County, California. *UCLA Archaeological Survey Annual Report* 7:19–80.

1991   Early Holocene Adaptations on Vandenberg Air Force Base, Santa Barbara County. In *Hunter-Gatherers of Early Holocene Coastal California*, edited by J. Erlandson and R. Colten, pp. 113–124. Institute of Archaeology, University of California, Los Angeles.

Glenn, B.

1990   Fish Exploitation: Analysis of Vertebrae and Otoliths. In Archaeological Investigations at *Helo'* on Mescalitan Island, edited by L. H. Gamble, pp. 17-1 through 17-34. Manuscript on file, Central Coast Information Center, Department of Anthropology, University of California, Santa Barbara.

Gobalet, K.

1990   Fish Remains from Archaeological Site LAN-229: Freshwater and Marine Fishes Exploited. In Archaeological Studies at Site CA-LAN-229: An Experiment in Inference Justification, edited by L. M. Raab, pp. 58–112. Northridge Center for Public Archaeology, California State University, Northridge.

Green, T.

1999   Spanish Missions and Native Religion: Contact, Conflict, and Convergence. Unpublished Ph.D. dissertation, Archaeology Program, University of California, Los Angeles.

Greenwood, R., and R. Browne

1969   *A Coastal Chumash Village: Excavation of Shisholop, Ventura, California*. Memoir No. 8, Southern California Academy of Sciences, Los Angeles.

Greenwood, R., J. Foster, and G. Romani (editors)

1986   Archaeological Study of CA-VEN-110, Ventura, California. Prepared for Corps of Engineers, Los Angeles District. Greenwood and Associates, Pacific Palisades, California.

Harrison, W., and E. Harrison

1966   An Archaeological Sequence for the Hunting People of Santa Barbara, California. *UCLA Archaeological Survey Annual Report* 8:1–90.

Hayden, B.

2001   Fabulous Feasts: A Prolegomenon to the Importance of Feasting. In *Feasts: Archaeological and Ethnographic Perspectives on Food, Politics, and Power*, edited by M. Dietler and B. Hayden, pp. 23–64. Smithsonian Institution Press, Washington, DC.

Hildebrandt, W., and K. McGuire

2002   The Ascendance of Hunting during the California Middle Archaic: An Evolutionary Perspective. *American Antiquity* 67(2):231–256.

Huddleston, R.

1985   Appendix F: Preliminary Investigations and Analysis of the Fish Remains from Mescalitan Island, CA-SBA-46, Site III. In SBa-46 Test Program, edited by R. Mason. Report prepared by Scientific Resource Surveys, Huntington Beach, California, for Goleta Sanitary District/Brown and Caldwell.

Huddleston, R., and L. Barker

1978   Otoliths and Other Fish Remains from the Chumash Midden at Rincon Point (SBa-1) Santa Barbara–Ventura Counties, California. *Contributions in Science* 289. Natural History Museum of Los Angeles County, Los Angeles.

Hudson, T., J. Timbrook, and M. Rempe (editors)

1978   *Tomol: Chumash Watercraft as Described in the Ethnographic Notes of John P. Harrington.* Anthropological Papers No. 9. Ballena Press, Socorro, New Mexico.

Johnson, J. R.

1980   Analysis of Fish Remains. In Cultural Resources Technical Report: Proposed Embarcadero Residential Development, edited by J. Serena, pp. 215–223. Office of Public Archaeology, Social Process Research Institute, University of California, Santa Barbara.

1982   Analysis of Fish Remains from the Late Period Chumash Village of *Talepop*. In Archaeological Investigations at *Talepop* (LAN-229), edited by C. King, pp. 12.1–12.29. Report prepared for California Department of Parks and Recreation. Office of Public Archaeology, University of California, Santa Barbara.

1993   Observations on Fish Remains from Five Santa Cruz Island Archaeological Sites. Report prepared for J. E. Arnold. Manuscript on file at Channel Islands Laboratory, UCLA.

Kennett, D. J., and J. P. Kennett

2000   Competitive and Cooperative Responses to Climatic Instability in Coastal Southern California. *American Antiquity* 65(2):379–395.

King, C. D.

1980   Prehistoric Background. In Cultural Resources Technical Report: Proposed Embarcadero Residential Development, edited by J. Serena, pp. 23–94. Office of Public Archaeology, Social Process Research Institute, University of California, Santa Barbara.

1982   Archaeological Investigations at *Talepop* (LAN-229). Report prepared for California Department of Parks and Recreation. Office of Public Archaeology, Social Process Research Institute, University of California, Santa Barbara.

1990   *Evolution of Chumash Society: A Comparative Study of Artifacts Used for Social System Maintenance in the Santa Barbara Channel Region before A.D. 1804.* Garland, New York.

King, C., T. Blackburn, and E. Chandonet

1968   The Archaeological Investigation of Three Sites on the Century Ranch, Western Los Angeles County, California. *UCLA Archaeological Survey Annual Report* 10:12–154.

Love, H.

1980   Marine Subsistence at Muwu—Ven-11. Unpublished Master's thesis, Archaeology Program, University of California, Los Angeles.

McKenna, J.

1985   Chronology. In SBa-46 Test Program, edited by R. Mason, pp. 226–243. Report prepared by Scientific Resource Surveys, Huntington Beach, California, for Goleta Sanitary District/Brown and Caldwell.

McLendon, S., and J. R. Johnson (editors)

1999   *Cultural Affiliation and Lineal Descent of Chumash Peoples in the Channel Islands and the Santa Monica Mountains.* Report prepared for the National Park Service, Washington, DC.

Moore, J. (editor)

1984   Archaeological Investigations at CA-SBA-1203: Results of Mitigation Excavations. Office of Pubic Archaeology, Social Process Research Institute, University of California, Santa Barbara.

Moore, J., B. Bowser, P. Lambert, and L. Sehgal

1988   Faunal Remains. In Archaeological Investigations at CA-SBa-1541: Prehistoric Settlement, Subsistence, and Economy, edited by J. Moore, pp. 84–102. Painted Cave Archaeological Associates, Santa Barbara, California.

Moss, M.

1983   Faunal Analysis: Fish Remains. In Archaeological Investigations at CA-SBa-1731: Final Report, edited by J. Moore and R. Luce, pp.77–107. Office of Public Archaeology, Social Process Research Institute, University of California, Santa Barbara.

Noah, A. C.

n.d.   Status and the Economy: The Role of Animals in a Historic Period Chiefdom on Santa Cruz Island, California. Ph.D. dissertation in progress. Department of Anthropology, University of California, Los Angeles.

Peterson, R.
1984   Early/Middle Period Subsistence Changes at SBA-1, Rincon Point, Coastal California. *Journal of California and Great Basin Anthropology* 6(2):207–216.

Pletka, S.
2001   The Economics of Island Chumash Fishing Practices. In *The Origins of a Pacific Coast Chiefdom: The Chumash of the Channel Islands*, edited by J. E. Arnold, pp. 221–244. University of Utah Press, Salt Lake City.

Porcasi, J. F., and H. Fujita
2000   The Dolphin Hunters: A Specialized Prehistoric Maritime Adaptation in the Southern California Channel Islands and Baja California. *American Antiquity* 65(3):543–566.

Rick, T. C., J. M. Erlandson, and R. L. Vellanoweth
2001   Paleocoastal Marine Fishing on the Pacific Coast of the Americas: Perspectives from Daisy Cave, California. *American Antiquity* 66:595–613.

Roeder, M.
1976   Fish Remains Collected from an Archaeological Site at the San Buenaventura Mission (Ven-87). In *The Changing Faces of Main Street: Ventura Mission Plaza Archaeological Project*, edited by R. S. Greenwood, pp. 555–578. Report prepared for the Redevelopment Agency, City of San Buenaventura, Ventura, California.

1979   Fish Remains, Primarily Centra, from an Inland Chumash Site in Ventura County, California. In *The Running Springs Site: Archaeological Investigations at Ven-65 and Ven-261*, edited by J. Pritchett and A. McIntyre, pp. 191–206. Monograph XII, Institute of Archaeology, University of California, Los Angeles.

1987   Archaeological Study of CA-VEN-110, Ventura, California: Fish Remains. Report prepared by Greenwood and Associates, Pacific Palisades, California, for Corps of Engineers, Los Angeles District.

Romani, G. R., J. M. Foster, and R. S. Greenwood
1987   Mitigation of Impacts on a Portion of CA-VEN-168, Ventura, California. Report prepared by Greenwood and Associates, Pacific Palisades, California, for Concrete Express, Ventura, California.

Salls, R. A.
1987   Fish Faunal Remains from Corral Canyon: LAn-311 and 1298. In Preliminary Summary of Archaeological Boundary Test Investigations on the Malibu Coast: CA-LAN-19, 210, 226, 264, 311, and 1298, Los Angeles County, California, edited by B. Dillon. Manuscript on file at South Central Coast Information Center, California State University, Fullerton.

1988   Prehistoric Fisheries of the California Bight. Unpublished Ph.D. dissertation, Archaeology Program, University of California, Los Angeles.

1992   Prehistoric Fishing at CA-SBA-27, Santa Barbara, California. In Cultural Resource Phase II Study: Harbor View Inn, 28 West Cabrillo Boulevard, Santa Barbara, California 93101, edited by L. Santoro, A. Toren, and T. Hazeltine, Appendix D. Report prepared by Ogden Environmental and Energy Services for the City of Santa Barbara, California.

1993   Prehistoric Fishing at the Arroyo Quemado Site (SBa-1900), Santa Barbara, California. In Archaeological Investigations Conducted along the Santa Barbara Coast from Gaviota to Las Flores Canyon for the All American Pipeline Project, edited by L. Santoro, T. G. Cooley, T. Hazeltine, and A. G. Toren. Report prepared by Ogden Environmental and Energy Services, Santa Barbara, California.

Santoro, L., T. G. Cooley, T. Hazeltine, and A. G. Toren (editors)
1993   Archaeological Investigations Conducted along the Santa Barbara Coast from Gaviota to Las Flores Canyon for the All American Pipeline Project. Report prepared by Ogden Environmental and Energy Services, Santa Barbara, California.

Serena, J. (editor)
1980   Cultural Resources Technical Report: Proposed Embarcadero Residential Development. Office of Public Archaeology, Social Process Research Institute, University of California, Santa Barbara.

Spaulding, A. C., and M. A. Glassow
n.d. Unpublished notes on excavations and radiocarbon dates at SCRI-240. On file at the Repository for Archaeological and Ethnographic Collections, University of California, Santa Barbara.

Susia, M. L.
1962 Soule Park Site (Ven-61). *UCLA Archaeological Survey Annual Report* 4:157–233.

Tartaglia, L. J.
1976 Prehistoric Maritime Adaptations in Southern California. Unpublished Ph.D. dissertation, Department of Anthropology, University of California, Los Angeles.

Wake, T.
2001 Bone Tool Technology on Santa Cruz Island and Implications for Exchange. In *The Origins of a Pacific Coast Chiefdom: The Chumash of the Channel Islands*, edited by J. E. Arnold, pp. 183–197. University of Utah Press, Salt Lake City.

Whitley, D. S., M. Schneider, J. Simon, and M. Drews
1979 Preliminary Excavations at CA-Ven-122. In *The Archaeology of Oak Park, Ventura County, California Vol. 3*, edited by C. W. Clewlow and D. S. Whitley, pp. 84–130. Monograph XI, Institute of Archaeology, University of California, Los Angeles.

Zimmer, J.
n.d. Patterns of Change in Chumash Fishing Technology. Unpublished paper, on file at the Repository for Archaeological and Ethnographic Collections, University of California, Santa Barbara.

4

The Role of Ritual Specialization in the Evolution of Prehistoric Chumash Complexity

Sandra E. Hollimon

The goal of understanding the emergence of organizational complexity in the prehistory of the Santa Barbara Channel area is of ongoing interest to archaeologists, as evidenced by the chapters in this volume. Although it may be tempting to simply project backward what we think we know about Chumash peoples at the time of European contact, Arnold (2001:287) notes that the search for the origins of complexity is not constituted by a search for specific "traits" we associate with prehistoric Late period society. Rather, it is a search for major organizational changes in economic, subsistence, and political systems, among others. In this chapter I examine one such change: the apparent shift from part-time, nonhereditary ritual specialists to the highly formal, institutionalized and exclusive 'antap religion that has been documented ethnohistorically and ethnographically. In simple terms we know that the emergence of Chumash complexity has something to do with the boats, as well as the beads, and, I would argue, with the "berdaches" ('aqi 'undertakers'). Our goal as archaeologists is to understand the linkages among these and other variables and how they combined to result in the form of Chumash organization that we know from the documentary record.

My examination of this topic is predicated on a number of assumptions. First is that the 'antap religion emerged during the later Middle period, developing from a less institutionalized shamanic system (see Bean and Vane 1992b; Hudson et al. 1981). Second is that the "original" religious system among Chumash peoples was essentially a shamanic one, based on personal ability to contact and manipulate supernatural power, rather than belonging to a secret society that restricted access to esoteric knowledge. It was believed that shamans acquired their supernatural power rather than having innate power, so this form of power lacks the moral authority that comes through birth (Blackburn 1975:23, 39, 41–42, 67; see also Applegate 1978). The third assumption is that when the moral authority of the chief (or other political leader) becomes linked to the power of the shaman, the chief then has the ability to control the labor and products of others (for aboriginal California examples see Aldenderfer 1993:25–26; Blackburn 1976:233–234; Gayton 1976; McKern 1922). The bases for these assumptions, and their implications, are addressed below.

ANTIQUITY OF SHAMANISM AMONG CHUMASH GROUPS

It is generally considered that the "original" religious practitioners throughout Native California were shamans, individuals who derived and manipulated supernatural power by making direct contact with it during altered states of consciousness (Bean and Vane 1992a:9–11, 1992b:34–35; see also Eliade 1964:4–8). This is in keeping with the anthropological observation that most foragers have shamanic religious systems and that in many of these ethnographically documented groups, the shaman, or analogous ritual specialist, is the only occupational specialist recognized (see Eliade 1964).

For the purpose of this discussion I regard the earliest ritual practitioners in Chumash prehistory as nonhereditary, part-time specialists. These persons would be freed from some subsistence activities in return for services rendered (by virtue of fees or other forms of compensation) but would not be on the "permanent payroll" of another individual or corporate entity, such as a chief. As such, these individuals would not be entirely freed from subsistence activity, which is a hallmark of full-time occupational specialization (see Arnold 1987 for a summary of sources).

In prehistoric California, as in North America generally, it is widely considered that shamanic systems have a great antiquity (Bean 1976a, 1976b; Bean and Vane 1992a:8–9; see also Hollimon 2001a for a summary of sources). The personal abilities and proclivities of an individual are (and most likely were in the past) considered a "sign" of shamanic potential (Bean and Vane 1992a:10–11). Among Chumash groups, folk practitioners were probably the earliest medical experts and healers (the shaman's primary duty), and named shaman specialists (including 'antap officials) developed later in prehistory (Timbrook 1987:172).

I have argued elsewhere that a possible precursor of Late period or contact-era occupational specialists was the guild of undertakers, called 'aqi (Hollimon 1997, 2000, 2001b). It is possible that these third-gender persons, who acted as intermediaries between the world of the living and that of the dead, were among the first named and organized occupational specialists in the prehistoric Santa Barbara Channel area. They performed the all-important function of ensuring the appropriate treatment and disposition of the dead and aided in the travel of deceased souls to the afterlife.

Bean (1992:55–56) has argued that the differentiation of ritual specialists into specific "niches" is an indication of the time depth of such religious and healing systems; what may have started as a relatively small number of "general practitioners" may have evolved into a collection of specialists whose powers were spe-

cific to snakebite remedies, granting propitious names to children, or interpreting astronomical and meteorological signs (see Green 1999:79; see also Kehoe's [2000:53–54] discussion of Daur Mongol and Guatemalan Maya ritual specialists). Oliver and Hyder (1983:55) suggest that the rapid depopulation during the postcontact period resulted in a conflation of what may have been distinct roles earlier in prehistory. If so, the number of named specialists in late prehistory may have been even larger than those documented in ethnohistoric and ethnographic sources.

ANTIQUITY OF THE 'ANTAP RELIGION

Several researchers have suggested that the 'antap religion, as understood from ethnographic and ethnohistoric information, was a protohistoric phenomenon, perhaps even a "crisis" religion along the same broad lines as have been hypothesized for the Chinigchinich religion of the Luiseño (Bean and Vane 1992b:46–47; Hudson et al. 1981:4, 11). The birthplace of the 'antap religion was part of the oral tradition recounted by Fernando Librado Kitsepawit to John Peabody Harrington in the early part of the twentieth century; the information was discussed in quasi-historical terms, suggesting that the religion may have been of relatively recent vintage (Hudson et al. 1981:100–119; see also Haley and Wilcoxon 1999).

In contrast, other researchers have suggested that major organizational changes in ritual systems occurred earlier in prehistory. On the basis of archaeological evidence, such as the standardization of deer tibia whistles, it is posited that such innovations took place during the Middle period (see Corbett, this volume). Items that were associated with 'antap ceremonialism during the Historic period have also been found as burial accompaniments in Early period cemeteries on Santa Cruz Island and the mainland (Hollimon 1990:141). These include deer tibia whistles, quartz crystals, and turtle-shell rattles, but of course their contexts of use at such early dates are unknown. Regardless of the specific timing of these changes, some researchers suggest that the formation of an elite and exclusionary society might have gone hand in hand with labor reorganization and establishment of chiefly authority (see Hudson et al. 1981:4, 11).

According to Harrington's early-twentieth-century consultants and other information that describes 'antap officials, not all ritual practitioners belonged to the society as initiated members (Green 1999:79). Some officials, such as the "astrologer" who named children, the person(s) who administered *Datura*, the "weather prophet," and the "master of herbs and keeper of poisons," were apparently 'antap members, whereas bear and rattlesnake shamans appear to have worked more or less independently of the society (Green 1999:78; Walker and Hudson 1993). One interpretation of mortuary evidence suggests that some of these positions, such as the astrologer, were probably not inherited (King 1990:57). One of the specialists, whose 'antap connections are unclear, was the person or persons who administered the hallucinogen *Datura* on various occasions; the person was referred to as "the one who causes intoxication" (Applegate 1975:3).

Old Woman Momoy: The Use of *Datura* among the Chumash

Study of aboriginal use of species of the narcotic plant *Datura* provides indirect evidence relevant to issues considered in this chapter. The antiquity of its uses by Native Californians, the training of practitioners who administered the drug, and its employment within medical and religious systems bear on the question of part-time specialists, and their time depth, in Chumash prehistory.

Anna Gayton's dissertation (1928) discussed the geographical distribution of *Datura* use in North and South America. Although its use was widespread in the New World, it appears that the Chumash had an exceptionally well-developed pharmacopoeia in which *Datura* was the most important plant (Applegate 1975; Baker 1994; Timbrook 1987; Walker and Hudson 1993). In the cosmology of the Chumash peoples, Old Woman Momoy (her native name) provides wisdom and supernatural visions to her grandson, the Chumash culture hero, by washing her hands in a bowl of water and giving it to him to drink. The dose depended on the depth to which she immersed her forearms in the bowl, with the elbow being the highest dose that she would administer. An entire corpus of Chumash oral narratives describes her activities and her ability to see the future. This allowed her to advise others about their future lives, explaining in part her great wealth and high social status depicted in the myths (see Blackburn 1975:36). Her prominence in the narrative tradition suggests long use of the plant by Chumash peoples (Blackburn 1975:36); apparently the only other groups with named mythological characters who are equivalent to Old Woman Momoy were the neighboring Yokuts and Western Mono (Gayton 1928:37, 1948) and the Tongva (Hudson and Blackburn 1978:228, 233).

The potentially lethal consequences of *Datura* use in part explain the necessity of trained specialists who could administer the correct dosage. The possibility of apprenticeship, and perhaps hereditary appointment to such a position, is of relevance to the present discussion; the antiquity of such a ritual office bears on the development of recognized specialists among Chumash groups.

Datura, Power, and Social Stratification

Throughout aboriginal California it was believed that knowledge was roughly equivalent to the control of supernatural power. Those who held and manipulated knowledge were therefore considered powerful and were treated with deference (Bean 1976b:411; see also Barnes 1988). Further, these persons were usually held accountable for the results of their actions in which power was manipulated; several mechanisms of social control applied to the power holder, and negative sanctions could be employed for those who broke culturally approved rules about the use of power (Bean 1976b:412). Among the Chumash, as among most aboriginal California societies, innate power was thought to be unevenly distributed in humans, as was the ability to acquire power. These concepts therefore reinforced a social structure in which monetary wealth, social authority, and control over the labor and products of others could be held by a relatively small elite (Bean 1976b:417).

While there were many avenues and techniques for acquiring power (see Bean 1976b:414–415), the use of *Datura* was of principal importance in the acquisition of power among the Chumash peoples (Applegate 1975, 1978; Blackburn 1975; Walker and Hudson 1993). The material correlates of *Datura* use and its associated "power objects" are of concern here, as their presence in the archaeological record potentially allows a determination of the antiquity of these beliefs and practices.

If we posit that there was a relationship between social mobility and acquiring power from a "dream helper" that was encountered during a *Datura* coma, then could there be some form of social control exerted by *Datura* specialists? If one could affect upward social mobility by acquiring many powerful supernatural guides by taking *Datura*, then there may have been a desire to have many hallucinogenic experiences. However, it appears that there were cultural proscriptions against taking too much *Datura* because it was believed to cause antisocial behavior, effectively putting a limit on how much upward social mobility one could attain. These ideas and cultural rules about taking *Datura* reinforce social stratification (see Baker 1994:270). Gayton (1976:413) discusses analogous principles among the Yokuts, the neighbors to the northeast of the Chumash region.

While ethnographic and ethnohistoric information describes specialized material culture associated with the preparation and consumption of *Datura*, archaeologists have yet to identify items specifically used in these practices. Undoubtedly, *Datura* use is of great antiquity among Chumash groups, but it is at present impossible to determine how ancient these practices are. Objects such as ceremonial mortars, drinking cups, and so on have not been differentiated from similar items used in secular contexts (see Hudson and Blackburn 1986), although the possibility of more sophisticated residue analyses in future research may address this issue.

Hudson and Blackburn (1982:20) discuss the difficulty of making a specific identification of certain items that may have functioned sequentially as secular and ritual items. The attribution of function is especially difficult with items referred to as wands (quartz crystal affixed to a stick), which may variously be described as sunsticks, hairpins, or other apparatus (Hoover 1975:107–109). One may ask, What is to stop a person from making such an item when the individual finds a crystal? When does such an artifact become a symbol of office, restricted to those who are "initiated" or otherwise sanctioned for possessing it?

Similarly, rock art that may have been produced during, or are depictions of, hallucinogenic experiences are not relevant in this discussion for two reasons. First, it is most likely that the majority of these images were produced during the contact era, perhaps as a "crisis" phenomenon (see, e.g., Benson and Sehgal 1987; Edberg 1985; Garvin 1978; Lee 1997; Oliver and Hyder 1983). Our examination of rock art and portable art should not necessarily assume the universalist position about who made it and why (viz. shamans; see Conkey 2001:277, 280–281), but at the very least, the presumed association between 'antap ritual practitioners and the extant rock art suggests that most rock art was produced late in prehistory. Second, the subject of Chumash rock art is so large that it is outside the strict purview of this chapter. Therefore, a more fruitful approach may be the examination of other material correlates of *Datura* use, such as the effigies known as "dream helpers" or talismans.

'Atiŝwɨn: Talismans of Power

One of the main purposes for taking *Datura* was to identify a person's spirit help while in the hallucinogenic coma. The 'atiŝwɨn, or dream helper, was a person's supernatural guardian and provided good luck and spiritual guidance throughout a person's life (Applegate 1975:8, 1978). According to ethnographic information, an 'atiŝwɨn could be obtained, and was actually sought, by all people, not just those who were shamanically gifted (Applegate 1978). Often, these dream helpers were carved in stone, as tangible talismans for the owner, and included zoomorphic and canoe forms (Lee 1997:71–84). Apparently Chumash peoples believed that the personal talisman acquired through a dream was of power only to the dreamer, so it was buried at death with the individual who had been its sole owner (Applegate 1978:53).

The existence of these material correlates of religious beliefs raises interesting issues for archaeologists. A long-standing debate among those who study Chumash prehistory has centered on the interpretation of burial accompaniments. While ethnographic information suggests that some burial accompaniments were not the property of the deceased (see King 1969, 1982, for summaries), there may have been specific items that were considered the property of only one person and therefore would be buried with that individual at death. The aforementioned talismans apparently fit this category and may therefore be burial accompaniments that actually reflect something about the deceased rather than his or her loved ones and mourners.

A possible implication of this principle might involve the identification of shamans or other ritual specialists in the archaeological record. As Blackburn (1975:87–88) has noted, Chumash oral narratives are replete with shamanic allegories, and in these sacred stories, most ritual practitioners seem to derive their powers from the possession of several 'atišwɨn or one of exceptional strength (see also Applegate 1978). The word 'atišwɨnic seems to be used as a kind of generic term for shaman. It is impossible to determine if all such practitioners ultimately derived their power from 'atišwɨn, although it does not seem unlikely. It is also unclear whether the acquisition of shamanistic powers was hereditary (Blackburn 1975:41, 51; King 1990:57). In some societies it is believed that hereditary shamanic powers can exist side-by-side with those attained personally (Eliade 1964:21); this belief is present in Chumash oral narratives (Blackburn 1975:23, 39).

Another implication for archaeological interpretation involves the personal ownership of ritual paraphernalia. Were these objects powerful in their own right or only in the hands of a powerful person? Does the power wane when buried? Can the power be transferred to a new owner? Smaller flutes or cane whistles could be acquired and used by anyone for personal or recreational use, but the controlled ritual disposal of deer tibia whistles suggests that their

use was restricted to 'antap members (Corbett 1999:54–56; also see Corbett, this volume). Certain kinds of talismans apparently were not considered powerful in their own right (see above), but the items recorded ethnographically as 'antap regalia and paraphernalia seem to have been recognized as powerful in and of themselves, not to be used by the "uninitiated" (Applegate 1978:54; Walker and Hudson 1993:45).

MEANS OF CONTROLLING ACCESS TO KNOWLEDGE

Controlled (or denied) access to esoteric knowledge is a major means by which elites can impose and reinforce a ruling ideology (Earle 1997:150, 153; see also Aldenderfer 1993:13). For example, among many Polynesian chiefdoms, commoners were not allowed to keep genealogies, which could serve to mark a person of distinction. Indeed, elites justified their positions by means of extensive genealogies, aided by memory specialists who were not available to the general population (Earle 1997:35–36). As Earle (1997:144; emphasis in original) notes, "Although other sources of power exist, it is *knowledge* of power (and powerlessness) as presented and experienced on a daily basis that makes it real to people and determines their actions."

A similar situation must have existed in precontact Chumash society, but rather than extensive genealogical information, an esoteric language full of metaphor and allegory appears to have been one of the mechanisms for reinforcing elite status (Blackburn 1975:26, 1976:236; Hudson and Underhay 1978:38; Hudson et al. 1981:5; Walker and Hudson 1993:41–45). Perhaps an analogy can be drawn between the glossolalia performed by (and unique to) an individual shaman who practiced independently and the speechifying by a Big Person who wishes to increase personal prestige, on the one hand, and the esoteric language and formal oration of 'antap initiates, including the chief, on the other hand (see Eliade 1964:96–97; Saladin D'Anglure 1994:208). In many societies organized as "Big Man" systems, skillful oration is a demonstration of power, and a person's unique turn of phrase is seen as control of knowledge. For example, among the Enga of Papua New Guinea,

Big Men often align themselves to supernatural power and thereby find religious reinforcement of their position; reciting "praise poetry" was one manifestation of this practice (Wiessner 2001:127–128).

Siberian shamans sometimes employ specific speech forms that other community members do not understand. In northern Siberia, *khorro*, or "shaman's language," is used during rituals. This is usually the language of a neighboring group that the shaman does not actually understand. For example, a Tungus shaman in an altered state of consciousness may speak Koryak, although this language is not understood by the shaman when he or she is in an unaltered state (Chadwick 1942:18).

Examples of this principle can be seen in Native North American societies as well. Among the Ojibway the shaman has conversations with the *manitou*, or guiding spirit, in an archaic form of the language, which is unintelligible to average people (Grim 1983:154). The Wintu of California also differentiate between personal glossolalia (i.e., unintelligible babbling [Samarin 1972:122]) spoken by anyone during prayer and the formal jargon of shamans (Shepherd 1992:200–201, 205). Although Shepherd (1992: 200) considers glossolalia and Wintu shamanic jargon to reside closely on a continuum, she notes that Wintu shamans were also frequently bilingual in a neighboring language and would use interpreters during rituals in order for the monolinguals in the audience to understand the ritual's meaning. During the first half of the twentieth century Wintu shamans and their interpreters would travel to neighboring groups, learning these adjacent languages; this was a palpable expression of the shaman's and interpreter's command of knowledge and supernatural power (Du Bois 1935: 107).

STATUSES IN CHUMASH GROUPS: ACQUIRED OR ASCRIBED?

Ethnographic, ethnohistoric, and archaeological information has been used to investigate various aspects of social and political organization among Chumash peoples during the prehistoric and historic periods. The timing and nature of a presumed shift from social status based prima-

rily on personal ability (achieved) to one based primarily on hereditary inequality (ascribed) are critical issues in these investigations. It is my contention that secular leaders gained some legitimacy by co-opting the supernatural power of the shaman by alignment to that person. At what point in time this form of sanction came to be considered a hereditary quality of chiefly persons remains to be identified, as well as do the particular factors that may have influenced such an ideological shift.

As Kehoe (2000:69) notes, anxious people who seek someone more capable than they believe themselves to be may find similarities between ritual practitioners and secular leaders, particularly in the notion that each has extraordinary powers (see also Aldenderfer 1993). "The common ascription of charisma to persons willing to make the effort to lead and help their fellows may be couched in terms of drawing upon spiritual power, or upon unusual intelligence" (Kehoe 2000:69).

Opportunistic or self-interested individuals who do not have direct access to supernatural power may try to co-opt someone else's, and the often-ambivalent feelings about the shaman can be exploited by such persons. The shaman has powerful (if not always positive) esteem in the community based on his or her ability to heal and to maintain the cosmological order. In such a scenario the almost entirely positive regard for the chief is backed up by the fear of the shaman. An array of ethnographic data from California describes just such circumstances (see Bean 1976a, 1976b, 1992; Bean and Vane 1992a, 1992b; Blackburn 1976). Among the Chumash during the contact period, it was widely believed that an executioner or "poisoner" was appointed from among the ranks of the 'antap. Although the identity of this individual, referred to as the "master of herbs and keeper of poisons" (*'altip'atišwin*), was a closely guarded secret, he or she could be distinguished by specific actions during large mourning ceremonies (Blackburn 1976:237–238). It was thought that rival chiefs would target each other for poisoning and that a wealthy man would begin to be poisoned some months before the mourning ceremony. The poisoner had the prerogative of ransoming the man for a cure or allowing him to die. If the latter occurred, the poisoner received a percentage of "the gate" from the chief at the subsequent mourning ceremony. This is a prime example of social control. Whether or not the poisoner frequently (or ever) killed someone is irrelevant; the belief that this person could do so "provided a chief with indirect coercive abilities that undoubtedly augmented his political power significantly" (Blackburn 1976:237–238; see also Arnold 1996a:6–7; 1996b:61–62; Bender 1989).

How and when does a chief form what Anna Gayton called the "unholy alliance" with the shaman? Gayton (1976:377) notes that among the Yokuts and Western Mono the chief was the ceremonial leader, despite the presence of shamans. Further, major ceremonies were actually underwritten by the community at large. When the chief puts the shaman "on the payroll," at least partially subsidizing the person, the chief appropriates or aligns himself/herself with the supernatural power of the shaman. Chumash specialists such as singers and dancers were "kept on a steady salary by the chief," at least partially legitimizing the chief's position (Blackburn 1976:237).

ARCHAEOLOGICAL IMPLICATIONS

How do we excavate an ideology or a language? As archaeologists we need to develop material correlates for these concepts that seem rather intangible. A number of researchers have noted that the effective promulgation of a ruling ideology must be materialized in widely witnessed ceremonial events and publicly displayed symbolic objects (DeMarrais et al. 1996; Earle 1997: 143–192). Ceremonial paraphernalia materializes ideology and communicates a standardized message among large audiences simultaneously and potentially over great distances sequentially

(Earle 1997:154–155). Elsewhere I have discussed similar concepts with regard to mourning ceremonialism as mechanisms that integrated Chumash groups at the local and regional levels (Hollimon 2001b). Analogous principles can be employed in our understanding of the roles played by ritual practitioners in various forms of ceremonialism, from the "medical" practice of an individual shaman to the regional integration of 'antap ceremonialism (Figure 4.1). Therefore, it should be possible to examine material objects and ceremonial structures in the archaeological record that may provide insight about the timing and nature of these shifts in ideology.

Innovative approaches to these tasks have recently been employed by archaeologists who study evidence of shamanic systems in the past. For example, excavations of megalithic structures in Europe and North America have examined the possible social implications of ritual behavior that may have taken place in these structures (Gulløv and Appelt 2001; Watson 2001). In an analysis of the acoustic properties of a Neolithic structure in Britain, Watson (2001: 180) notes that the use and control of sound not only separates an audience from performers or participants but also promotes the endurance of ritual procedures by minimizing the opportunity for aural interruption (see also Schafer 1993:36).

The use of sound and ritual space by Chumash groups could also be explored. As Corbett (1999) has demonstrated, a major factor in the standardization of the deer tibia whistle in Chumash prehistory was to increase its sonic potential. The human psychological responses to sounds could be compared cross-culturally to suggest some possible uses in ritual settings. At a minimum we can infer that the whistles were

Figure 4.1. Spectrum of Ceremonial Integration

Less integrated		More integrated
individual shaman	'aqi	'antap society
healing local patients	village burials	periodic mourning ceremony
local practice	local practice, possible extravillage practice	regional in scale

important in ritual contexts, given that only initiated 'antap could enter the ceremonial enclosure (siliyik in Ventureño Chumash, naxayilkiš in Barbareño and Ineseño Chumash) where the whistles were principally employed. If part of the demonstration of power exists in large ceremonial displays, then why would the 'antap assemble people just to have them stand outside the ceremonial enclosure? They could use sound, and the power of restricting visual access to knowledge, reinforcing their social distance from the common people, who were called 'emechesh. According to a twentieth-century ethnographic consultant, "the 'antap do not like the 'emechesh, for the 'emechesh will learn the secrets of their mysteries" (quoted in Hudson et al. 1981:19). Similarly, the tomol (plank canoe) builders restricted access to manufacturing information along the same lines as the 'antap (Hudson et al. 1978:40).

Another archaeological correlate of large-scale ceremonialism is the dance floor or ceremonial ground ('aqiwil in Ventureño Chumash, niwmu' in Barbareño Chumash, and 'axiwil in Ineseño Chumash [Hudson and Blackburn 1986: 50]). An analysis of possible archaeological examples of dance floors and their dimensions might shed light on the number of participants and audiences. This could serve as a proxy estimate of the size and level of integration of various ceremonies, especially those that were recorded ethnohistorically and ethnographically as large, intercommunity rituals (see Hollimon 2001b; Corbett, this volume).

I have suggested elsewhere that a possible template for later forms of occupational specialization could be found among the guild of undertakers, or 'aqi (Hollimon 2000; contra Flynn and Laderman 1994). Coordination of undertaking activity most likely happened earlier than other organized occupational specializations that were tied to locally available resources, and 'aqi may have had a specific supernatural sanction involving nonreproductive sexuality. The formal craft guilds, such as the "Brotherhood of the Tomol," apparently formed late in the prehistory of the Chumash peoples. Our examinations of archaeological features, such as ritual enclosures, cemeteries, and shrines, and of mate-

rial culture, such as ceremonial paraphernalia, will undoubtedly shed light on the nature and timing of significant ideological shifts among these groups. Future research should focus on the intersections of secular political leadership, hereditary inequality, and ideological reinforcement in the form of ceremonial activities. A better understanding of these relationships will benefit our interpretations of the archaeological record of these peoples.

In foraging societies there is inequality in access to ritual knowledge. "In many such societies the transmission of ritual 'knowledge' and control over it through initiation and other rites are one of the main social focuses of the people concerned. In fact, the control of cultural transmission of such knowledge is often the only legitimate locus for the generation of inequality among the members of forager societies, not the material goods or food with which anthropologists have been so obsessed. Furthermore, in some contexts such control is actually hereditary, again in complete contrast to what are usually asserted as the key characteristics of forager societies" (Shennan 1996:369).

REFERENCES CITED

Aldenderfer, M.
1993   Ritual, Hierarchy, and Change in Foraging Societies. *Journal of Anthropological Archaeology* 12:1–40.

Applegate, R. B.
1975   The Datura Cult among the Chumash. *Journal of California Anthropology* 2(1):7–17.
1978   *'Atišwin: The Dream Helper in South-Central California.* Anthropological Papers, No. 13. Ballena Press, Ramona, California.

Arnold, J. E.
1987   *Craft Specialization in the Prehistoric Channel Islands, California.* University of California Press, Berkeley.
1996a   Understanding the Evolution of Intermediate Societies. In *Emergent Complexity: The Evolution of Intermediate Societies*, edited by J. E. Arnold, pp. 1–12. International Monographs in Prehistory, Ann Arbor, Michigan.
1996b   Organizational Transformations: Power and Labor among Complex Hunter-Gather-

ers and Other Intermediate Societies. In *Emergent Complexity: The Evolution of Intermediate Societies*, edited by J. E. Arnold, pp. 59–73. International Monographs in Prehistory, Ann Arbor, Michigan.

2001   Social Evolution and the Political Economy in the Northern Channel Islands. In *The Origins of a Pacific Coast Chiefdom: The Chumash of the Channel Islands*, edited by J. E. Arnold, pp. 287–296. University of Utah Press, Salt Lake City.

Baker, J. R.
1994   The Old Woman and Her Gifts: Pharmacological Bases of the Chumash Use of *Datura*. *Curare* 17(2):253–276.

Barnes, B.
1988   *The Nature of Power*. Polity, Cambridge.

Bean, L. J.
1976a   Social Organization in Native California. In *Native Californians: A Theoretical Retrospective*, edited by L. J. Bean and T. C. Blackburn, pp. 99–123. Ballena Press, Socorro, New Mexico.

1976b   Power and Its Applications in Native California. In *Native Californians: A Theoretical Retrospective*, edited by L. J. Bean and T. C. Blackburn, pp. 407–420. Ballena Press, Socorro, New Mexico.

1992   California Indian Shamanism and Folk Curing. In *California Indian Shamanism*, edited by L. J. Bean, pp. 53–65. Ballena Press, Menlo Park, California.

Bean, L. J., and S. B. Vane
1992a   The Shamanic Experience. In *California Indian Shamanism*, edited by L. J. Bean, pp. 7–19. Ballena Press, Menlo Park, California.

1992b   California Religious Systems and Their Transformations. In *California Indian Shamanism*, edited by L. J. Bean, pp. 33–51. Ballena Press, Menlo Park, California.

Bender, B.
1989   The Roots of Inequality. In *Domination and Resistance*, edited by D. Miller, M. Rowlands, and C. Tilley, pp. 83–95. Unwin Hyman, London.

Benson, A., and L. Sehgal
1987   The Light at the End of the Tunnel. In *Rock Art Papers*, Vol. 5, edited by K. Hedges, pp.

1–16. San Diego Museum of Man, San Diego, California.

Blackburn, T. C.
1975   *December's Child: A Book of Chumash Oral Narratives*. University of California Press, Berkeley.

1976   Ceremonial Integration and Social Interaction in Aboriginal California. In *Native Californians: A Theoretical Retrospective*, edited by L. J. Bean and T. C. Blackburn, pp. 225–243. Ballena Press, Socorro, New Mexico.

Chadwick, N. K.
1942   *Poetry and Prophecy*. Cambridge University Press, Cambridge, UK.

Conkey, M. W.
2001   Hunting for Images, Gathering Up Meanings: Art for Life in Hunting-Gathering Societies. In *Hunter-Gatherers: An Interdisciplinary Perspective*, edited by C. Panter-Brick, R. H. Layton, and P. Rowley-Conwy, pp. 267–291. Cambridge University Press, Cambridge, UK.

Corbett, R.
1999   Chumash Bone Whistles and Flutes. Unpublished Master's thesis, Department of Anthropology, University of California, Los Angeles.

DeMarrais, E., L. J. Castillo, and T. Earle
1996   Ideology, Materialization, and Power Strategies. *Current Anthropology* 37:15–31.

Du Bois, C.
1935   Wintu Ethnography. *University of California Publications in American Archaeology and Ethnology* 36(1).

Earle, T.
1997   *How Chiefs Come to Power: The Political Economy in Prehistory*. Stanford University Press, Stanford, California.

Edberg, B.
1985   Shamans and Chiefs: Visions of the Future. In *Earth and Sky*, edited by A. Benson and T. Hoskinson, pp. 65–92. Slo'w Press, Thousand Oaks, California.

Eliade, M.
1964   *Shamanism: Archaic Techniques of Ecstasy*. Princeton University Press, Princeton, New Jersey.

Flynn, J. P., and G. Laderman
1994 Purgatory and the Powerful Dead: A Case Study of Native American Repatriation. *Religion and American Culture* 4(1):51–75.

Garvin, G.
1978 Shamans and Rock Art Symbols. In *Four Rock Art Studies*, edited by C. W. Clewlow, pp. 65–87. Ballena Press, Socorro, New Mexico.

Gayton, A. H.
1928 The Narcotic Plant Datura in Aboriginal American Culture. Unpublished Ph.D. dissertation, University of California, Berkeley.
1948 Yokuts and Western Mono Ethnography. *Anthropological Records* 10(1–2):1–302. University of California, Berkeley.
1976 Yokuts-Mono Chiefs and Shamans. In *Native Californians: A Theoretical Retrospective*, edited by L. J. Bean and T. C. Blackburn, pp. 175–223. Ballena Press, Socorro, New Mexico.

Green, T. M.
1999 Spanish Missions and Native Religions: Contact, Conflict, and Convergence. Unpublished Ph.D. dissertation, Archaeology Program, University of California, Los Angeles.

Grim, J. A.
1983 *The Shaman: Patterns of Siberian and Ojibway Healing*. University of Oklahoma Press, Norman.

Gulløv, H. C., and M. Appelt
2001 Social Bonding and Shamanism among Late Dorset Groups in High Arctic Greenland. In *The Archaeology of Shamanism*, edited by N. Price, pp. 146–162. Routledge, London.

Haley, B. D., and L. R. Wilcoxon
1999 Point Conception and the Chumash Land of the Dead: Revisions from Harrington's Notes. *Journal of California and Great Basin Anthropology* 21(2):213–235.

Hollimon, S. E.
1990 Division of Labor and Gender Roles in Santa Barbara Channel Area Prehistory. Unpublished Ph.D. dissertation, Department of Anthropology, University of California, Santa Barbara.
1997 The Third Gender in Native California: Two-Spirit Undertakers among the Chumash and Their Neighbors. In *Women in Prehistory: North America and Mesoamerica*, edited by C. Claassen and R. A. Joyce, pp. 173–188. University of Pennsylvania Press, Philadelphia.
2000 Archaeology of the 'Aqi: Gender and Sexuality in Prehistoric Chumash Society. In *Archaeologies of Sexuality*, edited by R. A. Schmidt and B. L. Voss, pp.179–196. Routledge, London.
2001a The Gendered Peopling of America: Addressing the Antiquity of Systems of Multiple Genders. In *The Archaeology of Shamanism*, edited by N. Price, pp. 123–134. Routledge, London.
2001b Death, Gender, and the Chumash Peoples: Mourning Ceremonialism as an Integrative Mechanism. In *Social Memory, Identity, and Death: Anthropological Perspectives on Mortuary Rituals*, edited by M. S. Chesson, pp. 41–55. Archeological Papers of the American Anthropological Association No. 10, Arlington, Virginia.

Hoover, R. L.
1975 Chumash Sunsticks. *Masterkey* 49(3):105–109.

Hudson, T., and T. C. Blackburn
1978 The Integration of Myth and Ritual in South-Central California: The "Northern Complex." *Journal of California Anthropology* 5(2):225–250.
1982 *The Material Culture of the Chumash Interaction Sphere*. Vol. I: *Food Procurement and Transportation*. Ballena Press Anthropological Papers No. 25. Ballena Press/Santa Barbara Museum of Natural History Cooperative Publication, Los Altos and Santa Barbara, California.
1986 *The Material Culture of the Chumash Interaction Sphere*. Vol. IV: *Ceremonial Paraphernalia, Games, and Amusements*. Ballena Press Anthropological Papers No. 30. Ballena Press/Santa Barbara Museum of Natural History Cooperative Publication, Menlo Park and Santa Barbara, California.

Hudson, T., T. C. Blackburn, R. Curletti, and J. Timbrook (editors)
1981 *The Eye of the Flute: Chumash Traditional History and Ritual As Told by Fernando Librado*

Kitsepawit to John P. Harrington. 2nd ed. Malki Museum/Santa Barbara Museum of Natural History, Santa Barbara, California.

Hudson, T., and E. Underhay
1978 *Crystals in the Sky: An Intellectual Odyssey Involving Chumash Astronomy, Cosmology, and Rock Art.* Ballena Press, Socorro, New Mexico.

Kehoe, A. B.
2000 *Shamans and Religion: An Anthropological Exploration in Critical Thinking.* Waveland Press, Prospect Heights, Illinois.

King, C. D.
1990 *Evolution of Chumash Society: A Comparative Study of Artifacts Used for Social System Maintenance in the Santa Barbara Channel Region before A.D. 1804.* Garland, New York.

King, L. B.
1969 The Medea Creek Cemetery (LAn-243): An Investigation of Social Organization from Mortuary Practices. *UCLA Archaeological Survey Annual Report* 11:23–68.
1982 Medea Creek Cemetery: Late Inland Chumash Patterns of Social Organization, Exchange, and Warfare. Unpublished Ph.D. dissertation, Department of Anthropology, University of California, Los Angeles.

Lee, G.
1997 *The Chumash Cosmos: Effigies, Ornaments, Incised Stones, and Rock Paintings of the Chumash Indians.* Bear Flag Books, Arroyo Grande, California.

McKern, W. C.
1922 Functional Families of the Patwin. *University of California Publications in American Archaeology and Ethnology* 13:235–258.

Oliver, M., and W. D. Hyder
1983 Meaning and Symbol: The Contribution of Social Organization to the Study of Chumash Rock Art. In *American Indian Rock Art*, Vol. 9, pp. 50–62. American Rock Art Research Association, El Toro, California.

Saladin D'Anglure, B.
1994 Brother Moon (*Taqqiq*), Sister Sun (*Siqiniq*), and the Direction of the World (*Sila*): From Arctic Cosmography to Inuit Cosmology. In *Circumpolar Religion and Ecology: An Anthropology of the North*, edited by T. Irimoto and T. Yamada, pp. 187–212. University of Tokyo Press, Tokyo.

Samarin, W. J.
1972 Variation and Variables in Religious Glossolalia. *Language in Society* 1:121–130.

Schafer, R.
1993 *Voices of Tyranny, Temples of Silence.* Arcana Editions, Indian River, Ontario.

Shennan, S.
1996 Social Inequality and the Transmission of Cultural Traditions in Forager Societies. In *The Archaeology of Human Ancestry: Power, Sex, and Tradition*, edited by J. Steele and S. Shennan, pp. 365–379. Routledge, London.

Shepherd, A.
1992 Notes on the Wintu Shamanic Jargon. In *California Indian Shamanism*, edited by L. J. Bean, pp. 185–210. Ballena Press, Menlo Park, California.

Timbrook, J.
1987 Virtuous Herbs: Plants in Chumash Medicine. *Journal of Ethnobiology* 7(2):171–180.

Walker, P. L., and T. Hudson
1993 *Chumash Healing: Changing Health and Medical Practices in an American Indian Society.* Malki Museum, Banning, California.

Watson, A.
2001 The Sounds of Transformation: Acoustics, Monuments, and Ritual in the British Neolithic. In *The Archaeology of Shamanism*, edited by N. Price, pp. 178–192. Routledge, London.

Wiessner, P.
2001 Of Feasting and Value: Enga Feasts in a Historical Perspective (Papua New Guinea). In *Feasts: Archaeological and Ethnographic Perspectives on Food, Politics, and Power*, edited by M. Dietler and B. Hayden, pp. 115–143. Smithsonian Institution Press, Washington, DC.

5

Chumash Bone Whistles

The Development of Ceremonial Integration in Chumash Society

Ray Corbett

This research proceeds from the premise that "material culture has a relevant history" (Schlanger 1994:144). If we perceive material objects as tools created to accomplish particular tasks, we can also understand ritual artifacts as tools produced to accomplish certain goals.

This chapter examines the archaeological record of bone whistle and flute artifacts from the Chumash region of central southern California. Ethnographic and ethnohistoric evidence indicates that certain types of these objects were exclusively associated with 'antap ritual specialists and were used in major Chumash religious ceremonies. By analyzing changes in form, configuration, and functional implications of these artifacts through time, my research has been able to identify significant temporal developments in ritual and ceremonial aspects of Chumash material culture. Based on ethnographic information, archaeological evidence, and replication experiments, I argue that significant changes in artifact form correlate with increasing levels of ceremonial integration in Chumash society. This suggests that ritual elaboration and increasing ceremonial integration were important sources of cultural change in Chumash society.

COMPLEX CHUMASH SOCIETY

The Malibu to San Luis Obispo coast at the time of the first European contact was occupied by a large, complex society of hunter-gatherer-fishers. At the time of Cabrillo's exploration in 1542, the Chumash were living in permanent coastal villages and were a noteworthy example of political complexity among hunter-gatherers in the western hemisphere. Their social structure featured ascribed status positions, an economic system with many occupational specializations, and an extensive regional trade network involving cross-channel exchanges of food resources and raw materials (Arnold 1991, 1992; King 1976:292). From the first protohistoric documents we have evidence indicating that the Chumash settlement system was hierarchically organized (Moriarty and Keistman 1968:12).

FUNCTION OF THE 'ANTAP INSTITUTION IN CHUMASH SOCIETY

At the center of the Chumash political hierarchy was an elite and powerful religious cult whose members were known as 'antap. Each Chumash town or substantial village had a number of 'antap members. All village chiefs and their families were required to be 'antap members. In addition, other important individuals of the community, such as shamans and canoe owners, were encouraged or required to become 'antap members (Blackburn 1976:236–237).

Chumash society is reported to have had an 'antap cult organized at the provincial level (Hudson and Underhay 1978). Presumably, it was formed by selecting representatives from locally based 'antap members. These members would be assembled together at a capital town in order to oversee and conduct important provincewide rituals and ceremonies (Hudson and Underhay 1978:29). At both the community and regional level it appears that the most important function of the 'antap cult was to organize and conduct the religious rituals and large public ceremonies that were instrumental in integrating Chumash society (Blackburn 1976: 237). Among the 'antap were certain ritual specialists who played key roles in these ceremonial events (Blackburn 1975:14).

The unique association of deer tibia whistles with the public expression of Chumash religious ceremonialism is the focus of this chapter. I also, however, examine the use of each type of whistle and flute in Chumash culture. Because the term *flute* is commonly incorrectly applied to artifacts that are actually whistles, I have included flutes in this study in order to identify and distinguish their significance in Chumash society in relation to whistles. First, I examine the functional usage of bone whistles and flutes as described in the ethnographic record. Next, I examine bone whistle artifacts from the Chumash region. I analyze this database of archaeological artifacts, describing and documenting the stylistic and functional changes in Chumash bone whistles over time. Finally, I correlate the results and other changes in the structuring of Chumash society to gain insight into the role of evolving ceremonial practice in relation to other aspects of Chumash sociopolitical evolution.

ETHNOGRAPHIC REFERENCES TO BONE WHISTLES

During the 1980s Travis Hudson and Thomas Blackburn compiled a five-volume work describing the corpus of Chumash material culture (Hudson and Blackburn 1982–1987). Their descriptions incorporate all known ethnographic references to specific types of objects. In the fourth volume Hudson and Blackburn (1986: 347–368) describe whistles and flutes of the Chumash and surrounding regions.

According to all available ethnographic and linguistic information, the Chumash used three different words to distinguish types of wind instruments. The Chumash word *towoli'lay* was the word for a flute. These were multiholed instruments, with either four or six holes, made of

a slender tube of either animal bone or elderwood. The word *'aqsiwo* referred to small, simple whistles made of either bone or carrizo, a type of reed. Finally, the Chumash word *'ich'unash* referred to a large whistle made from a deer tibia with the articular surface of the bone intact (Hudson and Blackburn 1986:349–363).

Following standard usage, for the purposes of this research flutes are defined as multiholed instruments that can produce multiple tones by varying finger placement over the holes. Whistles, on the other hand, are single-holed instruments that produce more or less one note. I will now briefly describe the functional distinctions and social context of these objects.

FUNCTIONAL DISTINCTION OF WHISTLE TYPES

Chumash flutes apparently had either four or six finger holes and were made from a slender tube of bone or, more commonly, wood. This instrument is ethnographically described as having been played for pleasure or recreation. One Chumash informant specifically indicated that flutes were *not* used in ceremonies "but at home, any time," and another said, "They were played for pleasure and for making love" (Hudson and Blackburn 1986:363). These statements are consistent with the ethnographically documented function of flutes among other California Indian groups, where they are most commonly associated with making music for romantic purposes.

It is interesting that all Chumash informants identify this instrument as made of wood. Not one account described a multiholed instrument made of bone. Yet after documenting six informants who identified towoli'lay flutes as made specifically of elderwood, Hudson and Blackburn illustrate seven examples made of bone. It is unclear whether these seven examples are archaeological or ethnologically collected specimens. The absence of examples of wooden flutes is probably best explained by limited preservation of wood in archaeological deposits, although some wooden flutes conceivably might still exist.

John Harrington's "Culture Element Distributions," published in 1942, reports the presence of *bone* flutes only for the Ventureño Chumash, but it records *elderwood* flutes present for all eight Chumash groups listed (Harrington 1942:29). Other than Harrington's trait list, there is little evidence that bone flutes were commonly used. One of the results of my research is that archaeological examples of flutes that can be confidently provenienced to the Chumash region are indeed very rare. In fact, because provoeniences for archaeological flute specimens are generally absent or very broad in scope, I could only include three flutes in my analysis, and none of these could be dated. Because of this and, more important, because of their private use rather than public function, flutes are not included in the rest of the analysis presented here.

Next are 'aqsiwo whistles. In Chumash culture they could have both secular and ritual functions. They were simple whistles made of either bone or carrizo reed (Figure 5.1). The same Chumash word refers to whistles of either material. In the ethnographic accounts, most informants identified the carrizo reed whistle as a bear-warning device for seed gatherers. Assuming that men and women were both routinely involved in seed-gathering activities, 'aqsiwo whistles of carrizo reed were probably used by both males and females. This secular use is interesting, as one of the more common contemporary uses of whistles in a broad range of societies is also as a warning device.

There is also evidence that 'aqsiwo whistles had a ceremonial role in certain dances. For example, the following description of their use in the Blackbird Dance was given by Chumash informant Fernando Librado (as recorded by Harrington): "The dancer imitated the blackbird with singing, whistling using a bone whistle.... [T]he dancers blew their whistles as the blackbirds do when they make a rumpus in the trees" (Hudson et al. 1981:84). This suggests that the sound produced by 'aqsiwo whistles was relatively high-pitched. This same informant goes on to indicate that these whistles were also used as a bear-warning device.

It is uncertain whether carrizo reed 'aqsiwo whistles were used in Chumash dances. I think it is probable that carrizo reed whistles were primarily used as bear-warning devices and not ceremonially. The citation above indicates that *bone*

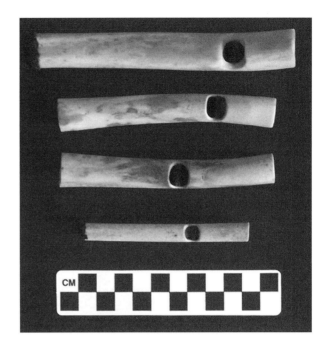

Figure 5.1. Simple whistles. Photo by author.

'aqsiwo whistles were used by individual blackbird dancers. However, in light of the fact that the same Chumash word refers to a whistle of either material, I do not think that this is an important (or resolvable) distinction for the purposes of this research. Similarly, Hudson and Blackburn note, "The term 'aqsiwo was apparently applied to any small whistle of whatever material" (Hudson and Blackburn 1986:350). In any case, Hudson and Blackburn claim that no archaeological examples of carrizo reed whistles exist, and I did not encounter any in my research.

Finally, we have 'ich'unash, the deer tibia whistle (Figure 5.2). Hudson and Blackburn (1986:354) describe this artifact as a large whistle made from the tibia of a deer. It is consistently described by ethnographic informants as made from a deer's leg bone or, more specifically, shinbone. One informant reported that "these whistles did not have holes in them like a flute. They had only two holes, one at one end, and the other at the side. The tibia was plugged with tar and the hole from which the marrow was removed was covered with an inlay of shell" (King 1982:384). This description clearly matches archaeological examples that fall into the distinctive category of the deer tibia whistle. My examination of the specimens in repositories

Figure 5.2. Deer tibia whistle. Photo by author.

clearly demonstrates how standardized deer tibia whistles are.

'Ich'unash are quite distinct from the small, simple 'aqsiwo whistle and the long, slender, multiholed towoli'lay (flute). However, confusion is rife in reference to the various instruments. Both informants and observers could be found to occasionally misapply the term *flute* when actually referring to a deer tibia *whistle*. For example, Harrington recorded the following statement from one of his informants: "MO [Magdalena Olivos] says that the *whistles* were made from the shinbone of the deer. MO knows well that it was called in V. [Ventureño Chumash] *'ich'unash*. The *flute* playing was always done by two only. They had between them a basket of water, into which they put the bone *flutes* when they finished playing" (Hudson and Blackburn 1986:356; emphasis mine).

This informant alternately calls the same object a *whistle* and a *flute*. Unfortunately, in the anthropological and archaeological literature this is also a common mistake and has led to considerable confusion about these important instruments. The current discussion should provide some clarification.

As this research is primarily concerned with the ceremonial use of whistles in Chumash culture, I now present the ceremonial association of these objects in more detail. Some Chumash ethnographic informants provided detailed information about the deer bone whistles used in 'antap rituals. Harrington recorded the following regarding the use of these whistles during a major Chumash ceremonial gathering: "The whistlers were stationed at the *siliyɨk* enclosure and always took part in every dance that was to be performed at the fiesta. . . . They had various

songs which were played according to the wishes of the *paha* [ceremony director]. The whistlers and their whistles were both called by the same name, *'ich'unash"* (Hudson et al. 1981:42).

The siliyɨk was a small sacred enclosure within a Chumash ceremonial ground. It was formed by a semicircle of poles and interwoven mat screens. This enclosure screened the ritual activities performed by 'antap from view by spectators. Only initiated 'antap members were allowed in the siliyɨk enclosure. Elsewhere it is recorded that there were no women allowed in the siliyɨk and that all of the males were old. So apparently deer tibia whistles were not used by females. Furthermore, as noted in a previous quote, the 'ich'unash whistlers kept the deer tibia whistles hidden in a basket between them when they were not being played. I suspect that this additional measure served to enhance the esoteric nature of the deer tibia whistle and the mystery and secrecy surrounding its use. It is also significant that the deer tibia whistle was apparently the musical backdrop for *all* ritual performances during these large ceremonies. This fact in itself suggests that deer tibia whistles, and the specialists who played them, occupied privileged positions in the most important religious rituals. All of these points indicate that 'ich'unash whistles were a highly specialized and prominent feature of the social ceremonial system in Chumash society.

In summary, bone whistles in general are associated with rituals, and deer tibia whistles in particular are associated exclusively with 'antap specialists in large public ceremonies. Now let us examine the archaeological record of Chumash bone whistles.

DATA COLLECTION

To obtain a representative sample of archaeological examples of whistles from the Chumash region, I examined museum and repository collections from Santa Barbara, Ventura, and Los Angeles counties. Through examining the collections of five institutions I have compiled a database of 177 bone whistles and flutes. For each artifact I recorded descriptive notes and dimensional measurements. After screening the available documentation, I selected 143 artifacts that could be confidently provenienced to Chumash contexts, and I used these as the primary database for analysis (Corbett 1999).

The geographical distribution of whistle-bearing sites in my sample ranges from San Luis Obispo in the north to western Los Angeles County in the south and includes San Miguel, Santa Rosa, and Santa Cruz islands. Temporal assignments and chronological sequencing of artifacts are based on radiocarbon dates and associations with time-sensitive shell bead types (Corbett 1999). These dates are correlated to Chester King's 1990 widely used regional chronology for the Santa Barbara Channel as modified by Jeanne Arnold in 1992.

ARTIFACT ANALYSIS

Analysis of the artifact database reveals two particularly interesting patterns. The first is that, in general, whistles increased in size through time. Figures 5.3 and 5.4 graph the average length and diameter of whistles by time period. This pattern is significant because of the relationship between whistle size and shape to sound production. After conducting replication experiments I learned that, simply stated, the larger the whistle, the louder the sound produced. This is due to both air volume and depth of pitch. More air can pass through a larger diameter whistle, and a longer length produces a lower-pitched sound. Moreover, lower-pitched sounds travel more efficiently and farther through the air. This is because sound is actually a longitudinal vibratory compression of some medium—be it air, water, or ground—and the longer wavelength (i.e., the lower pitch) travels more efficiently and with less obstruction than a shorter wavelength, which is associated with higher pitch (Terisa Green, personal communication 2002). Therefore, the observed change in whistle artifact form through time is toward increasingly effective sound projection. More people can hear the sounds produced from larger instruments, all

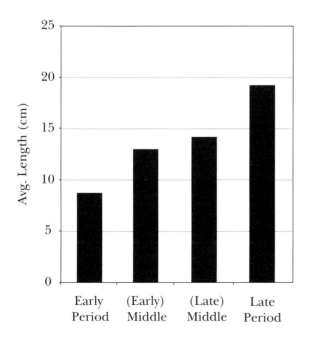

Figure 5.3. Whistle length through time.

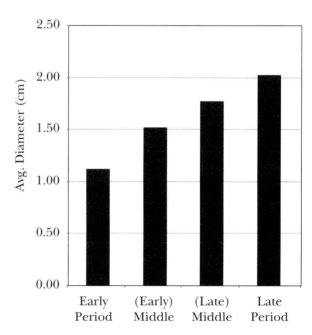

Figure 5.4. Whistle diameter through time.

Table 5.1. Artifact Size by Type

Artifact Type	Avg. Diameter in cm	Avg. Length in cm
Deer tibia whistle ('ich'unash)	2.34	23.89
Flute (towoli'lay)	—	19.75
Simple whistle ('aqsiwo)	1.50	12.00

other things being equal. So, then, if whistles are perceived as tools to accomplish a socioreligious task, whistle form can be interpreted as an index of the number of participants in ceremonial events. This evidence suggests strongly that the scale of ceremonial integration in Chumash society consistently increased through time.

Deer tibia whistles have the greatest average diameter and longest length of the three whistle and flute types (Table 5.1). Thus deer tibia whistles would have clearly produced the lowest-pitched, farthest carrying sound, making them the most effective instrument in a ceremonial context incorporating large numbers of people.

However, this increase in technological efficiency did not come without a price. Again, based on my replication experiments, deer tibia whistles are much more difficult to produce than simple whistles because of the added difficulty of removing the bone marrow from the proximal end of the bone. This is because access to the marrow cavity is restricted by the smaller diameter of the distal end and the distance necessary to reach the solidified marrow. In addition, it seems that the larger the whistle, the more critical the placement of the hole in order to obtain a clear sound.

As for the chronological pattern, my research indicates that the deer tibia whistle was developed in two developmental stages during the latter half of the Middle period, sometime between 1250 and 800 BP. It is important to note that the form of the deer tibia whistle did not change after the end of the Middle period, and its configuration remained remarkably stable through the Historic period.

This brings us to examine the significance of the two stages or types of deer tibia whistles. Temporal assignments for artifacts of each of these types are provided in Table 5.2. The first type of deer tibia whistle (Deer Tibia Whistle A) was a form with the distal end left intact and the

proximal end cut off (Figure 5.5). Leaving an articular end intact complicates the manufacturing process and was done quite deliberately. This development maximized the effective length of the remaining bone shaft and thus the effective length of the whistle.

The evolution of the second type of deer tibia whistle ("Deer Tibia Whistle" in Table 5.2 and Figure 5.2) demonstrates a continued effort toward intensifying sound production. By reversing the "working" end of the deer tibia, an artisan could effect a number of significant changes. In the first type of deer tibia whistle, the smaller distal (hoof) end was left intact, and the larger proximal (knee) end was cut off, and this was the end into which air was blown. This construction made the mouth end larger than the end that served as the resonating chamber. Conversely, when the ends were reversed—that is, when the larger proximal end was left intact while the smaller distal end was cut off—the mouth end was smaller, and the size of the resonating chamber increased greatly. This change also made the whistle less awkward to blow into and significantly lowered the pitch. Thus the development of the second type of deer tibia whistle represented a continued trend toward intensifying the sound production properties that related to effective sound projection.

Based on the data presented in Table 5.2, I suggest that some significant changes in ritual artifact form occurred during the later portion of the Middle period. The first was the development of the earlier type of deer tibia whistle. Second, we can see that the final phase of the Middle period marks the transition from the first to the second (and historically known) type of deer tibia whistle. This phase is where the deer tibia whistle proper first appears, and it is the only phase in which both forms co-occur. The tentative date for this phase spans from AD 900 to 1150 (King 1990:28).

It is interesting to note that this phase corresponds to the advent of *incipient* craft specialization in microblade and bead production on Santa Cruz Island (Arnold 1987:216, 223, 229; 1992; Arnold et al. 2001; Arnold and Munns 1994). Toward the end of the Middle period emerged the beginning stages of moderate volumes of microblade production at lithic quarry sites on the eastern end of Santa Cruz Island (see also Perry, this volume). Later the microblade industry developed into a legitimate economic specialization at specific sites, following the establishment of control over lithic resources during the Transitional and Late periods (Arnold 1987:216; 1992).

SIGNIFICANCE OF THE ADVENT OF DEER TIBIA WHISTLES

So what does this stylistic change in deer tibia whistles mean? If the development of deer tibia whistles reflected concerted efforts to integrate and incorporate increasingly large numbers of people into the Chumash ceremonial system,

Table 5.2. Temporal Assignments

ID #	Artifact Type	Site	Age of Site
29	Deer tibia whistle	Ojai	—
30	Deer tibia whistle	Ojai	—
31	Deer tibia whistle	Dry Cave	Late period
32	Deer tibia whistle	Dry Cave	Late period
33	Deer tibia whistle	Dry Cave	Late period
90	Deer tibia whistle	SBA-1279	Late/Historic
91	Deer tibia whistle	SBA-1279	Late/Historic
144	Deer tibia whistle	LAN-243	Late (L2b)
145	Deer tibia whistle	LAN-243	Late (L2b)
181	Deer tibia whistle A	SBA-72	M5
180	Deer tibia whistle A	SBA-72	M5
182	Deer tibia whistle	SBA-72	M5
75	Deer tibia whistle A	SBA-72	M5
109	Deer tibia whistle A	SCRI-257	M3–M5
113	Deer tibia whistle A	SCRI-257	M3–M5
114	Deer tibia whistle A	SCRI-257	M3–M5

Figure 5.5. Deer tibia A whistle. Photo by author.

and this in turn required increased organization by ritual specialists, then I suggest that the advent of deer tibia whistles marks a significant stage in socioreligious elaboration. This indicates that by the end of the Middle period, Chumash society had achieved a relatively advanced state of ceremonial integration, and there may have been politico-religious specialists who spurred these changes.

CONCLUSIONS

This chapter has examined the functions and social significance of bone whistles and flutes in Chumash society. The ethnographic and ethnohistoric records state that certain types of these objects were primarily used in religious rituals. Furthermore, available evidence indicates that deer tibia whistles were historically exclusively associated with 'antap ritual specialists and that they were used in the large public ceremonies that integrated significant numbers of people in Chumash society. Changes in the size, shape, and configuration of these artifacts through time increased their sound production efficiency. I suggest that the design changes over time in whistle forms correlate closely with increasing ceremonial elaboration and integration in Chumash society. Evidence presented here also suggests that significant developments in the integrative ritual and ceremonial aspects of Chumash culture occurred in the late Middle period. These immediately preceded transformations in specialization and labor organization (Arnold 1987, 1992, 2001) that occurred in the Transitional period. Thus, the results of this research also indicate that ritual elaboration and ceremonial integration were important sources of cultural change in Chumash society.

REFERENCES CITED

Arnold, J. E.
1987   *Craft Specialization in the Prehistoric Channel Islands, California.* University of California Press, Berkeley.
1991   Transformation of a Regional Economy: Sociopolitical Evolution and the Production of Valuables in Southern California. *Antiquity* 65(249):953–962.
1992   Complex Hunter-Gatherer-Fishers of Prehistoric California: Chiefs, Specialists, and Maritime Adaptations of the Channel Islands. *American Antiquity* 57:60–84.
Arnold, J. E. (editor)
2001   *The Origins of a Pacific Coast Chiefdom: The Chumash of the Channel Islands.* University of Utah Press, Salt Lake City.
Arnold, J. E., and A. Munns
1994   Independent or Attached Specialization: The Organization of Shell Bead Production in California. *Journal of Field Archaeology* 21:473–489.
Arnold, J. E., A. M. Preziosi, and P. Shattuck
2001   Flaked Stone Craft Production and Exchange in Island Chumash Territory. In *The Origins of a Pacific Coast Chiefdom: The Chumash of the Channel Islands,* edited by J. E. Arnold, pp. 113–131. University of Utah Press, Salt Lake City.
Blackburn, T. C.
1975   *December's Child: A Book of Chumash Oral Narratives.* University of California Press, Berkeley.
1976   Ceremonial Integration and Social Interaction in Aboriginal California. In *Native Californians: A Theoretical Retrospective,* edited by L. J. Bean and T. C. Blackburn, pp. 225–243. Ballena Press, Socorro, New Mexico.
Corbett, R.
1999   Chumash Bone Whistles: The Development and Elaboration of Ritual Activity and Ceremonial Integration in Chumash Society. Unpublished Master's thesis, Department of Anthropology, University of California, Los Angeles.
Harrington, J. P.
1942   Culture Element Distributions: XIX. Central California Coast. *University of California Anthropological Records* 7(1):1–42.
Hudson, T., and T. C. Blackburn
1982   *The Material Culture of the Chumash Interaction Sphere.* Vol. I: *Food Procurement and Transportation.* Ballena Press Anthropological Papers No. 25. Ballena Press/Santa Barbara Museum of Natural History Cooperative Publication, Los Altos and Santa Barbara, California.
1983   *The Material Culture of the Chumash Interaction Sphere.* Vol. II: *Food Preparation and Shel-*

ter. Ballena Press Anthropological Papers No. 27. Ballena Press/Santa Barbara Museum of Natural History Cooperative Publication, Los Altos and Santa Barbara, California.

1985 *The Material Culture of the Chumash Interaction Sphere*. Vol. III: *Clothing, Ornamentation, and Grooming*. Ballena Press Anthropological Papers No. 28. Ballena Press/Santa Barbara Museum of Natural History Cooperative Publication, Menlo Park and Santa Barbara, California.

1986 *The Material Culture of the Chumash Interaction Sphere*. Vol. IV: *Ceremonial Paraphernalia, Games, and Amusements*. Ballena Press Anthropological Papers No. 30. Ballena Press/Santa Barbara Museum of Natural History Cooperative Publication, Menlo Park and Santa Barbara, California.

1987 *The Material Culture of the Chumash Interaction Sphere*. Vol. V: *Manufacturing Processes, Metrology, and Trade*. Ballena Press Anthropological Papers No. 31. Ballena Press/Santa Barbara Museum of Natural History Cooperative Publication, Menlo Park and Santa Barbara, California.

Hudson, T., T. C. Blackburn, R. Curletti, and J. Timbrook (editors)

1981 *The Eye of the Flute: Chumash Traditional History and Ritual as Told by Fernando Librado Kitsepawit to John P. Harrington*. 2nd ed. Malki Museum/Santa Barbara Museum of Natural History, Santa Barbara, California.

Hudson, T., and E. Underhay

1978 *Crystals in the Sky: An Intellectual Odyssey Involving Chumash Astronomy, Cosmology, and Rock Art*. Ballena Press, Socorro, New Mexico.

King, C. D.

1976 Chumash Inter-Village Economic Exchange. In *Native Californians: A Theoretical Retrospective*, edited by L. J. Bean and T. C. Blackburn, pp. 288–318. Ballena Press, Socorro, New Mexico.

1990 *Evolution of Chumash Society: A Comparative Study of Artifacts Used for Social System Maintenance in the Santa Barbara Channel Region before A.D. 1804*. Garland, New York.

King, L. B.

1982 Medea Creek Cemetery: Late Inland Chumash Patterns of Social Organization, Exchange, and Warfare. Unpublished Ph.D. dissertation, Department of Anthropology, University of California, Los Angeles.

Moriarty, J., and M. Keistman

1968 Cabrillo's Log: 1542–1543, a Voyage of Discovery: A Summary by Juan Paez. *Western Explorer* 5(2 and 3). Cabrillo Historical Association, San Diego, California.

Schlanger, N.

1994 Mindful Technology: Unleashing the *Chaine Operatoire* for an Archaeology of Mind. In *The Ancient Mind: Elements of Cognitive Archaeology*, edited by C. Renfrew and E. B. Zubrow, pp. 143–151. Cambridge University Press, Cambridge, UK.

6

Cultural Transmission Processes and Change in Bead Types on Santa Cruz Island, California

Scott Pletka

The Transitional period (AD 1150–1300) was a time of tremendous climatic, environmental, economic, and social change on the northern Channel Islands (Arnold 1992a, 2001b). The production of beads, for example, increased dramatically in scale and changed greatly in organization after AD 1150, when craft specialists began to produce beads for exchange with groups on the mainland. Canoe-owning elites transported the specialists' wares across the Santa Barbara Channel in plank canoes. The types of beads made by craft specialists on the northern Channel Islands also changed. Before the Transitional period, bead makers produced *Olivella* beads made from the wall portion of the *Olivella* shell. By the end of the Transitional period, however, craft specialists made most *Olivella* beads from the callus portion of the *Olivella* shell. Changes in the scale and organization of bead production are reasonably well understood, as discussed below. In this chapter I focus on why the popularity of wall beads declined and the popularity of callus beads increased. This change is not as well understood. Many different processes could have caused changes in artifact frequencies. This chapter is intended to contribute to a growing body of theory on how different mechanisms of cultural transmission affect artifact frequencies, as well as to explore why bead makers in the northern Channel Islands made different types of beads.

AN EXAMPLE: BEAD PRODUCTION AT SCRI-191

Located at the western end of Santa Cruz Island, SCRI-191 is one of the few Santa Cruz Island sites to have been occupied from the late Middle period through the Late period (Arnold 2001a). The site lies on a low marine terrace near the mouth of Cañada Cervada Creek, one of the most important sources of fresh water on the island. The poor environmental conditions of the Transitional period disrupted settlement at many island sites. Occupation persisted only at those sites, such as SCRI-191, located near permanent and reliable water sources. Modern excavations at SCRI-191 focused on the deeper and denser deposits located in its southernmost third (Arnold 2001a). These excavated deposits provide a rare glimpse at the pace of changes in bead production.

Figure 6.1 and Table 6.1 show the changes in the proportion of *Olivella* wall and callus bead blanks and beads-in-production observed at this site. These data derive from Table 4.9 in Arnold and Graesch (2001), which reports the observed frequencies of bead blanks, beads-in-production, and finished beads for one excavated 1-x-1-m unit, labeled 35S, 3W. Bead blanks and beads-in-production are forms produced during the earlier stages in the *Olivella* bead production sequence. Their combined frequency in the

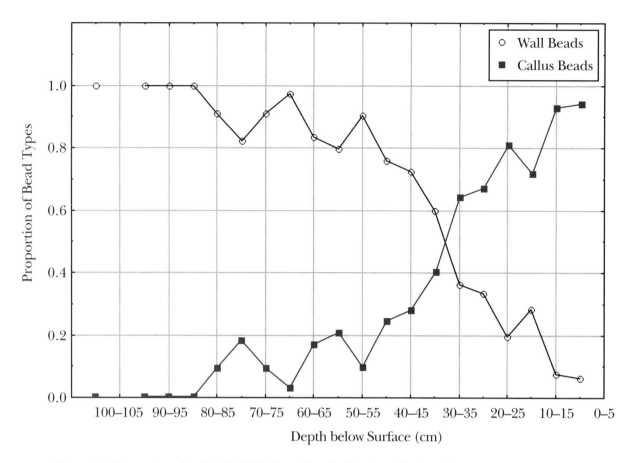

Figure 6.1. Proportion of unfinished *Olivella* wall and callus beads by level from Unit 35S, 3W at SCRI-191.

midden deposits from SCRI-191 provides an index of local bead production. The number of finished *Olivella* beads can be taken as an index of local bead consumption. The frequency with which *Olivella* wall beads were produced declined steadily during the period of occupation at SCRI-191, while the frequency of *Olivella* callus bead production increased. Although the sample sizes are much smaller, auger samples taken from various locations at the site depict trends similar to those from the unit excavation data.

Tivela stultorum, the Pismo clam, is the only other shellfish species from which beads were made with any appreciable regularity at SCRI-191. Although the production evidence for *Olivella* wall and callus beads demonstrates that these bead types have quite distinct histories at SCRI-191, I want to ignore these differences for a moment to highlight the pattern of change in

Tivela stultorum disk bead production. Figure 6.2 shows changes in the proportions of *Olivella* bead blanks and beads-in-production (including both wall and callus beads) and *Tivela stultorum* disk bead blanks and beads-in-production. Table 6.1 presents the raw data used to make this figure.

These data derive from Table 4.20 in Arnold and Graesch (2001). The number of *Tivela* beads recovered from these deposits is much lower than the number of *Olivella* beads. Comparisons that employ *Tivela* beads must be regarded as tentative, since the observed patterns of *Tivela* beads are subject to the possible effects of sampling error. *Tivela* beads are, nevertheless, second in frequency only to *Olivella* beads in the deposits from Unit 35S, 3W.

The observed changes in the proportion of unfinished *Tivela* disk beads (Figure 6.2) provide a useful contrast with the observed changes in

Table 6.1. Counts of Artifacts by Level from Unit 35S, 3W at SCRI-191

Level (cm)	Period	Unfinished Olivella Beads		Finished Olivella Beads		Tivela Disk Beads		Microdrills	
		Wall	Callus	Wall	Callus	Unfinished	Finished	Trapezoidal	Triangular
105–110	Middle	1	0	1	0	0	0	0	0
100–105	Middle	0	0	0	0	0	0	0	0
95–100	Middle	2	0	0	0	0	0	0	0
90–95	Middle	8	0	0	0	0	0	0	0
85–90	Middle	5	0	3	0	0	0	0	0
80–85	Middle	10	1	2	0	1	0	2	0
75–80	Middle	23	5	2	0	1	0	0	0
70–75	Middle	30	3	1	0	0	0	3	1
65–70	Middle	35	1	13	0	0	0	6	1
60–65	Middle	45	9	14	0	0	0	7	2
55–60	Middle	39	10	18	0	0	0	13	2
50–55	Middle	19	2	5	0	1	0	19	5
45–50	Transitional	75	24	6	4	1	1	95	34
40–45	Transitional	139	53	5	3	5	0	108	48
35–40	Transitional-Late	90	60	2	7	8	0	82	84
30–35	Late	43	76	6	1	25	1	19	131
25–30	Late	26	52	0	9	14	0	24	128
20–25	Late	14	58	0	9	11	0	4	79
15–20	Late	27	68	1	9	1	0	10	99
10–15	Late	3	37	2	3	2	0	1	18
5–10	Late	2	30	3	1	0	0	1	19
0–5	Late	0	0	0	0	0	0	2	12

Note: Data for beads from SCRI-191 were taken from Arnold and Graesch (2001:Tables 4.9, 4.20). Data for microdrills came from a database maintained in the Channel Islands Laboratory, Cotsen Institute of Archaeology, UCLA, and are used with the permission of Jeanne Arnold.

the proportion of unfinished Olivella bead types (Figure 6.1). The proportion of the Tivela beads does not change in the same fashion as the proportion of Olivella wall or callus beads. Distinct processes may thus be responsible for the manner in which the proportion of unfinished Olivella and Tivela beads varied through time. The question remains as to what those processes might have been. Overall, however, bead makers produced greater total numbers of both Olivella beads and Tivela beads during the Transitional period at SCRI-191 than they had previously, and such changes in bead production are easier to explain.

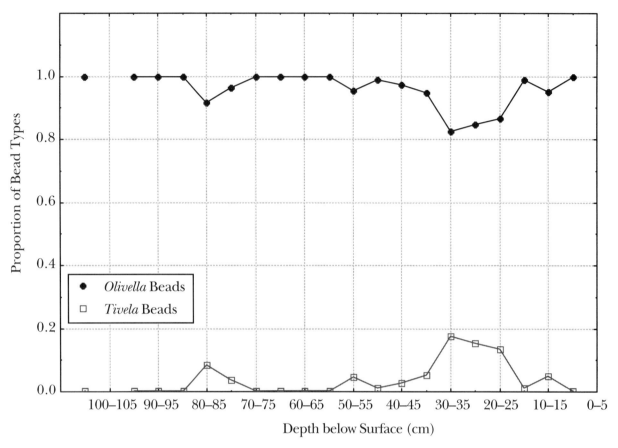

Figure 6.2. Proportion of unfinished *Olivella* beads (including wall and callus types) and unfinished *Tivela* disk beads from Unit 35S, 3W at SCRI-191.

THE ORGANIZATION OF THE CHUMASH ECONOMY

Prior to AD 1150, in the Middle period, shell bead and lithic tool production were relatively unspecialized (Arnold 1987, 1990; Arnold and Graesch 2001; Preziosi 2001). On the islands during the Middle period, bead making occurred on a scale only somewhat greater than that of the mainland (Arnold 1987, 1990). Economic activities on the whole were relatively uncoordinated (Pletka 2001).

Between AD 1150 and 1300, drought and changing sea temperatures stressed the population of Santa Cruz Island (Arnold and Tissot 1993; cf. Kennett and Kennett 2000). Islanders were especially vulnerable to these environmental changes because of the more limited array of plant foods and terrestrial game on the islands

and inhabitants' greater reliance on marine resources. Evidence for increased disease, malnutrition, and violence on the islands during this period attests to the effects of poorer environmental conditions (Lambert 1993, 1994; Lambert and Walker 1991; Walker 1986, 1989). Many island households apparently responded to their changing circumstances by specializing in the production of beads or other goods and by becoming involved in intensive mainland-island trade. The scale of bead making at SCRI-191 during the Transitional period—as measured by the density of bead blanks and beads-in-production—was an order of magnitude greater than the scale of bead making there during the Middle period (Arnold and Graesch 2001).

Bead consumption at this site did not increase at the same rate, however (Figure 6.3). Recall that the amount of finished beads pro-

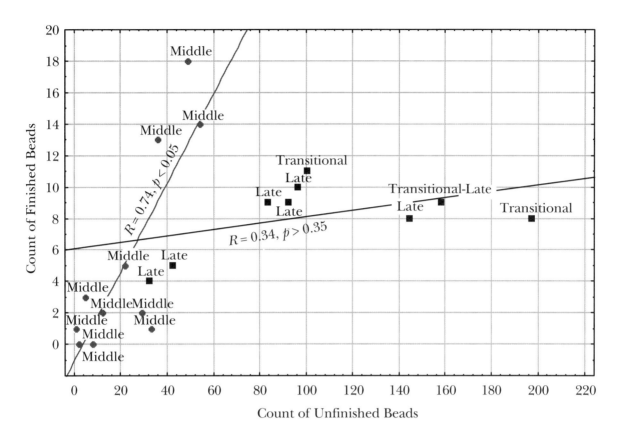

Figure 6.3. Relationship between the count of unfinished and finished *Olivella* and *Tivela* beads by level from Unit 35S, 3W at SCRI-191. Note that several levels had no data and so are not represented in this analysis. The graph shows two "best-fit" lines: one for Middle period levels and one for levels that postdate the Middle period. Statistical results depicted on the graph are for Spearman rank order correlation analyses, conducted separately for the Middle period and post-Middle period levels.

vides a measure of bead consumption. In the excavated deposits at SCRI-191 the number of finished *Olivella* and *Tivela* beads does not increase as rapidly through time as the increase in unfinished beads. A Spearman rank order correlation between the number of finished *Olivella* and *Tivela* beads and the number of unfinished *Olivella* and *Tivela* beads for all the levels from Unit 35S, 3W at SCRI-191 shows a modest but significant correlation between the two variables ($r = 0.63, p < 0.05$). This analysis did not include levels that lacked finished and unfinished beads. According to this preliminary analysis, bead consumption rose as bead production increased.

Figure 6.3, however, indicates that the relationship between bead production and consumption during the Middle period differed from the relationship that pertained after the Middle period. Including just the Middle period levels in the analysis, the correlation between the number of finished and unfinished beads is higher ($r = 0.74, p < 0.05$). When the Middle period levels have been excluded from the analysis, however, no significant relationship exists between the two variables ($r = 0.34, p > 0.35$). These results suggest that after the Middle period, bead makers exported many of the beads that they produced. Several additional lines of evidence support this conclusion (e.g., Arnold 1992b; Arnold and Graesch 2001; Arnold and Munns 1994). Craft specialists produced beads after the Middle period, and in return for these beads craft specialists received goods that were otherwise difficult to obtain on the islands.

The pattern of specialized production on the northern Channel Islands and the pattern of mainland-island exchange can be explained by invoking the principle of comparative advantage. Microlithic drill–making sites were located on the eastern end of Santa Cruz Island, near the source of the Monterey chert used to make the drills. Bead-making sites were mostly concentrated on the southern and western shores of Santa Cruz Island and on parts of Santa Rosa and San Miguel islands near sandy beaches where the *Olivella* shells used for making beads could be collected (Arnold 1991). Bead making seems to have occurred only rarely on the mainland in the Late period (Arnold 1992b:135–137; Erlandson 1993) and in limited quantities.

Specialists on the islands produced those goods that they were most able to manufacture: drills and beads. Their trading partners on the mainland specialized in the production of those goods that were harder to obtain on the islands. The list of goods that the mainlanders traded to the islands in the early Historic era includes acorns, seeds, and baskets (King 1976). So the increasing difficulty islanders faced in making a living by hunting, gathering, and fishing during the Transitional period spurred changes in economic organization, and these changes seem to make good economic sense.

The observed changes in *Olivella* bead type proportions may also make good economic sense. Assuming nothing about the characteristics of *Olivella* wall and callus beads, one possible hypothesis is that *Olivella* callus beads replaced *Olivella* wall beads because the callus beads are easier to make. This hypothesis must be rejected, however, once the characteristics of *Olivella* callus and wall beads are taken into consideration. The callus portion of the *Olivella* shell is thicker than the wall portion. The callus portion is thus more difficult to drill than the wall portion. Because the callus portion of the shell is also relatively small, many more wall beads than callus beads could be produced from a single *Olivella* shell. *Olivella* callus beads require more labor to produce than wall beads. Although bead makers certainly did not produce callus beads because they were easier to make, they might

have produced them because callus beads brought greater benefits as a trade good.

THE ROLE OF CALLUS BEADS

At the time of European contact *Olivella* callus beads served as a medium of exchange. Some archaeologists have suggested that the proportion and amount of *Olivella* callus beads increased because they began to serve this important function during the Transitional period (e.g., Arnold 2001b). Callus beads alone may have served as a medium of exchange, or they may have performed this role better than wall beads. If so, bead makers presumably realized the benefits of making callus beads rather than wall beads and adjusted their production accordingly. This explanation for the observed changes in bead production seems plausible, and some archaeological data support it.

Archaeological Evidence

Bead makers used microlithic drills, made by other craft specialists on the eastern end of Santa Cruz Island, to perforate beads. Drill makers mainly produced two different kinds of microlithic drills: drills with trapezoidal cross sections and drills with triangular cross sections. Triangular drills largely replaced the trapezoidal drills during the Transitional period (Arnold 1987, 1992b; Preziosi 2001). The rate of change in the proportion of *Olivella* bead types at SCRI-191 parallels the rate of change in the proportion of microlithic drill types (Arnold 1992b; Figure 6.4). These similarities suggest that the same process is responsible for changes in both artifact types. The proportion of *Tivela* beads does not, however, change in a corresponding manner, indicating that a different process may have produced changes in the proportion of *Tivela* beads produced at SCRI-191.

To verify these observations, I conducted a principal components analysis (PCA) on the frequencies of bead and drill types found in each level at SCRI-191. The PCA used the data presented in Figures 6.1, 6.2, 6.4, and Table 6.1. Only the proportion of unfinished *Olivella* wall beads, the proportion of trapezoidal microdrills, and

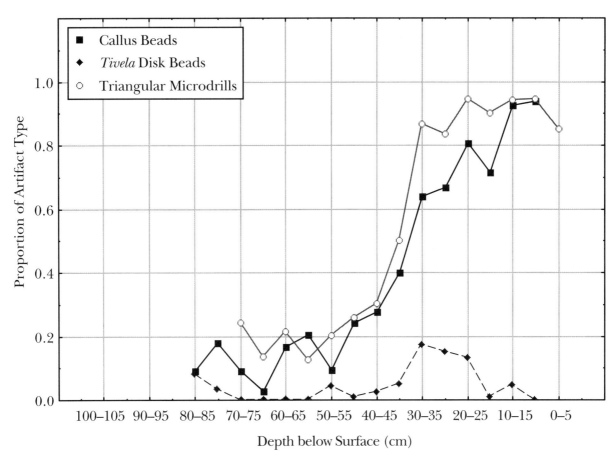

Figure 6.4. Comparison of unfinished *Olivella* callus bead, unfinished *Tivela* disk bead, and triangular microdrill proportions by level from Unit 35S, 3W at SCRI-191. The proportion of callus beads was calculated with respect to the total number of unfinished *Olivella* wall and callus beads. The proportion of unfinished *Tivela* disk beads was calculated with respect to the total number of unfinished *Olivella* callus and wall beads and unfinished *Tivela* disk beads; the proportion of triangular microdrills was calculated with respect to the total number of trapezoidal and triangular microdrills.

the proportion of unfinished *Tivela* disk beads provided data for this analysis.

Although these variables are proportions, they are not necessarily correlated with each other, since the variables are defined relative to artifact types not included in the analysis. The proportion of the unfinished *Olivella* wall beads is calculated relative to the total number of unfinished *Olivella* wall and callus beads in a level. Similarly, the proportion of trapezoidal drills is calculated relative to the total number of microlithic drills in a level. The proportion of unfinished *Tivela* disk beads is defined with reference to unfinished *Olivella* wall *and* callus beads and unfinished *Tivela* disk beads, so this proportion is not necessarily correlated with the proportion of *Olivella* wall beads alone. Thus,

the proportion of *Tivela* beads provides an additional case by which to evaluate how closely the changes in the proportion of *Olivella* bead types actually parallel the changes in the proportion of microlithic drill types. The PCA included the proportion of *Olivella* callus beads and triangular microdrills as supplementary variables. These variables contribute no data to the actual analysis, but the results of the PCA can be used to classify them.

Figure 6.5 and Tables 6.2 and 6.3 show the results of the PCA. The first factor in the PCA explains 71 percent of the variation in bead frequencies, and cumulatively the first two factors in the PCA explain 94 percent of the variation in bead frequencies (Table 6.2). The frequencies of wall beads and trapezoidal drills

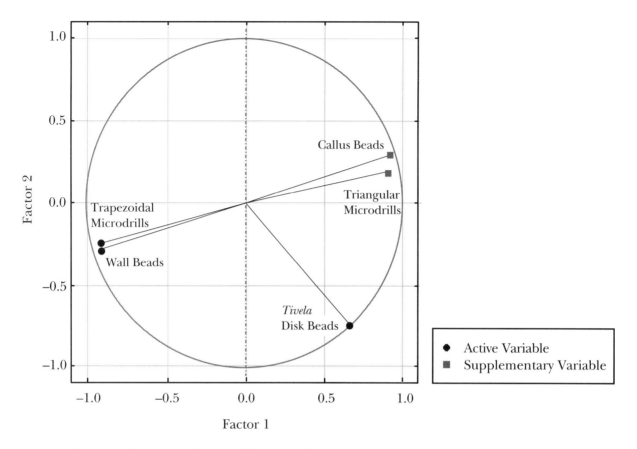

Figure 6.5. Projection of the variables on the factor plane. The proportions of trapezoidal microdrills, *Olivella* wall beads, and *Tivela* disk beads provided the data for this graph and the corresponding principal components analysis. The proportions of callus beads and triangular microdrills have been included as supplementary variables to show how they relate to the other, active variables.

score low on the first two factors, whereas the frequencies of callus beads and triangular drills score high on these factors (Table 6.3). *Tivela* beads fall between these two sets of artifact types on the first factor and score considerably lower than all the other artifact types on the second factor (Table 6.3). In other words, the proportions of callus beads and triangular drills within the SCRI-191 midden deposit increased at the same rate, and the proportions of wall beads and trapezoidal drills decreased at the same rate. *Tivela* bead frequencies do not mirror the observed changes in the other artifact types. These results are illustrated in Figure 6.5. In this figure the distance between the variables shows how similar or different the observed sequences of changes in artifact proportions are. If the same process is in fact responsible for causing changes in *Olivella*

bead types and microlithic drill types, what was that process?

Detailed studies of the production of the microlithic drills suggest an answer to this question. Triangular drills are more efficiently produced than the trapezoidal drills. Flint knappers experienced a lower rate of production errors when making the triangular drills as compared to the trapezoidal drills (Arnold 1987). The higher efficiency of triangular drill production undoubtedly helps to explain the observed changes in microdrill type proportions. As the activities of craft specialists became an increasingly important part of the island economy, these specialists employed more cost effective ways of producing their wares. This line of evidence also indicates that bead makers produced greater numbers of cal-

Table 6.2. Eigenvalues for the First Two Factors

Factor Number	Eigenvalue	% Total Variance	Cumulative Eigenvalue	Cumulative %
1	2.12	70.70	2.12	70.70
2	0.71	23.78	2.83	94.48

Table 6.3. Factor Loadings on the First Two Factors

Artifact Type	Factor 1	Factor 2
Trapezoidal drills	−0.92	−0.25
Wall beads	−0.92	−0.28
Tivela disk beads	0.66	−0.75
Triangular drills	0.89	0.18
Callus beads	0.92	0.28

lus beads because they were better than wall beads in some way. The exact advantages of callus beads may not be ascertainable, but the processes responsible for their increase in popularity may leave distinctive signatures in the archaeological record.

Like many hypotheses employed in archaeology, the hypothesis that callus beads increased in popularity because of their perceived advantages implicitly invokes a model of cultural transmission. Bead makers consciously or unconsciously evaluated the costs and benefits to different activities and arrived at some decision about what to do (Arnold 2000). To see why bead frequencies changed, we need to understand this decision-making process.

THEORETICAL BACKGROUND

Understanding how humans select among different traits requires an examination of the mechanisms of cultural transmission. Humans have evolved an extensive capacity for culture, because the mechanisms of cultural transmission facilitate the rapid acquisition of adaptive (and nonadaptive) traits. Cultural transmission allows individuals to circumvent the process of trial-and-error learning, which can be costly, difficult, and time consuming. Suppose, for example, that you had to independently decide whether to drive on the right-hand side of the road or the left-hand side of the road. Either choice seems plausible, but the best choice is the one that other drivers adopt. Picking the wrong side of the road would obviously have drastic consequences. Mechanisms of cultural transmission provide one means by which people could acquire the appropriate norm (but see also Sugden 1986). These assertions find support in a growing body of theoretical and empirical research (Boyd and Richerson 1985).

Previous Research

Some archaeologists have begun the task of thinking about how mechanisms of cultural transmission might affect artifact frequencies. These archaeologists have typically followed the tenets of evolutionary archaeology, which views the archaeological record as the result of the action of processes like selection and drift on inherited lineages of artifact types (Dunnell 1978; O'Brien and Holland 1990). Cultural change occurs as selection acts on functional variability, and driftlike processes act on non-functional or "stylistic" variability (e.g., Dunnell 1978; Lipo et al. 1997; Neiman 1995; O'Brien and Holland 1990, 1992). Driftlike cultural transmission processes in particular have been the focus of recent research (Lipo et al. 1997; Neiman 1995; Shennan and Wilkinson 2001).

In the modeling of the driftlike transmission rule individuals acquire a particular trait in the following manner (Neiman 1995). Assume that each individual in a population of size N possesses one variant from a mutually exclusive set of variants for a particular cultural trait. With probability $1 - d$ (where typically $d = [N-1]/N$), an individual retains the original variant. With probability d, however, that individual picks another person from the population at random and copies that person's cultural variant.

The effects of the driftlike transmission rule on artifact type diversity have been explored in some depth (Neiman 1995; Shennan and Wilkinson 2001). The driftlike mechanism of cultural transmission leads to changes in the popularity of artifact styles (such as ceramic types) that can produce the battleship-shaped curves used in frequency seriation (Neiman 1995). Selection-like processes, on the other hand, could produce steady changes in artifact frequencies until one type predominates (O'Brien and Holland 1992). However, selection-like processes and other cultural transmission processes may also produce battleship-shaped frequency distributions (Bettinger et al. 1996; Shennan and Wilkinson 2001). Driftlike transmission rules can create rapid change in type frequencies among small populations, causing a particular style to predominate (Neiman 1995). Distinguishing among the effects of different cultural transmission processes may not be easy, particularly when population sizes are small (Shennan 2000).

Furthermore, the driftlike transmission rule is not necessarily a realistic model of cultural transmission for many of the traits of interest. Although the driftlike rule has the virtue of simplicity, most cultural transmission probably does not employ such a rule. Undoubtedly people often adopt the behaviors and traits of those individuals in the population who seem successful. Boyd and Richerson (1985) call similar kinds of

cultural transmission "indirect bias." Critical to the success of this mechanism is the ability to recognize and then imitate those individuals who are truly successful. The likelihood that people adopt a particular trait is partly a function of that trait's effects on the success of the people who carry it. The strength of this transmission rule on a particular trait thus depends on how much the environment favors those who possess it. In this way indirect bias resembles the kind of selection discussed by many evolutionary archaeologists (e.g., Dunnell 1978; O'Brien and Holland 1990, 1992). Limitations of space here preclude a more detailed discussion of the other similarities and differences.

For the indirect bias rule suppose that each individual picks a random sample of people of size x from the population of size N, where $2 < x < N$. These individuals then evaluate how well people in their sample are doing, given the type of artifact that they are making. Each person in the sample could be assigned some number between 0 and 1 that quantifies their perceived quality of life or well-being. If indirect bias favors a particular cultural variant for the type of artifact made, those individuals possessing the favored variant get an additional value of size s added to this quantity. The parameter, s, thus measures the strength of indirect bias for this trait. Individuals should adopt a cultural variant when individuals with that trait have the highest average well-being. Although the form of this rule is quite distinct from the form of the driftlike rule, its effects on artifact frequencies in small populations may sometimes be quite similar.

Other mechanisms of cultural transmission that differ greatly from the driftlike and selection-like forces discussed by evolutionary archaeologists may also produce rapid change in artifact frequencies. Boyd and Richerson (1985) have described a mechanism that they call "frequency-dependent biased transmission" or "conformist transmission." In this transmission rule people are *disproportionately* likely to adopt the common type. Individuals take a random sample of size x from a population of size N, where $2 < x < N$. The proportion of the common type in the population is p. In the analytical model developed by Boyd and Richerson (1985) individuals adopt the common trait in the sample with a probability of $p + [(1–p)(2p–1)c]$, where c is the strength of conformist transmission. Boyd and Richerson (1985) provide both empirical and theoretical support for the existence of a transmission rule like conformist transmission among humans. In small populations sampling error could cause individuals to mistakenly identify a rare cultural variant as a common cultural variant and adopt it. The effects of conformist transmission could potentially be confused with those of drift or indirect bias.

Goals of This Study

To return to the ultimate goal of this chapter, I would like to be able to determine which cultural transmission process may be responsible for the changes in observed bead frequencies on the northern Channel Islands. This goal requires the development of middle level (middle range) theory to identify the effects of different processes. In the absence of long-term studies of material culture change among modern human groups, I decided to develop a computer simulation of several different transmission processes, including drift, indirect bias, and conformist transmission. These simulations are intended to provide a qualitative picture of how these different processes affect artifact frequencies in small populations such as lived on the northern Channel Islands. To make the simulations as realistic as possible, I have tried to design them to model the kind of changes in bead type frequencies observed from excavated shell midden deposits at SCRI-191.

THE SIMULATIONS

I simulated the effects of three different transmission rules—drift, conformist transmission, and indirect bias—separately. Each simulation included three parameters: population size, sample size, and a rule-specific parameter. The simulations were conducted at populations of size 10 and 30, which are reasonable estimates for the minimum and maximum number of bead makers in the community at SCRI-191 (Jeanne Arnold, personal communication 2002).

In the simulations of the driftlike rule individuals pick only one person from the population as a model for purposes of deciding what bead type to make. In the simulations of conformist transmission and indirect bias individuals pick larger samples to determine what type of bead to make. When the population was size 10, the simulations were run with sample sizes of 3, 5, and 7. When the population was size 30, the simulations were run with sample sizes of 3, 5, 6, 7, 9, 15, and 21. Thus, the simulations at this larger population size included samples of both the same size and proportion as the simulations with a population of 10 individuals in order to fully capture potential effects of a larger population size on the outcome of the simulation.

The rule-specific parameters varied at regular intervals of 0.05 from 0.05 to 0.95, but I also conducted some simulations at values of 0.01 and 0.025. For the driftlike rule the rule-specific parameter is d, the probability of picking another person from the population at random and copying their bead type. For conformist transmission the rule-specific parameter is c, the factor by which people disproportionately favor the common type. For indirect bias the rule-specific parameter is s, the parameter that quantifies how much better off callus bead makers are compared to wall bead makers.

Although the rule-specific parameters have been defined in each case to run from 0 to 1, they have very specific meanings. In some of the figures below I have graphed the results from the simulations of different transmission rules onto a single graph to facilitate comparison. The x-axis in these figures refers to the value of the simulation-specific parameters, but keep in mind that the interpretation of the rule-specific parameters is quite distinct from one rule to the next.

Simulating an Increase in Callus Bead Makers

Every simulation begins in the same manner. Each individual in the population makes one of two bead types, callus or wall beads. The starting proportion of callus bead makers in the simulated population is always 10 percent, because that number is roughly the percentage at which callus beads first appeared relative to wall beads at SCRI-191 (Figure 6.1). Each individual in the population then takes a turn deciding about what kind of bead to make in the next interval of time. In the case of drift the individual either picks another person from the population at random to emulate with probability d or does the same thing as he or she did before with probability $1- d$. In the case of both conformist transmission and indirect bias the focal individual takes a sample from the population and uses the sample to decide what to do. The conformist transmission rule operates exactly as described above. The indirect bias transmission rule requires some additional explanation.

In the simulations of the indirect bias transmission rule, each individual in the sample is assigned a random number between zero and one, following a uniform distribution. An amount s or nothing is added to this random number, depending on whether the sampled individual makes callus beads or wall beads. The number assigned to an individual during the simulation, the well-being of that individual, is meant to reflect the cumulative impact of all the things an individual does that might lead to a perceptible difference in his or her quality of life. Bead makers did not just make beads. They ate, slept, raised families, and probably engaged in many other economic activities. The manner in which bead makers conducted these additional activities also probably influenced how other individuals in their community regarded them. The larger the value of s, the more callus bead production contributes positively to the bead maker's quality of life in a manner that is obvious to an observer. Once a sample has been chosen and observations made, the focal individual then adopts the bead type made by the individuals—wall bead makers or callus bead makers—who have the highest average well-being.

In all of the simulations, each individual in the population applies the same transmission rule and decides what type of bead to make. Once these decisions have been made, all individuals adopt the bead type that they have chosen. This process starts over again until one of two things happens. A particular run of the sim-

ulation ends when either the proportion of callus bead makers in the population is 0 or when the proportion of callus bead makers in the population is greater than or equal to 0.93. This latter number was the proportion of callus beads relative to wall beads attained in the uppermost level of the shell midden at SCRI-191 before it was abandoned early in the Late period (AD 1300–1782). The simulations were repeated at a particular combination of parameter values until the proportion of callus bead makers had increased to at least 0.93 in 100 simulation runs.

Assumptions and limitations of the simulations. Like any effort to model the real world, the simulations provide—at best—a caricature of the phenomenon that they are meant to illustrate. This simplification is desirable to a certain extent, since a truly accurate model of the real world would likely be no more comprehensible than the real world itself. The simulations allow a few variables of interest to be explored to see how they operate. I highlight a few important points where the simulations incorporate significant simplifications.

The simulations assume that the selective environment remains constant. Our current understanding of the level of stress and violence experienced by the Island Chumash clearly contradicts this assumption (e.g., Lambert 1994; Lambert and Walker 1991; Walker 1986, 1989). Nevertheless, the simulations should provide insight as to how transmission processes like indirect bias operate under particular environmental conditions.

The simulations assume that bead makers make one type of bead only. Of course, bead makers probably made more than one type of bead. Certainly, individual households produced multiple bead types during the Historic period (Graesch 2000). This assumption may not be particularly crucial; simulations in which individuals decide what proportion of bead types to make would probably not produce a dramatically different result, although I did not verify this intuition. Such a simulation would require further assumptions about how individuals choose among various bead types in deciding what to make. I chose to start with the simplest simulation possible.

In the current simulations the bead makers are assumed to discard or lose all of their unfinished beads in the same midden. The results of augering at SCRI-191 have shown a fair amount of consistency in midden constituents and rates of change in bead frequencies across the site. These results suggest that this assumption may not be terribly unrealistic, either. Thus, the simulation results may well help to identify the processes that caused artifact frequencies to change at SCRI-191.

As mentioned previously, the simulations will be used to develop middle level theory for distinguishing the effects of different cultural transmission processes on callus bead frequencies. The exact quantitative results are not as important as the qualitative results. I do not know, for example, how strongly the environment might have favored callus bead makers during the Transitional period, nor do I know the typical proportion of the population that people sample when making decisions about what traits to adopt. Nevertheless, different cultural transmission processes may cause bead frequencies to change in distinctive patterns.

The limitations of midden data. The data set that inspired this work, the shell beads from the stratified levels of midden at SCRI-191, is a data set in which slight perturbations in bead frequencies are not likely to be preserved. The data from an excavated 5-cm-deep level of midden represent the aggregate result of independent decisions made by many individuals over a relatively long period. Thus, broad trends are likely to be preserved in this data set, but minor fluctuations around that trend are not likely to be preserved. For this reason I chose to focus on whether or not differences in such broad trends could be distinguished among the different transmission rules.

Analysis of the Simulations

I analyzed only those simulations that successfully increased the proportion of callus bead makers to 0.93. The goal of the simulations is to distinguish the effects of the three different

transmission rules. I know that some process caused the proportion of callus bead makers to increase. My hope in conducting the simulations was that some aspect of *how* they change artifact frequencies could distinguish these transmission processes. To that end I looked at two aspects of the simulation results.

First, I looked at the rate of change over time in artifact frequencies. I measured the rate of change by the slope of a regression line running from the last time interval that the proportion of callus bead makers was as low as 0.1 to the point in time at which the proportion was greater than 0.93. The rate of change was averaged for each 100 successful simulation runs conducted at a particular combination of parameter values. I chose to investigate the rate of change because it would have been most likely to be archaeologically visible in the kind of data sets with which I was working.

Second, the simulations recorded the last point during an individual trial run that the proportion of callus bead makers in the population dipped as low as 0.1 before the proportion reached 0.93 or greater, called the "last low point." At SCRI-191 the proportion of callus beads rises fairly steadily relative to the proportion of wall beads (Figure 6.1), while the proportion of *Tivela* beads drops back down to around 0.1 before increasing to its maximum proportion of 0.25 (Figure 6.2). I hoped that the simulations of some of the cultural transmission processes would manifest the kind of steady increases in proportion observed at SCRI-191 whereas other processes would not, allowing me to distinguish them.

I therefore calculated the average point in the simulation runs at which the proportion was last 0.1 or less. This point was calculated as a proportion of the total number of generations in the simulation run. I identified the last generation in a simulation run that the proportion was less than or equal to 0.1 and divided it by the total number of generations in that simulation run. Smaller values of the last low point indicate that the proportion of callus bead makers in the population stayed greater than 0.1 from an early point in the simulation run. High values of the last low point, on the other hand, indicate that the proportion of callus bead makers in the population was not sustained at a high proportion until late in the simulation run. The last low point thus provides a measure of how recently a group vacillated between making virtually no callus beads and making a modest amount of them prior to the overwhelming adoption of callus bead manufacture by group members. The results of the foregoing analyses are reported below.

RESULTS OF THE SIMULATIONS

I have illustrated the results of the simulations by looking primarily at the simulation runs with a population of size 10 for brevity's sake. With one exception, the outcomes resulting from simulations that were conducted with populations of size 10 and 30 are qualitatively similar. Where the results of the simulations at these population sizes differ, I discuss the results of both sets of simulation runs.

The Average Rate of Change

Comparing the average rate of change among the three transmission rules, two observations are striking (Figure 6.6). First, compared to the variation among the transmission rules, the simulation trials at various parameter values for any particular transmission rule show relatively little variation. Second, these transmission rules can generally be distinguished by how fast they cause change in bead type proportions. Indirect bias clearly causes greater rates of change as long as the strength of indirect bias, s, is not too weak. The intuition that selection-like processes can be distinguished from other transmission processes because such processes produce steady, directional change in artifact proportions (O'Brien and Holland 1992) is thus largely borne out in these simulations. In the case where indirect bias is weak, however, indirect bias may be difficult to distinguish from the other transmission rules.

This last conclusion warrants further discussion. The strength of indirect bias can be regarded as the degree to which the type of beads that individuals make confers obvious benefits to those individuals. As I suggested earlier, humankind's dependence on culture evolved to obviate the

need to acquire most traits through individual, trial-and-error learning. Individual learning is typically too difficult and error-prone to facilitate the acquisition of complex cultural adaptations. For these reasons I would expect the strength of indirect bias for most traits to be weak.

Distinguishing Weak Indirect Bias from Other Transmission Processes

The effects of strong indirect bias should be clear, but weak indirect bias may be more difficult to identify. When indirect bias is weak, the effects of sampling error should play a prominent role in determining the proportion of callus bead makers. Weak selection-like processes may be confused with drift or similar transmission processes as a consequence (Shennan and Wilkinson 2001). I focused on a different aspect of the simulation results in order to distinguish weak indirect bias from the other transmission processes, using the last low point results.

When the population size was 10, this characteristic of the simulation runs distinguished the three cultural transmission processes fairly well (Figure 6.7). When indirect bias was very weak, the last low point occurred quite late in the simulation runs. The last low point for the conformist transmission and drift simulations was much earlier in comparison. When the strength of indirect bias was at least moderately high, however, the last low point was the first generation in the simulation runs; the proportion of callus bead makers increased steadily under these circumstances. The last low point never occurred so consistently early for the conformist transmission and drift simulations.

Very weak indirect bias and fairly strong (or stronger) indirect bias are thus both readily distinguishable from drift and conformist transmission. The last low point for drift and conformist transmission did not vary much, regardless of the simulation's parameter values. The last low point for these two transmission rules occurred fairly early in the simulation runs but not as early as when the force of indirect bias was moderately strong or stronger. Moderately weak indirect bias may be confused with the other transmission process using this characteristic. Such confusion, however, may only occur when populations are quite small.

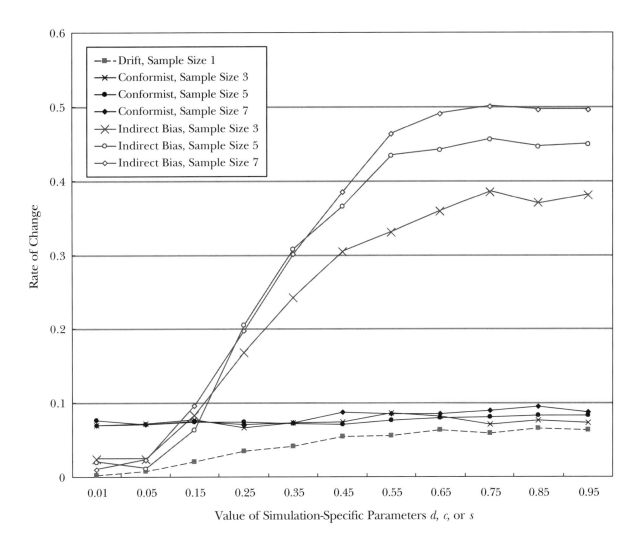

Figure 6.6. Rate of change in bead proportions for populations of size 10. Simulations at three different sample sizes shown where applicable.

When the population was size 30, the last low point was almost always near the very start of the simulation run for the simulations of the indirect bias rule, while the simulations of drift and conformist transmission had much higher average last low points (Figure 6.8). The last low point was always less than 0.02 during the indirect bias simulation runs. If the population size is moderately large, the last low point will almost certainly be a reliable means of distinguishing the effects of indirect bias from the effects of other transmission processes. Although these results are promising, they require explanation. I focus first on explaining why the last low point occurred so early for populations

of size 30 who were following the indirect bias rule.

Recall that when the force of indirect bias was weak (the value of s was low), the indirect bias rule took a long time to increase the proportion of callus bead makers in the population to 0.93 or more. Yet the proportion of callus bead makers rarely dropped back down to 0.1 (or lower) once the simulations of weak indirect bias got underway. To account for these patterns requires an understanding of how sampling error influences the expression of the indirect bias rule.

Reviewing the rule might be useful at this point. Under the indirect bias rule, individuals observe a sample of the population and compare

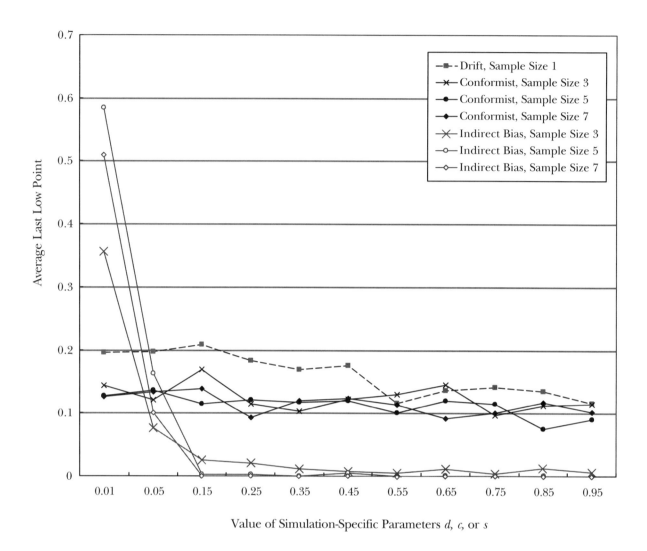

Figure 6.7. Average last low point for populations of size 10. Simulations at three different sample sizes shown where applicable.

how well callus bead makers and wall bead makers are doing. I quantified "how well" bead makers were doing in the simulations by assigning each bead maker in a sample a random number between zero and one. Callus bead makers get an additional value, s, to reflect the effect of making callus beads on the well-being of those craftspersons. The size of s relative to the random number measures the extent to which bead making contributes to the perceived quality of life enjoyed by a bead maker. In the simulation each individual then picks a sample of bead makers at random from the population. The individual taking the sample compares the average value of well-being for the sampled callus

bead makers and for the sampled wall bead makers. The individual adopts the bead type of the group that had the highest average value.

At the start of the simulations, callus bead makers are rare, making up only 10 percent of the population. A few individuals in that population, however, will almost certainly take a sample that includes a rare callus bead maker when the population is relatively large. Most of the individuals in the sample will be wall bead makers. The expected value of "well-being" for a wall bead maker is 0.5, since the random values generated in the simulation follow a uniform distribution and range from zero to one. When the sample of wall bead makers is relatively large,

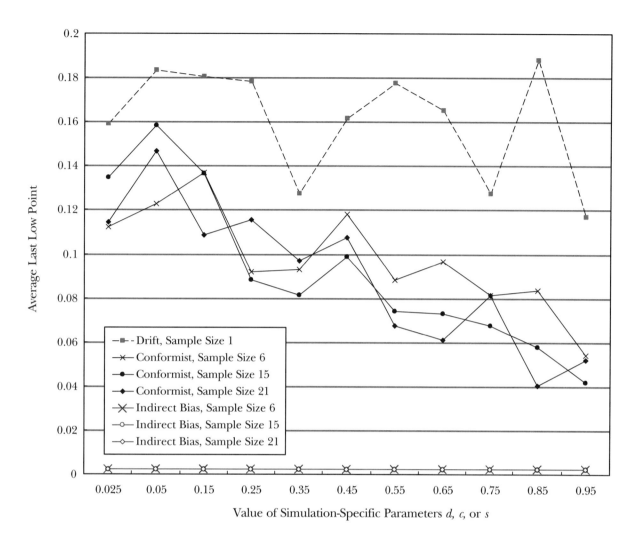

Figure 6.8. Average last low point for populations of size 30. Simulations at three different sample sizes shown where applicable. Note that the indirect bias simulation trials had average last low points near zero for all the sample sizes depicted in this figure. For purposes of clarity, these data have been shown at a slightly higher value.

the *average* value of "well-being" will probably be fairly close to the expected value.

The expected value of "well-being" for a callus bead maker is 0.5 plus the value of s. Even though s may be small, the actual value of "well-being" for a callus bead maker in a sample could be high just because the random component of their "well-being" is high. The well-being of callus bead makers could also be less than 0.5 for the same reason. Callus bead makers are rare at the beginning of a simulation run, so the actual average value of callus bead makers' "well-being" in an individual's sample should vary around 0.5 considerably. The information that

can be obtained by observing a small sample of callus bead makers is noisy.

Consequently, some wall bead makers will be induced to switch to making callus beads whether or not the advantage conferred by callus bead manufacture is very strong. The random component of the perceived quality of life enjoyed by bead makers will significantly influence each individual's decision when those individuals are comparing small samples of wall and callus bead makers. In other words, when callus bead makers are rare, some individuals may think that the callus bead makers in their sample are doing really well just because the callus bead makers in that small sample happen *by chance* to be doing really well. These individuals will switch to producing callus beads. Other individuals will pick the rare callus bead maker, and that callus bead maker will—by chance—not appear to be doing well. Individuals who have picked such samples will not switch to making callus beads. Overall, some wall bead makers should switch to making callus beads. The low sample size of callus bead makers should produce "noisy" information about them, causing callus bead makers to increase when rare.

As callus bead makers increase in proportion, both wall bead makers and callus bead makers should be relatively common in any given individual's sample. Thus, the average value of "well-being" for callus bead makers in the sample should be fairly close to 0.5 + *s*, and the average value of "well-being" for wall bead makers should be fairly close to 0.5. Although *s* may be small, it should have a noticeable effect when both bead makers are well represented in the population. As the proportion of callus bead makers increases further, the wall bead makers become rare in samples, and sampling error should play the same prominent role as it did when callus bead makers were rare. Individuals should switch between making wall beads and callus beads again and again.

The overall proportion of callus bead makers in the population should fluctuate around 0.5 for a long time before chance events increase the proportion of callus bead makers when the population size is 30. My observations on the proportion of callus bead makers in the population during individual simulation runs suggest that this is exactly what happens. In the populations of size 10, however, the last low point was quite high in the simulations of weak indirect bias. These simulation runs require a different explanation.

When population sizes are very small, the potential sample sizes of both callus bead makers and wall bead makers are generally low. Information about the well-being of callus bead makers and wall bead makers should almost always be "noisy" under these circumstances. The proportion of callus bead makers should therefore fluctuate greatly, dipping to as low as 0.1 many times before increasing to fixation. My

observations on the proportion of callus bead makers in the population during individual simulation runs also support this interpretation.

I now consider the factors that affect the last low point for the other two transmission rules, the drift rule and the conformist transmission rule. Under the drift rule each individual samples only one other person in the population. The proportion of callus bead makers will only increase if a wall bead maker happens to pick a callus bead maker to imitate. Since callus bead makers are rare at the start of a simulation run, this situation does not occur very often. The proportion of callus bead makers should stay low for quite a while, so the last low point in the simulations of the drift rule should be relatively high.

Under the conformist transmission rule, individuals compare the proportion of callus and wall bead makers in their sample. Individuals disproportionately favor the common type when deciding which type to make. For this reason callus bead makers rarely increased in proportion when they were uncommon at the start. The last low point typically occurred relatively late in the simulation runs when a chance event caused individuals to adopt the rare type.

DISCUSSION AND CONCLUSIONS

Referring back to Figure 6.1, the proportion of callus beads at SCRI-191 increased fairly steadily after fluctuating at a low proportion for a considerable period. The question remains: what process caused the proportion of callus beads to increase in this fashion? Three different explanations could account for the observed changes in bead frequencies.

In the first explanation changes in the selective environment account for the manner in which the proportion of callus beads increased. The invention of callus beads occurred sometime around AD 1150. Only a very few people adopted this innovation at first. The stresses of the Transitional period, however, drove bead makers to produce goods for exchange, and callus beads may have been an obviously better type of bead to produce for this purpose than other beads. Thus, bead makers made an increasingly larger proportion and number of callus beads. Prior to the Transitional period, processes like drift and conformist transmission influenced the proportion of callus bead makers in the population. Indirect bias determined the proportion of callus bead makers during and after the Transitional period. This explanation accounts for why the proportion of callus beads at SCRI-191 changed slowly at first and then increased rapidly.

In the second explanation I assume that the selective environment remained constant, and I make the further assumption that the effective population of bead makers at SCRI-191 was nearer to 10 than to 30. Weak indirect bias is more likely to have caused the observed changes in callus bead frequencies under these conditions. When the population size was low and the strength of indirect bias was weak, the last low point occurred quite late in the simulations. This explanation also assumes that observed changes in callus bead frequencies cannot be characterized as very rapid. In the simulations weak indirect bias changed the proportion of bead makers at a lower rate than the other processes did. Unfortunately, experimental and ethnographic studies have not yet quantified how often people make decisions about what traits to adopt and thus how rapidly change in trait frequencies can occur.

In the third explanation I again assume that the selective environment remained constant, and I assume that the effective population of bead makers was closer to 30 than to 10. Indirect bias is unlikely to have been the transmission process that caused the proportion of callus bead makers to increase in this case. The last low point occurred quite early in the simulations of indirect bias at population size 30. Some other process, like drift or conformist transmission, would better account for the observed changes in bead type proportions under these circumstances.

The hypothesis that indirect bias or a similar selection-like process increased the proportion of callus beads cannot be rejected. I favor the first explanation of the three proposed explanations. Available evidence does suggest that much greater stresses afflicted Island Chumash populations during the Transitional period than before this time. Under those conditions any ad-

vantage that the manufacture of callus beads might have conferred in exchange would have become much more salient and obvious.

In the end, however, the simulations have allowed me to advance only a little way toward my goal of identifying the cultural transmission process responsible for the observed changes in bead types. The biggest obstacle to a better understanding of how these processes change bead types is my inability to characterize the observed rates of change in bead proportions as fast or slow. Selection can often be distinguished by how quickly it changes artifact frequencies. We need better studies of how artifact type frequencies changed over comparable time scales. Fortunately, archaeologists are well positioned to develop such studies and thus to make substantive contributions to cultural and evolutionary theory.

Acknowledgments. Jeanne Arnold provided access to the data that inspired this study and supported my efforts to complete it. I benefited greatly during the formative stages of research from the advice and assistance offered by Rob Boyd and Richard McElreath. Thanks also go to Nicole Pletka.

REFERENCES CITED

Arnold, J. E.

1987   *Craft Specialization in the Prehistoric Channel Islands, California.* University of California Press, Berkeley.

1990   Lithic Resource Control and Economic Change in the Santa Barbara Channel Region. *Journal of California and Great Basin Anthropology* 12(2):158–172.

1991   Transformation of a Regional Economy: Sociopolitical Evolution and the Production of Valuables in Southern California. *Antiquity* 65:953–962.

1992a   Complex Hunter-Gatherer-Fishers of Prehistoric California: Chiefs, Specialists, and Maritime Adaptations of the Channel Islands. *American Antiquity* 57:60–84.

1992b   Cultural Disruption and the Political Economy in Channel Islands Prehistory. In *Essays on the Prehistory of Maritime California,* edited by T. L. Jones, pp. 129–144. Center for Archaeological Research Publication 10, University of California, Davis.

2000   The Origins of Hierarchy and the Nature of Hierarchical Structures in Prehistoric California. In *Hierarchies in Action: Cui Bono?* edited by M. W. Diehl, pp. 221–240. Center for Archaeological Investigations, Occasional Paper 27. Southern Illinois University, Carbondale.

2001a   The Channel Islands Project: History, Objectives, and Methods. In *The Origins of a Pacific Coast Chiefdom: The Chumash of the Channel Islands*, edited by J. E. Arnold, pp. 21–52. University of Utah Press, Salt Lake City.

2001b   Social Evolution and the Political Economy in the Northern Channel Islands. In *The Origins of a Pacific Coast Chiefdom: The Chumash of the Channel Islands*, edited by J. E. Arnold, pp. 287–296. University of Utah Press, Salt Lake City.

Arnold, J. E., and A. P. Graesch

2001   The Evolution of Specialized Shellworking among the Island Chumash. In *The Origins of a Pacific Coast Chiefdom: The Chumash of the Channel Islands*, edited by J. E. Arnold, pp. 71–112. University of Utah Press, Salt Lake City.

Arnold, J. E., and A. Munns

1994   Independent or Attached Specialization: The Organization of Shell Bead Production in California. *Journal of Field Archaeology* 21:473–489.

Arnold, J. E., and B. Tissot

1993   Measurement of Significant Marine Paleo-temperature Variation Using Black Abalone Shells from Middens. *Quaternary Research* 39:390–394.

Bettinger, R. L., R. Boyd, and P. J. Richerson

1996   Style, Function, and Cultural Evolutionary Processes. In *Darwinian Archaeologies*, edited by H. G. D. Maschner, pp. 133–164. Plenum, New York.

Boyd, R., and P. J. Richerson

1985   *Culture and the Evolutionary Process*. University of Chicago Press, Chicago.

Dunnell, R. C.

1978   Style and Function: A Fundamental Dichotomy. *American Antiquity* 43:192–202.

Erlandson, J. M.

1993   Summary and Conclusions. In *Archaeological Investigations at CA-SBA-1731: A Transitional Middle-to-Late Period Site on the Santa Barbara Channel*, edited by J. Gerber, pp. 187–196. Submitted to Exxon Company, Goleta, California. Prepared by Dames and Moore, Santa Barbara, California.

Graesch, A. P.

2000   Chumash Houses, Households, and Economy: Post-Contact Production and Exchange on Santa Cruz Island. Unpublished Master's thesis, Department of Anthropology, University of California, Los Angeles.

Kennett, D. J., and J. P. Kennett

2000   Competitive and Cooperative Responses to Climatic Instability in Coastal Southern California. *American Antiquity* 65:379–395.

King, C. D.

1976   Chumash Inter-Village Economic Exchange. In *Native Californians: A Theoretical Retrospective*, edited by L. J. Bean and T. C. Blackburn, pp. 288–318. Ballena Press, Socorro, New Mexico.

Lambert, P. M.

1993   Health in Prehistoric Populations of the Santa Barbara Channel Islands. *American Antiquity* 58:509–522.

1994   War and Peace on the Western Front: A Study of Violent Conflict and Its Correlates in Prehistoric Hunter-Gatherer Societies of Coastal Southern California. Unpublished Ph.D. dissertation, Department of Anthropology, University of California, Santa Barbara.

Lambert, P. M., and P. L. Walker

1991   Physical Anthropological Evidence for the Evolution of Social Complexity in Coastal Southern California. *Antiquity* 65:963–973.

Lipo, C. P., M. E. Madsen, R. C. Dunnell, and T. Hunt

1997   Population Structure, Cultural Transmission, and Frequency Seriation. *Journal of Anthropological Archaeology* 16:301–334.

Neiman, F.

1995   Stylistic Variation in Evolutionary Perspective: Implications for Middle Woodland Ceramic Diversity. *American Antiquity* 60:7–36.

O'Brien, M. J., and T. D. Holland

1990 Variation, Selection, and the Archaeological Record. In *Archaeological Method and Theory,* Vol. 2, edited by M. B. Schiffer, pp. 31–79. University of Arizona Press, Tucson.

1992 The Role of Adaptation in Archaeological Explanation. *American Antiquity* 57:36–59.

Pletka, S.

2001 Bifaces and the Institutionalization of Exchange Relationships in the Chumash Sphere. In *The Origins of a Pacific Coast Chiefdom: The Chumash of the Channel Islands*, edited by J. E. Arnold, pp. 133–150. University of Utah Press, Salt Lake City.

Preziosi, A. M.

2001 Standardization and Specialization: The Island Chumash Microdrill Industry. In *The Origins of a Pacific Coast Chiefdom: The Chumash of the Channel Islands*, edited by J. E. Arnold, pp. 151–164. University of Utah Press, Salt Lake City.

Shennan, S. J.

2000 Population, Culture History, and the Dynamics of Culture Change. *Current Anthropology* 41:811–845.

Shennan, S. J., and J. R. Wilkinson

2001 Ceramic Style Change and Neutral Evolution: A Case Study from Neolithic Evolution. *American Antiquity* 66:577–593.

Sugden, R.

1986 *The Economics of Rights, Co-operation, and Welfare*. Basil Blackwell, Oxford.

Walker, P. L.

1986 Porotic Hyperostosis in a Marine Dependent California Indian Population. *American Journal of Physical Anthropology* 69:345–354.

1989 Cranial Injuries as Evidence of Violence in Prehistoric Southern California. *American Journal of Physical Anthropology* 80:313–323.

7

Social and Economic Dynamics on Late Holocene San Miguel Island, California

Torben C. Rick

Southern California contains a remarkable archaeological record of coastal hunter-gatherers and emergent complexity (Arnold 1996, 2000, 2001; Lightfoot 1993; Moss and Erlandson 1995). Ethnohistoric and archaeological data indicate that Chumash and Tongva (Gabrielino) peoples in the region often lived in large villages or towns, had hierarchical sociopolitical organization, and used standardized shell bead currency to purchase a variety of goods and services. Archaeologists and anthropologists have long focused on explaining the development of cultural complexity in California (e.g., Arnold 1992; Arnold et al. 1997; Colten 1993; Colten and Arnold 1998; Gamble 2002; Gamble et al. 2001; Johnson 2000; Kennett 1998; Kennett and Kennett 2000; King 1990; Raab 1996; Raab and Larson 1997). Researchers have explored changes in sociopolitical organization by investigating human responses to various environmental perturbations, such as changes in sea surface temperature and drought, as well as changes in human population growth, declines in resource productivity, and human agency. Although the precise timing is debated, most agree that the Chumash achieved heightened levels of cultural complexity by at least 1,000 to 800 years ago (see Arnold 1992, 2001; Munns and Arnold 2002), with some researchers arguing for key sociopolitical developments by roughly 2,500 years ago (e.g., King 1990).

The unique geography of coastal southern California, including eight offshore islands and a relatively sheltered and protected coastline, along with the incredible cultural diversity of the region, provides an exciting area for archaeological studies of cultural complexity. However, a number of gaps persist in the regional archaeological record, including a dearth of research into Late Holocene (ca. 3,500 years ago to the present) cultural developments on San Miguel Island. San Miguel, the most isolated of the northern Channel Islands, contains an archaeological record spanning roughly 12,000 calendar years, with more than 600 archaeological sites and several housepit villages. Ethnohistoric records describe two villages on San Miguel (*Tuqan* and *Niwoyomi*), and in recent years a number of additional sites with Late and/or Historic period occupation have been documented. The significance and scope of this Late Holocene record, however, remain poorly understood.

Kennett and Conlee (2002) recently provided an update on the Late Holocene archaeology of Santa Rosa and San Miguel islands, relying primarily on data from column samples and surface survey. In this chapter I expand on their study by presenting preliminary data from three archaeological sites excavated during 2000 and 2001 (Figure 7.1). My intent is to provide a brief synthesis of San Miguel's role in the development of cultural complexity in the larger Santa Barbara Channel region, focusing on subsistence strategies and evidence for craft production and exchange. Ultimately, I examine the possibility that San Miguel's relatively isolated location led to unique social and economic trajectories. I begin with a brief discussion of San Miguel environments and then discuss trends in Late Holocene settlement and demography.

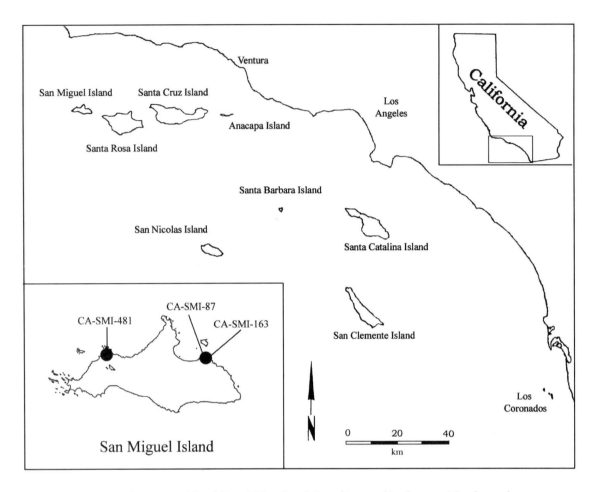

Figure 7.1. Location of San Miguel Island and sites discussed in the text. Map by author.

ENVIRONMENTAL CONTEXT

San Miguel is the western and northernmost of California's eight Channel Islands, roughly 42 km off the mainland coast. The island has a maximum elevation of 253 m and is bisected by numerous ravines, gullies, and dune sheets that cover roughly 37 km² in area. San Miguel Island has a Mediterranean climate, with mild summers and cool, wet winters, averaging about 14° C and only 356 mm of rain annually. The island is dominated by low-lying coastal sage scrub, reflecting its exposure to wind, aridity, and proximity to the ocean (Schoenherr et al. 1999). San Miguel is also home to one of the largest pinniped rookeries in the Americas and contains abundant rocky intertidal and kelp bed habitats

that provided a wealth of marine resources for people to exploit. These productive marine environments have fostered human occupation spanning the last 12,000 calendar years (Erlandson et al. 1996).

San Miguel Island was heavily impacted by more than a century of overgrazing by introduced sheep, horses, and cattle (see Johnson 1980). This overgrazing denuded vegetation over much of the island, promoted deflation of many archaeological sites (Rick 2002), and impacted the island's hydrology. The dearth of vegetation and water on San Miguel has often led to the erroneous assumption that the island is little more than a windswept sand dune.

Since the 1980s, San Miguel Island vegetation communities have been stabilizing and rejuvenating under the management of Channel Islands National Park. This vegetation recovery has had a profound impact on the island's hydrology and terrestrial flora and fauna. Numerous springs not noted during previous hydrological and archaeological studies are also once again flowing. Many of the island's larger archaeological sites are clustered around these seeps, springs, and creeks, and new seeps are documented each year. These changes in San Miguel's terrestrial environment, along with the island's rich marine habitats, are helping to reshape perceptions of San Miguel Island's ancient human occupation.

DEMOGRAPHY AND SETTLEMENT

Understanding human population fluctuations and demography is crucial to documenting developments in sociopolitical organization. Erlandson et al. (2001) recently presented evidence of Late Holocene demographic changes on the Channel Islands based on radiocarbon date frequencies. Although focused on developments during the Protohistoric and Historic periods, their data show a clear increase in human population over the last 2,000 years, with the most dramatic changes occurring during the last 700 years. Specifically, their estimates indicate that human occupation of the islands may have reached its zenith between AD 1300 and 1500 but was also relatively high around AD 750 (Erlandson et al. 2001). As human populations increased, so did human impact on the landscape, with a gradual occupation of most available land and increased territoriality. This demographic pressure had a significant impact on human sociopolitical organization in the region (Erlandson and Rick 2002; Glassow 1996).

The San Miguel Island data in many ways mirror the general Channel Islands radiocarbon curves, with the highest number of dated components on the island falling during the Late Holocene (61 percent). This may underestimate population growth, however, since as of this writing only about 7.5 percent (*n* = 46) of the island's roughly 615 documented sites have been radiocarbon dated, and Early and Middle Holocene sites tend to be much smaller. Similar problems also plague nearby Santa Cruz Island

(Munns and Arnold 2002). Of the 46 dated sites on San Miguel Island, 28 have components dated to the last 3,500 years. Fourteen of these have components dated to between 2,000 and 1,000 years ago and 13 to the last 1,000 years.

Arnold (1992), Jones et al. (1999), Kennett and Conlee (2002), Munns and Arnold (2002), Raab and Larson (1997), Yatsko (2000), and others have argued that there appears to be a decline in archaeological sites dated to the Middle-to-Late Transition (AD 1150–1300) or Medieval Climatic Anomaly, roughly corresponding with a period of intense drought. Kennett and Conlee (2002) suggest that there was partial abandonment of the outer islands at this time. Interestingly, of the 13 site components dated to the last 1,000 years, four sites (31 percent) have components that date to the Transitional period (SMI-261, -264, -464, and -468), and several others bracket this interval. Since only one of these components (SMI-468) has been tested, and analysis is ongoing, it is difficult to determine the precise implications of this trend. However, these data illustrate that human responses to climatic perturbations of the Transitional period were more variable than previously recognized (Rick and Erlandson 2001). While population increases during the Late Holocene were probably dramatic, further radiocarbon dating is needed to more accurately evaluate these developments.

LATE HOLOCENE CASE STUDIES

During 2000 and 2001, as part of my dissertation research, I investigated three archaeological sites on San Miguel Island that span the last 3,000 years (Rick 2004). Here I briefly report on preliminary findings from excavations at SMI-87, a roughly 3,000-year-old village complex; SMI-481, a dense shell midden dated to about 1,200 years ago; and SMI-163, the probable historic Chumash village of *Tuqan* (Johnson 1999; Kennett 1998). I focus on reconstructing general subsistence patterns and the importance of bead making and exchange at these and other Channel Islands sites.

Field methods for each of the sites are described individually below. Laboratory identifications were performed using faunal collections housed at the Departments of Anthropology at the University of Oregon and University of California, Santa Barbara, following procedures described by Erlandson (1994), Glassow (1996), and Kennett (1998). Sea mammal bones were identified using collections housed at the National Marine Mammal Laboratory in Seattle and the Department of Anthropology at the University of Oregon. Similar to procedures outlined by Kennett (1998) and Moss (1989), all of the shellfish from the 1/4-inch and larger fraction were sorted, while the 1/8-inch fraction is based on projections of 25 percent subsamples that were completely processed. All vertebrate remains from the 1/8-inch and larger fraction were completely processed.

To determine the importance of various faunal classes, I used dietary reconstructions based on the weight method (see Erlandson 1994:57–58). These dietary reconstructions were calculated using multipliers obtained from Erlandson (1994), Kennett (1998), and Vellanoweth et al. (2000). Shell and bone weights from presumably nondietary taxa (e.g., acorn barnacles, small rodents) were excluded from the present analysis. While a number of problems are known to bias dietary reconstructions based on the weight method (diagenesis, differential processing and preservation, etc.), similar complications also affect other methods of zooarchaeological quantification (i.e., NISP, MNI, weight). When this method is used cautiously and applied to sites from the same geographical region, it provides an important analytical tool for understanding past human subsistence. Nonetheless, these reconstructions should be treated as approximations rather than absolute dietary determinations.

SMI-87

Located on the eastern side of Cuyler Harbor, SMI-87 contains several stratified archaeological deposits, dating from roughly 4,500 to 2,300 years ago (Rick 2002). Radiocarbon dates suggest that most of the site occupation occurred between roughly 3,100 and 2,500 calendar years ago (Table 7.1). This is currently one of the most underrepresented periods in the Santa Barbara Channel cultural sequence.

SMI-87 measures roughly 170 x 270 m and is located in a series of mostly unvegetated dunes at the beginning of an area called the wind tunnel. Although intact deposits are present at the

site, deflated areas are visible across most of the dunes, and wind has heavily impacted the archaeological materials (Rick 2002). SMI-87 contains several unique archaeological features and artifacts, including large rock clusters or pavements, numerous pieces of porpoise bone, bone gorges, stone projectile points, and shell beads. The assemblage also includes the oldest directly dated single-piece shell fishhook in the region (2450 cal BP; Rick et al. 2002). The extensive rock features and diverse faunal and artifact assemblages suggest that SMI-87 was an extensive Middle and Late Holocene residential site. The site is also situated adjacent to a spring on the edge of Cuyler Harbor, providing easy access to fresh water.

Fieldwork in 1999 and 2000 included excavation of two 0.5-x-1-m units in midden areas on top of the two main dune ridges and surface collection of sea mammal remains and diagnostic artifacts from deflated site areas. The two units were excavated as contiguous 50-x-50-cm units, following natural stratigraphy to sterile sediments at a depth of roughly 50 cm. The first two units (West Unit 1 and East Unit 1) were screened over 1/16-inch mesh, and all residuals were collected. The other units (West Unit 2 and East Unit 2) were screened over 1/8-inch mesh, and only vertebrate faunal remains, artifacts, and whole shell valves were collected. The vertebrate and invertebrate remains from 1/8-inch and larger residuals of West Unit 1, with a total volume of 0.141 m^3, are the focus of this chapter. Radiocarbon dates from the top and bottom of the unit suggest that it most likely dates to a relatively brief window of time between about 3110 and 2990 cal BP (Table 7.1). Eolian disturbances were particularly severe in the upper 20 cm of the unit (Rick 2002). Consequently, I focus on materials from the lower, buried strata (1D and 1E, volume = .066 m^3), which provide a more accurate picture of the overall site economy.

Preliminary analysis suggests that fish, including rockfish (*Sebastes* spp.), mackerel (*Scomber japonicus* or *Trachurus symmetricus*), perch (Embiotocidae), cabezon (*Scorpaenichthys marmoratus*), and California sheephead (*Semicossyphous pulcher*), were the most important component of the diet at SMI-87 (46 percent of total meat yield; Table 7.2). Shellfish, primarily

Table 7.1. Radiocarbon Chronology for Late Holocene Components from Three San Miguel Island Sites

Site	Provenience	Lab No.	Material	Uncorrected ^{14}C Age	^{13}C/^{12}C Adjusted Age	Calibrated Age, cal BP (1 sigma)	Calibrated Age, BC/AD (1 sigma)
SMI-87	East Unit Top	Beta-146120	Black abalone	2530 ± 60	2960 ± 60	2540 (2420) 2340	590 (470) 390 BC
	East Dune Surface	OS-26071	Abalone hook	—	2980 ± 35	2540 (2450) 2350	590 (500) 400 BC
	East Dune Rock Feature	OS-27236	Charred twig	2510 ± 55	—	2740 (2610) 2470	790 (660) 520 BC[a]
	East Dune Top	Beta-134832	CA mussel	2660 ± 70	3090 ± 70	2730 (2690) 2490	780 (740) 540 BC
	East Unit Bottom	Beta-145425	Black abalone	2830 ± 60	3260 ± 60	2860 (2780) 2740	910 (830) 790 BC
	West Dune, Tar Feature	Beta-134831	CA mussel	2990 ± 80	3420 ± 80	3130 (2980) 2860	1180 (1030) 910 BC
	West Unit Top	Beta-146121	CA mussel	3000 ± 90	3430 ± 90	3150 (2990) 2860	1200 (1040) 910 BC
	Uppermost West Dune	Beta-145426	CA mussel	3030 ± 60	3460 ± 60	3160 (3050) 2940	1210 (1100) 990 BC
	West Unit Bottom	Beta-145427	Black abalone	3070 ± 50	3500 ± 50	3200 (3110) 3000	1250 (1160) 1050 BC
SMI-163	Top of Unit 2, House 5	OS-27183	Black abalone	—	655 ± 60	270 (150) 0	AD 1690 (1800) 1950[b]
	House 1, 25 cm	Beta-145428	CA mussel	330 ± 60	760 ± 60	270 (150) 0	AD 1690 (1800) 1950
	House 3, Auger C, 43 cm	OS-33376	CA mussel	—	830 ± 25	290 (270) 240	AD 1660 (1680) 1710
	House 6, Auger D, 64 cm	OS-33375	CA mussel	—	880 ± 35	320 (290) 270	AD 1630 (1660) 1680
	Unit 2, 110 cm	OS-33417	CA mussel	—	880 ± 30	320 (290) 270	AD 1630 (1660) 1680
	House 2, Auger B, 29 cm	OS-33377	CA mussel	—	885 ± 35	330 (290) 270	AD 1630 (1660) 1680
	House 5, 67 cm	Beta-138430	Black abalone	510 ± 70	950 ± 70	450 (380) 290	AD 1500 (1570) 1670
	Auger 2, 40 cm	OS-37142	CA mussel	—	955 ± 50	440 (390) 300	AD 1510 (1560) 1650
	House 4, 10 cm	CAMS-14365	Charcoal	310 ± 60	310 ± 60	470 (380) 300	AD 1490 (1570) 1650[a]
	Unit 3, 27-28 cm	OS-34805	CA mussel	—	1060 ± 35	500 (470) 440	AD 1480 (1450) 1510
	Unit 3, 52-54 cm	OS-33374	CA mussel	—	1790 ± 25	1170 (1130) 1060	AD 780 (820) 890
	Duplicate of OS-33374	OS-33420	CA mussel	—	1930 ± 30	1290 (1260) 1230	AD 660 (690) 720

Table 7.1. Radiocarbon Chronology for Late Holocene Components from Three San Miguel Island Sites (continued)

Site	Provenience	Lab No.	Material	Uncorrected ^{14}C Age	^{13}C/^{12}C Adjusted Age	Calibrated Age, cal BP (1 sigma)	Calibrated Age, BC/AD (1 sigma)
SMI-481	Upper Dune, East Margin	OS-33353	CA mussel	—	1000 ± 35	470 (430) 380	AD 1480 (1520) 1570
	Top of Vertical Face	Beta-139977	Red abalone	860 ± 60	1290 ± 60	670 (640) 560	AD 1280 (1310) 1390
	Eastern Middle Dune	Beta-180925	CA mussel	1120 ± 80	1540 ± 80	940 (880) 760	AD 1010 (1070) 1200
	Unit 1: Stratum 1E, Base	Beta-145429	Black abalone	1230 ± 60	1660 ± 60	1050 (960) 920	AD 900 (990) 1040
	Unit 1: Stratum 1E, Base	Beta-150317	CA mussel	1400 ± 60	1830 ± 60	1240 (1170) 1070	AD 710 (780) 880
	Unit 1: Stratum 1A, Top	OS-27182	Black abalone	—	1870 ± 35	1260 (1220) 1160	AD 690 (730) 790
	Vertical Exposure: Base	Beta-139978	Black abalone	1550 ± 70	1980 ± 70	1360 (1290) 1240	AD 590 (660) 710
	West Stratum 1, Top	Beta-139980	Black abalone	1560 ± 60	1990 ± 60	1370 (1300) 1260	AD 580 (650) 690
	West Stratum 1, Bottom	Beta-139979	Black abalone	1600 ± 60	2030 ± 60	1410 (1330) 1280	AD 540 (620) 670
	Middle Dune Complex	OS-38218	Abalone fishhook	—	2150 ± 50	1530 (1480) 1400	AD 420 (470) 550
	Southern Dune Complex	Beta-180924	CA mussel	1820 ± 50	2250 ± 50	1680 (1580) 1520	AD 270 (370) 430
	Stratum 2, 4 m deep	Beta-148498	Black abalone	3180 ± 70	3610 ± 70	3340 (3250) 3160	1390 (1300) 1210 BC
	Stratum 4, 7 m deep	Beta-148500	CA mussel	3280 ± 100	3710 ± 100	3470 (3360) 3250	1520 (1410) 1300 BC

Note: All dates were calibrated using Calib 4.3 (Stuiver and Reimer 1993, 2000) and applying a ΔR of 225 ± 35 years for all shell samples (see Kennett et al. 1997). ^{13}C/^{12}C ratios were determined by the radiocarbon labs, or an average of + 430 years was applied (Erlandson 1988).

[a]Sample with multiple intercepts. The average is provided.

[b]This date is just beyond the calibration range of CALIB 4.3. The age range provided is an estimate based on the most recent possible calibrated range (i.e., Beta-145428).

rocky intertidal species including California mussel (*Mytilus californianus*), platform mussel (*Septifer bifurcatus*), and abalone (*Haliotis* spp.), make up roughly 40 percent of the overall meat yield. Sea mammals contributed roughly 12 percent of the meat yield, with birds contributing only about 2 percent. Although only a few small, undiagnostic sea mammal bones were recovered in the units, a diverse assemblage of pinniped and small cetacean bones, associated with several large projectile points and bone barbs, was also recovered from the site surface. Analysis of the marine mammal bones is ongoing, but small cetaceans (porpoise or dolphin), sea otter (*Enhydra lutris*), California sea lion (*Zalophus californianus*), and fur seal remains have been identified. The marine mammal and fish bones, along with projectile points, bone

Table 7.2. Estimated Meat Yields for Three Late Holocene Sites on San Miguel Island

Taxon	Multi-plier[a]	SMI-87			SMI-481			SMI-163		
		Raw Wt.	Meat	% Meat	Raw Wt.	Meat	% Meat	Raw Wt.	Meat	% Meat
Chiton undif.	1.15	90.6	104.2	3.1	79.5	91.4	0.1	546.8	628.8	0.4
Haliotis cracherodii (black abalone)	0.944	228.1	215.3	6.5	953.1	899.7	0.9	2,510.5	2,369.9	1.5
Haliotis rufescens (red abalone)	1.36	42.5	57.8	1.7	1,283.6	1,745.7	1.7	947.4	1,288.5	0.8
Haliotis spp. (abalone)	1.15	18.8	21.6	0.6	194.2	223.3	0.2	311.6	358.3	0.2
Lottia gigantea (owl limpet)	1.36	—	—	—	390.9	531.6	0.5	317.0	431.1	0.3
Mytilus californianus (California mussel)	0.298	2,073.6	617.9	18.6	8,411.9	2506.7	2.5	70,452.8	20,994.9	13.0
Septifer bifurcatus (platform mussel)	0.364	287.5	104.7	3.1	161.3	58.7	0.1	758.8	276.2	0.2
Strongylocentrotus spp. (sea urchin)	0.583	92.0	53.6	1.6	958.1	558.6	0.6	467.1	272.3	0.2
Tegula spp. (turbans)	0.365	314.1	114.6	3.4	861.5	314.4	0.3	4,101.2	1,496.9	0.9
Other shell[b]	0.724	72.4	52.4	1.6	99.5	72.0	0.1	1,040.7	753.5	0.5
Shellfish subtotal	—	3,219.6	1,342.1	40.3	13,393.6	7,002.1	6.9	81,453.9	28,870.4	17.9
Fish	27.7	55.0	1,523.5	45.7	771.2	21,362.2	21.1	4,322.3	119,727.7	74.3
Bird	15.0	4.4	66.0	2.0	11.4	171.0	0.2	127.7	1,915.5	1.2
Sea mammal	24.2	16.5	399.3	12.0	2,997.1	72,529.8	71.8	443.3	10,727.9	6.7
Vertebrate subtotal	—	75.9	1,988.8	59.7	3,779.7	94,063.0	93.1	4,893.3	132,371.1	82.1
Total	—	3,295.5	3,330.9	—	17,173.3	101,065.1	—	86,347.2	161,241.5	—

[a]All values obtained from Vellanoweth et al. (2000) and sources cited therein.

[b]Mostly mussel and abalone nacre fragments. Multiplier is an average of the two.

barbs, gorges, and a single-piece fishhook, suggest people were actively hunting marine mammals and fishing, probably using boats, by 3,000 years ago. A billfish vertebra recovered from the site surface also provides tantalizing but speculative evidence for communal hunting and boat use.

Beads and ornaments are relatively rare at SMI-87, but several *Olivella* spire lopped and barrel beads were recovered. Analysis of *Olivella* detritus suggests that there are only about 75 g/m³ of detritus in West Unit 1 (Table 7.3). This low density is relatively common for other Channel Islands sites of this age (Kennett and Conlee 2002). Although bead densities at the site are relatively low, the subsistence data suggest a relatively balanced economy, with people collecting shellfish, fishing, and hunting sea mammals.

Table 7.3. *Olivella* Bead Detritus Densities (g/m³) for Late Holocene Sites on San Miguel Island

Site	Age (calibrated intercept)[a]	*Olivella* (g/m³)
SMI-602[b]	AD 1820	11,875
SMI-163	AD 1730[c]	5,510
SMI-470	AD 1600[c]	7,044
SMI-485[b]	AD 1430	5,100
SMI-481	AD 800[c]	520
SMI-503[b]	560 BC	375
SMI-488[b]	700 BC	275
SMI-87	1100 BC	75

[a]All dates calibrated using Calib 4.3.
[b]Obtained from Kennett and Conlee (2002).
[c]Date is an average of multiple dates for same strata.

SMI-481

SMI-481, located on Otter Point, is a large dune complex with an associated cave, containing roughly ten discrete archaeological deposits spanning nearly 7,500 years. Thirteen radiocarbon dates suggest that the site was occupied for most of the last 3,500 years. This remarkable sequence provides a unique case study for understanding long-term human interactions with the environment and the Holocene history of dune building on the island (see Erlandson et al. n.d.). Like SMI-87, this is one of the larger archaeological sites on San Miguel, covering an area roughly 600 x 420 m (Greenwood, unpublished 1977 site record). Two sandy coves (Amphitheater Cove and Otter Harbor) provide beaches for safely landing a boat. There is also abundant kelp bed and rocky intertidal habitat adjacent to the site, and fresh water is available in Otter Creek on the eastern site boundary and at a series of springs in Simonton Cove to the east and Running Springs to the west. The site lacks surface house depressions, but its enormous, stratified deposits suggest it was a large Chumash occupational site for several millennia.

My research at SMI-481 focused on dense shell midden deposits on the top of the roughly 30-m-high dune on the western site margin. Excavation of a 0.4-x-0.8-m unit and systematic surface collection during the summer of 2000 yielded large faunal samples, including the re-

mains of sea mammals, billfish, small nearshore fishes, and a variety of shellfish. The unit was excavated in an erosional exposure on top of the dune. It was excavated as two contiguous 40-x-40-cm units (Unit 1a and Unit 1b) in a series of five natural strata (1A–1E). The first of these units was screened over ¹/16-inch mesh, and all screen residuals were retained. The second unit (Unit 1b) was screened over ¹/8-inch mesh, and only vertebrate faunal remains, artifacts, and whole shell valves were collected. Although wind appears to have impacted portions of SMI-481, preservation in Unit 1 was excellent (see Rick 2002). The vertebrate and invertebrate faunal data from the ¹/8-inch and larger residuals of Unit 1a (0.08 m³) are discussed in this chapter.

Three radiocarbon dates from Unit 1 bracket the deposits between roughly 1220 and 960 cal BP (AD 730–990) near the end of the Middle period (see Table 7.1). Additional dates obtained by Kennett from the top of the dune extend the occupation back about 150 years to roughly 1400 cal BP. However, the most likely date for the occupation represented by Unit 1 is based on the dates obtained from the actual unit (ca. AD 730 to 990). Since these dates are statistically similar, the most accurate age for the site deposits is probably the average of the three dates from Unit 1 (see Rick 2004). Averaging these dates using Calib 4.3 provides a 1 sigma age range of roughly AD 700–900, with an average of about

AD 800. Because of this relatively narrow time span and the similar constituents in the five strata, all of the materials from Strata 1A–1E have been lumped together for the present analysis.

Shellfish remains identified in the assemblage include California mussel, red and black abalone, turbans (*Tegula* spp.), and other rocky intertidal taxa. Fish remains from the unit are dominated by rocky intertidal and kelp bed species, including rockfish, perch, lingcod (*Ophiodon elongatus*), sheephead, and clupeids (sardines or herring). Four billfish vertebrae and several barracuda (*Sphyraena argentea*) remains were also recovered from Unit 1a and 1b. This unit produced a dense assemblage of sea mammal bones. Preliminary identifications include sea otter (*Enhydra lutris*), California sea lion (*Zalophus californianus*), Steller's sea lion (*Eumetopias jubatus*), Guadalupe fur seal (*Arctocephalus townsendi*), Northern fur seal (*Callorhinus ursinus*), elephant seal (*Mironga angustirostris*), and harbor seal (*Phoca vitulina*). Walker and Snethkamp (1984) presented data on sea mammal remains from SMI-481, indicating the presence of harbor seal, Guadalupe fur seal, elephant seal, and sea lion (see also Colten 2002:16).

Dietary reconstructions of faunal remains from Unit 1 suggest that pinnipeds (72 percent), followed by fish (21 percent), provided most of the edible meat yield represented by this sample (see Table 7.2). Shellfish (7 percent) and birds (0.2 percent) appear to have been supplemental parts of the diet. Other than shell fishhooks, expedient chipped stone tools, and a few bone tools, no direct evidence of hunting technology was recovered.

Although *Olivella* wall, barrel, and spire lopped beads were recovered from the site, *Olivella* bead production appears to have been relatively minor at SMI-481, with only about 520 g/m³ of detritus. This low density is similar to other values for late Middle period sites reported by Kennett and Conlee (2002:160). The high proportion of sea mammal remains in the site raises the possibility that some of these animals may have been procured for exchange. Further analysis of skeletal element distributions will help test this possibility.

SMI-163

SMI-163, a village complex just east of Cuyler Harbor, contains at least six visible house depressions. The site was occupied primarily during the Protohistoric and Historic periods and was probably *Tuqan*, one of two named historic villages on San Miguel (Johnson 1999; Kennett 1998). Two recent dates from the western site margin also identified a discrete late Middle period component (1260 to 1130 cal BP). The site contains archaeological deposits well over 1 m deep, with abundant evidence of bead making, marine fishing, and other activities. The six house depressions are highly variable in size, and surface exposures, auger holes, and excavation of three test units also demonstrate variability in the site constituents. Ethnohistoric records suggest that one chief, Cristóbal Mascál, resided at *Tuqan* (Johnson 1999:66). Radiocarbon dating of samples from each of the six houses suggests that they were occupied primarily between about AD 1570 and 1800.

During 2000 and 2001 I excavated three units at the site: Unit 1 located in Housepit 1, Unit 2 located on the rim of Housepit 5 in dense midden deposits, and Unit 3 located on the edge of Housepit 1. Two of these units (Units 1 and 2) produced radiocarbon dates for the Historic or Protohistoric periods. Here I present data from Unit 2, a dense deposit, radiocarbon dated to between about AD 1660 and 1800, with an average of roughly AD 1730 (see Table 7.1). This 50-x-50-cm unit was excavated to a depth of roughly 120 cm, and augering indicates that the deposit goes down at least another 80 cm. Stratigraphic variation in the deposits was minimal, and consequently this unit was excavated in arbitrary 10-cm levels, with all residuals screened over 1/16-inch mesh. I focus on data from 1/8-inch residuals of levels 0–100 cm (0.269 m³).

The deposits throughout the unit are relatively homogeneous. The shellfish assemblage includes large California mussel shells, red and black abalone, turbans, and other rocky intertidal shellfish taxa. Similar to SMI-87 and -481, the fish remains are dominated by rockfish, perch, California sheephead, and other rocky intertidal and kelp bed taxa. Barracuda and mackerel remains were also recovered, and several fragments of a probable billfish beak were recently identified during laboratory analysis. While sea mammal remains were recovered, unlike SMI-481, they constitute a relatively small percentage of the faunal assemblage. The SMI-163 sea mammal assemblage, however, includes the remains of sea otters, Guadalupe fur seal, Northern fur seal, and harbor seal.

Dietary reconstructions for this unit indicate an economy dominated by fish (74 percent), followed by shellfish (18 percent), with sea mammal (7 percent) and bird (1 percent) as supplemental parts of the diet. The dominance of fish in this deposit is similar to patterns noted by Kennett and Conlee (2002), where fish in Late or Historic period sites on the outer islands often constitute about 80 to 90 percent of the overall meat yield.

Beads and ornaments are extremely common at SMI-163, and production of both *Olivella* and red abalone beads has been identified. The density of *Olivella* bead detritus (5,510 g/m^3) is roughly 10 times greater than at SMI-481, suggesting that bead production was an important activity for people at SMI-163. Red abalone beads appear to have been another important item for trade (see Rick 2004).

DISCUSSION AND CONCLUSIONS

When combined with other data from San Miguel Island, my preliminary analysis of these three sites reveals interesting trends in Chumash social, political, and economic dynamics over the last 3,000 years. To contextualize the data from these sites, I offer a brief synthesis of changes in human subsistence, craft production, and exchange on San Miguel Island.

The link between human subsistence strategies and social organization has long been recognized by archaeologists. In coastal southern California, archaeologists have correlated periods of resource intensification with growing human populations and concomitant political, social, and technological changes (e.g., Glasgow 1996; Raab et al. 1995). A dominant trend noted by many Santa Barbara Channel archaeologists is a dramatic increase in the importance of fishing and a decrease in shellfish collecting beginning roughly 3,000 years ago (Glassow 1993; Kennett and Conlee 2002; Vellanoweth et al. 2000; and

others). The ratios of fish and shellfish meat yields from SMI-87, -163, and -481 clearly illustrate this trend (Figure 7.2). Kennett and Conlee (2002) also present data from Late Holocene sites on San Miguel that lend further support to the increased reliance on marine fishing. Middle and Late Holocene data from Cave of the Chimneys and Daisy Cave on San Miguel Island also document this development (Vellanoweth et al. 2000).

When sea mammals are factored into these dietary reconstructions, it becomes clear that they were also an important resource, raising the possibility that some San Miguel Island sites (e.g., SMI-481) may have been special pinniped hunting/processing localities (Figure 7.3). The decrease in pinniped remains late in time, however, may reflect declines in the number of sea mammals on San Miguel Island during the last 1,000 years (see Walker et al. 2000). This may also, in part, account for the relatively small number of pinniped bones at SMI-163.

At least six Late Holocene archaeological sites (SMI-9, -87, -163, -470, -481, and -485) on San Miguel Island are known to contain billfish remains (see also Bernard 2001 and this volume). Given the relatively limited excavations on the island, this is a high percentage that suggests San Miguel islanders may have acquired these important fish for trade or ceremony. With the intensive sea mammal hunting on San Miguel, it is likely that pinniped parts that could be used for nonfood purposes (e.g., bone tools, oils, and hides) may have also been important trade items. Forthcoming analysis of pinniped element distributions from these sites should help evaluate this possibility. The available subsistence data suggest that a balanced economy, including fishes, sea mammals, shellfish, and birds, was important by the onset of the Late Holocene. Through time, subsistence strategies appear to have become increasingly specialized and focused on fishing, as people worked to feed larger populations with dwindling amounts of shellfish and pinnipeds. At SMI-163, however, shellfish still account for roughly 18 percent of the overall meat yield, suggesting they were an important supplemental part of the diet.

In addition to subsistence the production of craft items was fundamental to changing socio-

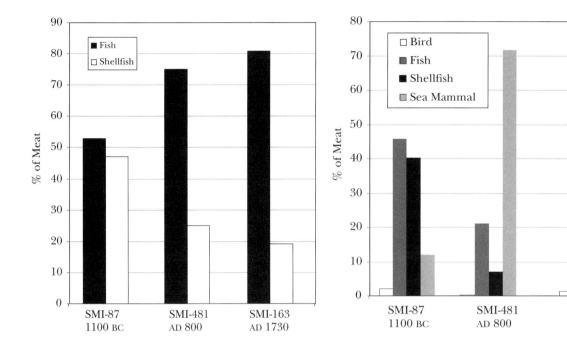

Figure 7.2. Fish and shellfish dietary reconstructions for three Late Holocene San Miguel Island sites. Dates presented are calibrated intercepts or average of multiple dates from same strata.

Figure 7.3. Dietary reconstruction for three Late Holocene shell middens on San Miguel Island. Dates presented are calibrated intercepts or average of multiple dates from same strata.

political systems in the southern California Bight (Arnold 1987, 1991, 1992). The Island Chumash appear to have dramatically intensified bead and microblade production by roughly AD 1150–1300 on Santa Cruz Island (Arnold 1991; Arnold and Graesch 2001; Arnold and Munns 1994). Beads were primarily produced on the islands to be traded with mainlanders and other islanders to acquire resources and services not readily available locally. Kennett and Conlee (2002:157–158) recently presented data from Santa Rosa and San Miguel islands that suggest bead production may have intensified at some locations by roughly AD 650, but bead detritus densities remain highly variable among sites. On San Miguel current data indicate that microblades were never produced in the same abundance as on Santa Cruz Island, but production of *Olivella* and red abalone beads was relatively intensive at certain localities. For example, at SMI-163 *Olivella* detritus densities exceed 5,500 g/m³. SMI-163 also contains an extensive red abalone bead production industry (see Rick 2004). These

densities of *Olivella* detritus fall in the middle range of Late Holocene bead production for the area, ranging from about 54 to 48,700 g/m³ (Figure 7.4; see Arnold and Munns [1994] and Kennett and Conlee [2002:160] and sources cited therein). Kennett (1998:569; Kennett and Conlee 2002:160) indicated that *Olivella* bead detritus densities at SMI-602 on Point Bennett approach 12,000 g/m³, rivaling some of the higher values for the Channel Islands. SMI-470, a Protohistoric and Historic period site on the northwest coast of the island, which may be the village of *Niwoyomi*, has bead detritus densities of over 7,000 g/m³, further illustrating the variability of bead making at various sites on San Miguel Island.

Conlee (2000) recently updated evidence for prehistoric bowl production on San Miguel Island, suggesting that intensive bowl production began around AD 600. At a Late Holocene site on Point Bennett, Doug Kennett, Phil Walker, and others recently uncovered evidence for abalone fishhook production (Doug Kennett, personal communication 2002). XRF

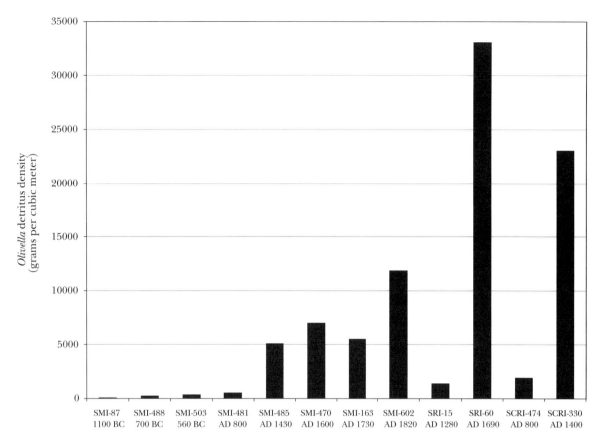

Figure 7.4. Bead detritus densities for northern Channel Islands archaeological sites. Santa Rosa data obtained from Kennett and Conlee (2002) and Santa Cruz data obtained from Arnold and Munns (1994). Dates presented are calibrated intercepts or average of multiple dates from same strata.

source characterization of obsidian artifacts from San Miguel Island by Rick et al. (2001), including at least four artifacts dated to the Late Holocene, illustrates that San Miguel islanders participated in broader exchange systems throughout California and western North America.

Recent archaeological research is helping to change perceptions of Chumash cultural complexity on San Miguel Island. Regeneration of island flora and watersheds provide evidence of a more hospitable environment than previously presumed. Although only two villages are documented in ethnohistoric records, archaeological projects on the island have located over 600 sites, including numerous Late Holocene sites. People on San Miguel produced *Olivella* and red abalone beads and stone bowls for exchange, lived in large, multiple-house villages, and ex-

ploited a diverse array of marine resources, with an increasing trend toward subsistence specialization and craft production during the latter half of the Late Holocene. Similar to the general Channel Islands trend, San Miguel islanders likely developed intensive trade relations and production of craft items to combat their relatively remote location and dearth of terrestrial resources. This strategy may have been very significant for people on San Miguel Island since they were the most isolated of all the northern Channel Islanders, a pattern also described for San Nicolas Island (see Vellanoweth et al. 2002). The growing body of data suggests that although relatively geographically isolated, Chumash peoples of San Miguel Island were not peripheral; they appear to have played an important role in the development of cultural complexity throughout the Santa Barbara Channel region. Future research into changing social and economic patterns on San Miguel Island should further illuminate the rich cultural traditions of the Island Chumash and their ancestors and will help to test and refine the ideas presented in this chapter.

Acknowledgments. This research was funded by a National Park Service Grant (1443CA8120-00-007), a National Science Foundation Dissertation Improvement Grant (SBR-0201668), funds from the US Naval Weapons Station, Point Mugu, California, and a Western National Parks Association Grant awarded to Rick and Jon Erlandson. I am indebted to the generous support and encouragement of Ann Huston, Don Morris, Georganna Hawley, Ian Williams, and Steve Schwartz. I also thank Bob DeLong and Sharon Melin for logistical support on San Miguel Island, access to the NMML comparative collections in Seattle, and information on San Miguel Island natural history. I thank Jeanne Arnold and Anthony Graesch for organizing the SAA symposium and allowing me to present this work. Finally, I thank Jeanne Arnold, Gary Coupland, Jon Erlandson, and three anonymous reviewers for comments that greatly improved this chapter.

REFERENCES CITED

Arnold, J. E.

1987   *Craft Specialization in the Prehistoric Channel Islands, California.* University of California Press, Berkeley.

1991   Transformation of a Regional Economy: Sociopolitical Evolution and the Production of Valuables in Southern California. *Antiquity* 65:953–962.

1992   Complex Hunter-Gatherer-Fishers of Prehistoric California: Chiefs, Specialists, and Maritime Adaptations of the Channel Islands. *American Antiquity* 57:60–84.

1996   The Archaeology of Complex Hunter-Gatherers. *Journal of Archaeological Method and Theory* 3:77–126.

2000   The Origins of Hierarchy and the Nature of Hierarchical Structures in Prehistoric California. In *Hierarchies in Action: Cui Bono?* edited by M. Diehl, pp. 221–240. Center for

Archaeological Investigations, Occasional Paper 27. Southern Illinois University, Carbondale.

2001   Social Evolution and the Political Economy in the Northern Channel Islands. In *The Origins of a Pacific Coast Chiefdom: The Chumash of the Channel Islands,* edited by J. E. Arnold, pp. 287–296. University of Utah Press, Salt Lake City.

Arnold, J. E., R. H. Colten, and S. Pletka

1997   Contexts of Cultural Change in Insular California. *American Antiquity* 62:300–318.

Arnold, J. E., and A. P. Graesch

2001   The Evolution of Specialized Shellworking among the Island Chumash. In *The Origins of a Pacific Coast Chiefdom: The Chumash of the Channel Islands,* edited by J. E. Arnold, pp. 71–112. University of Utah Press, Salt Lake City.

Arnold, J. E., and A. Munns

1994   Independent or Attached Specialization: The Organization of Shell Bead Production in California. *Journal of Field Archaeology* 21:473–489.

Bernard, J.

2001   The Origins of Open-Ocean and Large Species Fishing in the Chumash Region of Southern California. Unpublished Master's thesis, Department of Anthropology, University of California, Los Angeles.

Colten, R. H.

1993   Prehistoric Subsistence, Specialization, and Economy in a Southern California Chiefdom. Unpublished Ph.D. dissertation, Archaeology Program, University of California, Los Angeles.

2002   Prehistoric Marine Mammal Hunting in Context: Two Western North American Examples. *International Journal of Osteoarchaeology* 12:12–22.

Colten, R. H., and J. E. Arnold

1998   Prehistoric Marine Mammal Hunting on California's Northern Channel Islands. *American Antiquity* 63:679–701.

Conlee, C. A.

2000   Intensified Middle Period Ground Stone Production on San Miguel Island. *Journal of California and Great Basin Anthropology* 22:374–391.

Erlandson, J. M.

1988   Cultural Evolution and Paleogeography on the Santa Barbara Coast: A 9600-Year [14]C Record from Southern California. *Radiocarbon* 30: 25–39.

1994   *Early Hunter-Gatherers of the California Coast.* Plenum, New York.

Erlandson, J. M., D. J. Kennett, B. L. Ingram, D. A. Guthrie, D. P. Morris, M. A. Tveskov, G. J. West, and P. L. Walker

1996   An Archaeological and Paleontological Chronology for Daisy Cave (CA-SMI-261), San Miguel Island, California. *Radiocarbon* 38:355–373.

Erlandson, J. M., and T. C. Rick

2002   Late Holocene Cultural Developments along the Santa Barbara Coast. In *Catalysts to Complexity: Late Holocene Societies of the California Coast*, edited by J. M. Erlandson and T. L. Jones, pp. 166–182. Cotsen Institute of Archaeology, University of California, Los Angeles.

Erlandson, J. M., T. C. Rick, D. J. Kennett, and P. L. Walker

2001   Dates, Demography, and Disease: Cultural Contacts and Possible Evidence for Old World Epidemics among the Island Chumash. *Pacific Coast Archaeological Society Quarterly* 37(3):11–26.

Erlandson, J. M., T. C. Rick, and C. Peterson

n.d.   A Geoarchaeological Chronology for Holocene Dune Building on San Miguel Island, California. *The Holocene*, in review.

Gamble, L. H.

2002   Archaeological Evidence for the Origin of the Plank Canoe in North America. *American Antiquity* 67:301–315.

Gamble, L. H., P. L. Walker, and G. S. Russell

2001   An Integrative Approach to Mortuary Analysis: Social and Symbolic Dimensions of Chumash Burial Practices. *American Antiquity* 66:185–212.

Glassow, M. A.

1993   Changes in Subsistence on Marine Resources through 7,000 Years of Prehistory on Santa Cruz Island. In *Archaeology on the Northern Channel Islands of California: Studies of Subsistence, Economics, and Social Organization*, edited by M. A. Glassow, pp. 75–94.

Archives of California Prehistory 34. Coyote Press, Salinas, California.

1996   *Purisimeño Chumash Prehistory: Maritime Adaptations along the Southern California Coast.* Harcourt Brace, Fort Worth, Texas.

Johnson, D. L.

1980   Episodic Vegetation Stripping, Soil Erosion, and Landscape Modification in Prehistoric and Recent Historic Time, San Miguel Island, California. In *The California Islands: Proceedings of a Multidisciplinary Symposium*, edited by D. M. Power, pp. 103–121. Santa Barbara Museum of Natural History, Santa Barbara, California.

Johnson, J. R.

1999   The Chumash Sociopolitical Groups on the Channel Islands. In *Cultural Affiliation and Lineal Descent of Chumash Peoples in the Channel Islands and the Santa Monica Mountains*, edited by S. McLendon and J. R. Johnson, pp. 51–66. Report prepared for the National Park Service, Washington, DC.

2000   Social Responses to Climate Change among the Chumash Indians of South-Central California. In *The Way the Wind Blows: Climate, History, and Human Action*, edited by R. J. McIntosh, J. A. Tainter, and S. K. McIntosh, pp. 301–327. Columbia University Press, New York.

Jones, T. L., G. M. Brown, L. M. Raab, J. L. McVickar, W. G. Spaulding, D. J. Kennett, A. York, and P. L. Walker

1999   Environmental Imperatives Reconsidered: Demographic Crises in Western North America during the Medieval Climatic Anomaly. *Current Anthropology* 40(2):137–170.

Kennett, D. J.

1998   *Behavioral Ecology and the Evolution of Hunter-Gatherer Societies on the Northern Channel Islands, California.* Ph.D. dissertation, University of California, Santa Barbara. University Microfilms International, Ann Arbor, Michigan.

Kennett, D. J., and C. A. Conlee

2002   Emergence of Late Holocene Sociopolitical Complexity on Santa Rosa and San Miguel Islands. In *Catalysts to Complexity: Late Holocene Societies of the California Coast*, edited by J. M. Erlandson and T. L. Jones, pp. 147–

165. Cotsen Institute of Archaeology, University of California, Los Angeles.

Kennett, D. J., B. L. Ingram, J. M. Erlandson, and P. L. Walker
1997   Evidence for Temporal Fluctuations in Marine Radiocarbon Reservoir Ages in the Santa Barbara Channel, Southern California. *Journal of Archaeological Science* 24:1051–1059.

Kennett, D. J., and J. P. Kennett
2000   Competitive and Cooperative Responses to Climatic Instability in Coastal Southern California. *American Antiquity* 65:379–396.

King, C. D.
1990   *Evolution of Chumash Society: A Comparative Study of Artifacts Used for Social System Maintenance in the Santa Barbara Channel Region before A.D. 1804.* Garland, New York.

Lightfoot, K. G.
1993   Long-Term Developments in Complex Hunter-Gatherer Societies: Recent Perspectives from the Pacific Coast of North America. *Journal of Archaeological Research* 1:167–201.

Moss, M. L.
1989   *Cultural Ecology of the Prehistoric Angoon Tlingit.* Ph.D. dissertation, University of California, Santa Barbara. University Microfilms International, Ann Arbor, Michigan.

Moss, M. L., and J. M. Erlandson
1995   Reflections on North American Pacific Coast Prehistory. *Journal of World Prehistory* 9:1–45.

Munns, A. M., and J. E. Arnold
2002   Late Holocene Santa Cruz Island: Patterns of Continuity and Change. In *Catalysts to Complexity: Late Holocene Societies of the California Coast*, edited by J. M. Erlandson and T. L. Jones, pp. 127–146. Cotsen Institute of Archaeology, University of California, Los Angeles.

Raab, L. M.
1996   Debating Prehistory in Coastal Southern California: Resource Intensification versus Political Economy. *Journal of California and Great Basin Anthropology* 18:64–80.

Raab, L. M., and D. O. Larson
1997   Medieval Climatic Anomaly and Punctuated Cultural Evolution in Coastal Southern California. *American Antiquity* 62:319–336.

Raab, L. M., J. Porcasi, K. Bradford, and A. Yatsko
1995   Debating Cultural Evolution: Regional Implications of Fishing Intensification at Eel Point, San Clemente Island. *Pacific Coast Archaeological Society Quarterly* 31(3):3–27.

Rick, T. C.
2002   Eolian Processes, Ground Cover, and the Archaeology of Coastal Dunes: A Taphonomic Case Study from San Miguel Island, California, U.S.A. *Geoarchaeology* 17:811–833.

2004   Daily Activities, Community Dynamics, and Historical Ecology on California's Northern Channel Islands. Unpublished Ph.D. dissertation, Department of Anthropology, University of Oregon.

Rick, T. C., and J. M. Erlandson
2001   Late Holocene Subsistence Strategies on the South Coast of Santa Barbara Island, California. *Journal of California and Great Basin Anthropology* 23:297–307.

Rick, T. C., C. E. Skinner, J. M. Erlandson, and R. L. Vellanoweth
2001   Obsidian Source Characterization and Human Exchange Systems on California's Channel Islands. *Pacific Coast Archaeological Society Quarterly* 37(3):27–44.

Rick, T. C., R. L. Vellanoweth, J. M. Erlandson, and D. J. Kennett
2002   On the Antiquity of the Single-Piece Fishhook: AMS Radiocarbon Evidence from the Southern California Coast. *Journal of Archaeological Science* 29:933–942.

Schoenherr, A., C. R. Feldmath, and M. Emerson
1999   *Natural History of the Islands of California.* University of California Press, Berkeley.

Stuiver, M., and P. J. Reimer
1993   Extended [14]C Data Base and Revised Calib 3.0 [14]C Age Calibration Program. *Radiocarbon* 35:215–230.

2000   *Calib 4.3 Radiocarbon Calibration Program 2000.* Quaternary Isotope Lab, University of Washington, Seattle.

Vellanoweth, R. L., P. Martz, and S. Schwartz
2002   The Late Holocene Archaeology of San Nicolas Island. In *Catalysts to Complexity: Late Holocene Societies of the California Coast*, edited by J. M. Erlandson and T. L. Jones, pp. 82–100. Cotsen Institute of Archaeology, University of California, Los Angeles.

Vellanoweth, R. L., T. C. Rick, and J. M. Erlandson
2000   Middle and Late Holocene Maritime Adaptations on Northeastern San Miguel Island, California. In *Proceedings of the Fifth California Islands Symposium* (CD Publication), edited by D. Brown, K. Mitchell, and H. Chaney, pp. 607–614. U.S. Department of the Interior, Minerals Management Service, Washington, DC.

Walker, P. L., D. J. Kennett, T. Jones, and R. Delong
2000   Archaeological Investigations of the Point Bennett Pinniped Rookery on San Miguel Island. In *Proceedings of the Fifth California Islands Symposium* (CD Publication), edited by D. Brown, K. Mitchell, and H. Chaney, pp. 628–632. U.S. Department of the Interior, Minerals Management Service, Washington, DC.

Walker, P. L., and P. Snethkamp
1984   Archaeological Investigations on San Miguel Island, 1982. Prehistoric Adaptations to the Marine Environment. Report on File, Central Coast Information Center, Department of Anthropology, University of California, Santa Barbara.

Yatsko, A.
2000   Late Holocene Paleoclimatic Stress and Prehistoric Human Occupation on San Clemente Island. Unpublished Ph.D. dissertation, Department of Anthropology, University of California, Los Angeles.

8

Quarries and Microblades

Trends in Prehistoric Land and Resource Use on Eastern Santa Cruz Island

Jennifer E. Perry

Of major concern to archaeologists are the mechanisms underlying the development of complex socioeconomic and political organization among prehistoric agricultural and hunter-gatherer-fisher societies. In particular, Arnold (1987, 1992a, 1992b, 1995, 2001; ed. 1996), Glassow (1993, 1997, 1999), Kennett (1998), King (1981), and others have attempted to document temporal trends in behavioral strategies among the inhabitants of Santa Cruz Island in relation to other Chumash populations in the Santa Barbara Channel region. To understand complexity, some researchers have focused specifically on dramatic changes that occurred during the late Middle (1050–800 BP) and Transitional periods (800–650 BP) (Kennett and Kennett 2000). These periods have been characterized as episodes of environmental degradation, potentially related to sustained elevated sea surface temperatures (possibly like extended El Niño-Southern Oscillation events) and/or drought, among other environmental and demographic factors (Arnold et al. 1997; Raab and Larson 1997). Island communities experienced severe periods of resource stress, based on osteological evidence for health decline and increased competition and violence (Lambert 1993, 1994; Lambert and Walker 1991; Walker 1996), as well as site abandonment (Arnold 1991:956; Kennett 1998:320; Yatsko 2000). Besides fishing intensification, one of the primary responses to population-resources imbalances was to increase trade interaction between the islands and mainland to obtain supplemental resources. Intensified cross-channel exchange and associated specialization are regarded as providing the basis for subsequent social ranking, wealth accumulation, and leadership and control (Arnold 1995:744; Johnson 2000).

Increased island-mainland exchange during and after the Transitional period was facilitated by earlier technological innovations, including circular fishhooks, plank canoes, and microdrills. As early as 1500 BP, plank canoe technology allowed for kelp bed and midchannel fishing, as well as transportation for cargo and people (Arnold 1995:739). Around 1050 BP microdrills began to be made of chert from eastern Santa Cruz Island (East End) to manufacture shell beads for socioeconomic transactions (Arnold 1987). Trapezoidal microdrills were manufactured of chert exposed in quarries along El Montañon, although production was conducted at dispersed locations throughout the Channel Islands and on the mainland (Arnold 1987). Triangular microdrills with dorsal retouch (TDR) became the dominant form during the Late period. They were made exclusively on the East End and then distributed to other parts of the island to produce callus beads from purple olive (*Olivella biplicata*) shells, used as a regional exchange currency after 650 BP. Callus beads were more expensive with respect to raw material and labor investment than other bead types and, therefore, held more economic value (Kennett 1998:337; King 1981:254). In conjunction with callus beads, TDR microblades were made in much higher densities, with increased standardization and success rates, suggesting some degree of organized or regulated production (Arnold 1987; Preziosi 2001).

In this chapter I assess the changing role of microblade production with the goal of identifying regional trends in land and resource use as indicators of changes in prehistoric behavioral strategies. The main question underlying my research is, How, if at all, did microblade production and associated activities influence prehistoric subsistence and settlement activities on the East End? To answer this question, I conducted surveys, surface collections, and limited subsurface excavations in a range of environmental contexts on the East End to assess the impact of increased exchange and specialization (Perry 2003). I discuss six East End sites (SCRI-406, -423, -506, -507, -647, and -753) to illustrate some of the general interpretations made with respect to site location and distribution, temporal assignment, and surface artifact types and distribution. Time-sensitive artifacts and radiocarbon samples were recovered with the intention of selecting sites dating throughout the Middle period to document the transition to microblade production and associated organizational changes. However, it is also important to situate these interpretations within the larger chronological framework of human habitation on the East End, commencing from its earliest occupation.

THEORETICAL CONTEXT AND THE ROLE OF CHERT RESOURCES

For my dissertation I generated hypotheses and expectations regarding land and resource use on the East End based on several theories and models applied to the Channel Islands, particularly by Arnold (1987, 1992a, 1992b, 1995) and Kennett (1998). Evolutionary ecology, including optimal foraging models such as patch choice, diet breadth, and central place; economic game theory; and political economy models were utilized to generate expectations for and interpretations of temporal trends in behavioral strategies on the East End. By invoking natural selection as the prime motivator of human action, fitness and self-interest are viewed as the ultimate goals of human decisions and strategies. Individuals have finite amounts of time and energy to invest in foraging and nonforaging activities, based on the perceived relative values of alternative op-

tions (Bettinger 1991:166). What strategies are selected at any given time depend on the specific environmental and social opportunities and constraints operating during the period being investigated, existing organizational structures and technologies, and individual perceptions (Kantner 1996:45; Winterhalder and Smith 1992:8).

During episodes of population-resource imbalances, as interpreted for the late Middle and Transitional periods, risk-minimization strategies require cooperation among individuals and within groups to mediate stressful conditions through intensified resource acquisition (Arnold et al. 1997; Raab and Larson 1997). Larson et al. (1994:270) discuss risk-minimization strategies, of which the following have been documented or inferred for the Channel Islands: "1) intensify existing subsistence strategies, 2) practice new technologies, 3) reorganize labor and political activities, 4) engage in raiding and warfare to establish and protect territories, 5) increase ritual and ceremonial activities for the purpose of integrating regional settlements, and 6) increase dependence on manufactured items that you can exchange for food." Most of these strategies necessitate the formation of groups to mobilize labor to accomplish specific tasks such as fish netting, canoe construction, microblade and bead production, and organized warfare, all of which require investments in material resources.

Several criteria make particular resources more lucrative and worthy of investment with respect to labor and materials, including their relative abundance, distribution, and storability (Boone 1992:317). First, abundant and predictable resources in concentrated or circumscribed areas, such as chert quarries on and around the ridges of El Montañon, are the most probable ones to be defended (Kennett 1998:46). Dispersed and unpredictable resources, such as terrestrial plants, tend not to be protected or defined territorially because the amount of energy required to protect them is much greater than the potential yield. Second, storable and transportable goods including chert microdrills and olive shell beads are easier to defend and exchange when compared to heavy, large, or perishable items (Kantner 1996:47). During episodes of resource stress, exchange may be channeled through reciprocal relationships between groups with differential access to resources, such as exchange relationships between inhabitants of the islands and mainland (Minc and Smith 1989:10). At times when there are conflicts in resource scheduling, payments for goods received are delayed, and exchange currencies are used as measures of value. Currencies, namely callus beads made of olive shell, and the raw materials used to manufacture them, island chert, satisfy the criteria for defendable resources.

Individuals will attempt to control different stages of resource extraction, production, and/ or distribution through one or more of the following strategies: resource ownership, finance of enhanced procurement technology and manufacturing activities, and control over distribution through regional exchange networks (Hayden 1995). In contexts of high population density the resulting hierarchical organization may become essential to the regulation of socioeconomic interactions and conflict (Larson et al. 1994:277). Although individuals may be acting out of self-interest, the strategies they select through time in response to shifting environmental and historical conditions may become formalized, thereby stimulating changes promoting complex socioeconomic and political organization (see Feinman 1995:257).

METHODS: A REGIONAL APPROACH

In light of these theoretical considerations, I implemented a stratified judgmental sampling strategy on the East End to survey comparable land units in different environmental zones (Figure 8.1). The East End is defined as the region east of El Montañon, the prominent northwest-southeast trending ridge that serves as the major natural barrier between this area and the rest of the island. According to this definition the East End encompasses approximately 25 km² of land composed geologically of Santa Cruz Island volcanics and Monterey formation shales. However, given that chert quarries and other resources are easily accessible from both sides of El Montañon, its western flanks and nearby ridges on the north side of the isthmus were included in this analysis. Therefore, the overall area addressed encompasses about 30 km², with

15 percent of that surveyed systematically at 10-m intervals during fieldwork conducted between February 2001 and July 2002.

I divided the East End into five major environmental zones (referred to as *land areas*) based primarily on topographic and resource-related variables. The land areas are beaches, which include all locales with direct coastal access (0–100 ft), canyons (0–500 ft), coastal bluffs and terraces (100–300 ft), upland plateaus or elevated landforms (300–800 ft) (see Clifford 2001; Kennett 1998), and El Montañon and adjacent interior ridges (800–1,800 ft). The major variables are fresh water, plant communities, marine resources, chert, protection from the elements, and viewshed or degree of visibility. Their current and prehistoric distributions were evaluated based on personal observations; discussions with Channel Islands archaeologists, botanists, and geologists/soil scientists; and relevant archaeological and botanical publications (Arnold 1987; Glassow 1993; Junak et al. 1995; Kennett 1998; Timbrook 1993). Specific survey areas were selected to collectively encompass interior and coastal environmental zones, northern and southern exposures, and cross sections of current plant communities, including oak woodland, coastal sagebrush, coastal bluff scrub, grasslands, coniferous forest, and riparian habitat (see Junak et al. 1995).

Emphasis was placed on the eastern and southern areas of the East End, given that most previous work has been conducted on El Montañon (Arnold 1987) and in the massive Scorpion watershed (Clifford 2001; Kennett 1998), which extends east and north from seven drainages into Scorpion Anchorage. Despite the major contributions of earlier projects, gaps remained in our understanding of the East End because of the sparse data for elevated landforms in the interior and areas south of Scorpion Canyon. Regarding the Smugglers watershed, most previous archaeological data had been obtained from coastal sites, whereas little was known about the rest of the watershed including in the canyon itself. Furthermore, with some exceptions, most prior research was conducted at sites located at elevations lower than 300 feet or above 1,000 feet. In attempting to assess changes in behavioral strategies through time, I thought

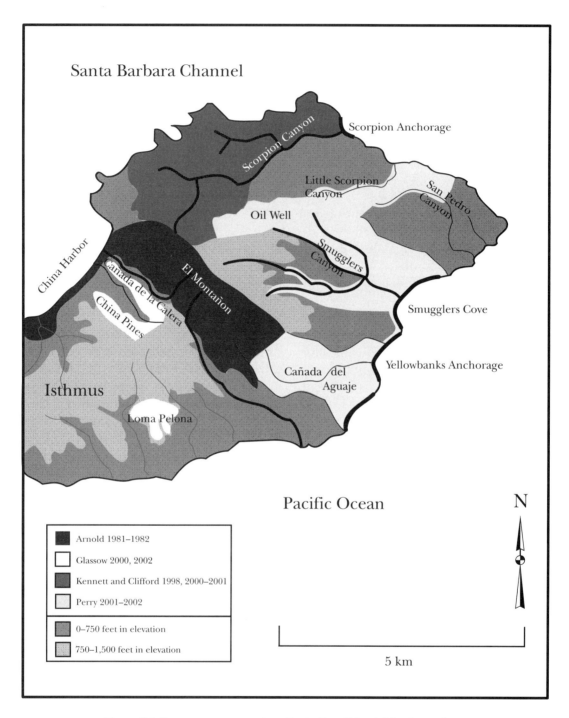

Figure 8.1. Survey areas on eastern Santa Cruz Island. Map by author.

that the intermediate elevations should be investigated, given observed differences in topography, plant communities, and fresh water availability, among other factors.

I surveyed the following units: (1) major ridges east of El Montañon above 800 feet; (2) Little Scorpion and San Pedro Canyons and the land in between, including the sea cliff; (3) Smugglers Cove and the elevated areas to the north and south; and (4) Yellowbanks Anchorage, La Cañada del Aguaje, and ridges to the north and south (Perry 2003). Site distribution, radiocarbon dates, and other relevant data regarding sites in Scorpion Canyon and Anchorage were derived from Kennett (1998) and Clifford (2001), whereas evaluations of El Montañon and China Harbor were based primarily on Arnold (1987), as well as my own site investigations. Interpretations of the East End and isthmus were also based on conversations with Michael Glassow, Sam Spaulding, Jeanne Arnold, Doug Kennett, and other researchers (personal communications 2001–2002).

Temporal assignments were based on radiocarbon dates and the two dominant forms of microblades, trapezoidal and triangular with dorsal retouch (TDR), with unprepared triangular microblades not being temporally diagnostic (see Preziosi 2001:152–153). Although there is overlap with respect to when both microblade forms were manufactured, the trapezoidal form dominated the late Middle period, whereas TDR microblades were produced in significantly higher quantities and increased consistency in form during the Late period (Arnold 1987). Given that only one of the forms was found at each of the sites inspected during this research, it seemed reasonable to assign sites to each period based on the form observed, while simultaneously not ruling out the possible presence of the other form. Other time-sensitive artifacts were considered but not included in the present discussion, given the comparatively small quantity that has been collected on the East End and given the current focus on microblades and their role in island-mainland exchange networks. However, when deemed relevant, the significance of artifact types and their distribution, including mortars and pestles, were considered and included in this discussion.

GENERAL RESULTS AND INTERPRETATIONS

In total, 66 sites with 90 distinct temporal components were incorporated into the current study, representing 50 percent of all recorded sites on the East End and eastern portion of the isthmus (Perry 2003). These sites were selected for analysis based primarily on the presence of two chronological criteria: calibrated radiocarbon dates and trapezoidal and TDR microblades

and microcores (Table 8.1). Of the 40 sites identified and documented during this research and 90 previously recorded sites, I selected 12 for further investigation through systematic surface collections, radiocarbon dating, and limited subsurface testing including the excavation of auger and column samples. Excavation and interpretation of these 12 sites formed an integral part of this research because they provided significant insights into land and resource use throughout the East End landscape, especially on elevated landforms in the interior, thereby filling the regional gaps noted above.

Chi-square tests were conducted to assess whether there are significant differences in East End site distributions by period and by land area. The results of these tests indicate a highly significant temporal pattern with respect to habitation in different land areas (χ^2 = 43.032, $p \leq$ 0.0005, 12 df). To address the relatively small sample size, Kruskal Wallis tests were also conducted, yielding similarly significant results (χ^2 = 14.739, $p \leq$ 0.005, 4 df). In more detailed analyses two clear patterns emerge that meet more specific expectations with respect to trends in site location and site type distribution (Table 8.2). First, there was a major shift from seasonal emphasis on coastal terraces and elevated landforms during the Early period (15 sites) to increasingly permanent habitation primarily along the coastline in the Late period (13 sites). Conversely, there is limited evidence for coastal habitation during the Early period (1 site) and fewer Late period sites at higher elevations relative to those situated near the shoreline. Second, the dual emphasis on quarries on El Montañon (17 sites) and nearby elevated landforms (10 sites), as well as beach areas (6 sites), highlights the importance of microblade production and maritime activities, respectively, during the late Middle and Transitional periods.

Early Period (9500–2500 BP)

Of the 66 archaeological sites considered on the East End, components at 18 sites date to the Early period, of which 14 date to between 5000 and 2700 cal BP (Figure 8.2). The majority of these radiocarbon dates are from shell middens dispersed along coastal terraces and elevated landforms (83.3 percent), including on top of El

Table 8.1. Recent Radiocarbon Dates from Eastern Santa Cruz Island

Site Number	Lab No.	Unit and Depth (cm)	RCYBP[a]	Corrected $^{13}C/^{12}C$ Years BP	Calibrated Age Range (1 sigma)	Calibrated Age Range (2 sigma)
SCRI-406	Beta-164526	A 3SE/29NE, 19–25	5040 ± 80	4820 ± 90	3320 BC–3010 BC	3370 BC (3120) 2890 BC
SCRI-406	Beta-164527	A 3SE/34NE, 32–40	6380 ± 70	6160 ± 80	4720 BC–4540 BC	4800 BC (4660) 4450 BC
SCRI-647	Beta-164528	A 5S, 29–39	1520 ± 60	1300 ± 70	AD 1030–1190	AD 980 (1080) 1260
SCRI-647	Beta-172037	A 15E, 27–38	1690 ± 60	1470 ± 70	AD 870–1020	AD 780 (950) 1060
SCRI-649	Beta-164529	A 5NE, 39–45	3720 ± 80	3500 ± 90	1520 BC–1350 BC	1630 BC (1420) 1220 BC
SCRI-649	Beta-172038	A 25NW, 15–23	3980 ± 80	3760 ± 90	1870 BC–1620 BC	1960 BC (1730) 1510 BC
SCRI-698	Beta-167971	CS 1, 20–30	5800 ± 50	5580 ± 60	4040 BC–3950 BC	4160 BC (3990) 3910 BC
SCRI-699	Beta-172034	A 10NE/10SE, 28–39	3700 ± 70	3480 ± 80	1490 BC–1320 BC	1600 BC (1400) 1220 BC
SCRI-699	Beta-164525	A 10NE/10SE, 63–75	4200 ± 80	3980 ± 90	2140 BC–1900 BC	2280 BC (2020) 1770 BC
SCRI-706	Beta-167976	A 5E/5S, 30–42	4210 ± 60	3990 ± 70	2130 BC–1940 BC	2230 BC (2030) 1870 BC
SCRI-741	Beta-172033	A 15E, 24–35	4000 ± 70	3780 ± 80	1870 BC–1670 BC	1960 BC (1740) 1560 BC
SCRI-741	Beta-164524	A 15E, 58–66	4330 ± 70	4110 ± 80	2320 BC–2110 BC	2440 BC (2200) 1970 BC
SCRI-746	Beta-172035	A 15E, 17–27	4220 ± 80	4000 ± 90	2180 BC–1920 BC	2300 BC (2040) 1810 BC
SCRI-746	Beta-167972	A 15E, 53–63	4660 ± 60	4440 ± 70	2760 BC–2560 BC	2860 BC (2630) 2460 BC
SCRI-747	Beta-167975	CS 1, 40–50	1220 ± 50	1000 ± 60	AD 1310–1420	AD 1290 (1390) 1450
SCRI-751	Beta-172036	A 15E/14N, 20–30	3990 ± 70	3770 ± 80	1870 BC–1650 BC	1950 BC (1740) 1530 BC
SCRI-751	Beta-167973	A 155E/5N, 29–39	4740 ± 50	4520 ± 60	2860 BC–2670 BC	2890 BC (2790) 2580 BC
SCRI-751	Beta-167974	A 15E/14N, 77–85	4830 ± 50	4610 ± 60	2910 BC–2840 BC	3010 BC (2870) 2740 BC
SCRI-752	Beta-168346	A 5S, 30–40	4370 ± 60	4150 ± 70	2380 BC–2160 BC	2460 BC (2270) 2050 BC
SCRI-753	Beta-168347	10–15 below surface	1180 ± 50	960 ± 60	AD 1340–1440	AD 1300 (1410) 1470

[a]Radiocarbon dates obtained from California mussel (*Mytilus californianus*) samples.

Table 8.2. Temporal Distribution of Sites by Land Area

	Early	Middle	Late Middle	Late	Total
Beach	1	3	6	13	23
Canyon	1	2	4	4	11
Coastal terrace	7	1	3	2	13
Elevated landform	8	1	10	5	24
El Montañon	1	0	17	1	19
Total	18	7	40	25	90

Montañon and adjacent ridges. The remainder includes one rockshelter in Scorpion Canyon (SCRI-614) and one situated on a rocky headland just east of Little Scorpion Anchorage (SCRI-698). As also documented elsewhere on Santa Cruz Island and the mainland north of Point Conception (Glassow 1993), the faunal constituents from each of the Early period sites that I analyzed were dominated by shellfish, specifically California mussel (*Mytilus californianus*), one of the most abundant, high-ranking shellfish species in the area. Contributions from fish and sea mammal vary among sites, and these faunal assemblages potentially correlate with differences in the natural distribution of marine species along the north-facing and southeastern-oriented coastlines of the East End.

In considering the relative abundance and locations of Early period sites, Glassow (1997) and others have suggested that population growth was promoted at this time because of favorable climatic conditions and subsistence intensification, including the adoption of mortars and pestles to process acorns and other foods. Based on paleoenvironmental data, oak woodlands were distributed most extensively between 4,500 and 3,300 years ago, when the "warmest and most climatically variable intervals during the Holocene occurred" (Kennett 1998:245). It is possible that these Early period sites are representative of the mobile foraging strategies of expanding island populations moving into the East End, populations that seasonally exploited marine resources and collected various plant species in coastal sagebrush, grassland, and oak woodland habitats distributed along coastal terraces and elevated landforms.

The potential role of plant resources is indicated not only by site location but also by the presence of mortars, pestles, digging stick weights, manos, and ground-stone fragments at all of the Early period sites investigated. Although it is possible that these artifacts may date to later periods (given their surface locations), the quantity of ground-stone artifacts recovered at sites dating to this period and the landforms on which they are found are suggestive. In recent years researchers have argued that mortars and other milling implements may not have been used strictly for plant foods; rather, their uses may have included the pulverizing and processing of small animals, shellfish, and other materials (Glassow 1996). Nevertheless, the abundance of mortars and pestles in archaeological sites near present-day oak stands is compelling with respect to at least one of their dominant uses (plant processing). Other implements traditionally associated with plant collection and processing, such as manos and digging stick weights, also have been identified. In particular, digging stick weights indicate the collection of various roots, tubers, and bulbs such as blue dicks (*Dichelostemma capitatum*), which are available in coastal sagebrush and grassland regions in the spring and represent significant sources of carbohydrates (Timbrook 1993:56).

One of the most well-dated Early period sites on the East End is SCRI-406, a small shell midden located immediately west of a prominent oak stand on El Montañon at an elevation of 1,500 feet. The site was originally recorded in 1981 by Jeanne Arnold (unpublished site record), and intensive site mapping, systematic surface collection, and auger sampling were

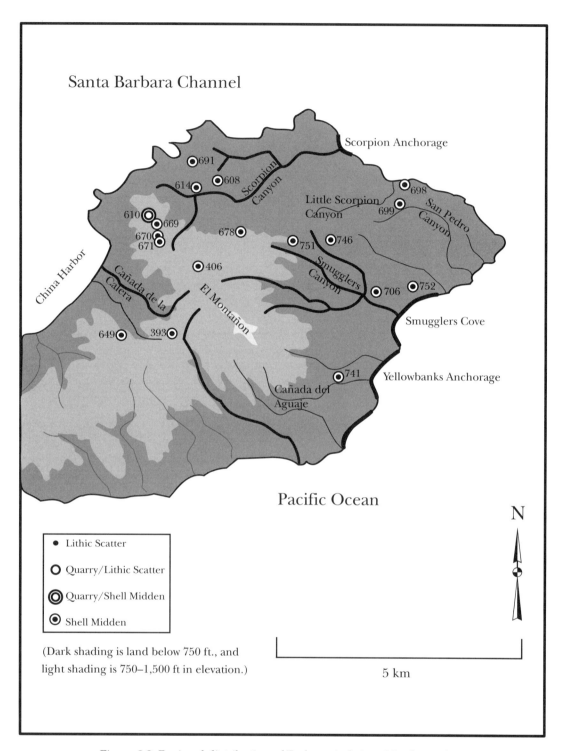

Figure 8.2. Regional distribution of Early period sites. Map by author.

conducted in September 2001 as part of my dissertation research (Perry 2003). Three calibrated radiocarbon dates indicate sporadic occupation from 6760 to 3500 cal BP (2 sigma values), taken from California mussel (*Mytilus californianus*) fragments at depths of 32 to 40 cm, 18.5 to 24.5 cm, and 0 to 5 cm, respectively. Surface artifacts on the shell midden at SCRI-406 are limited to the following: one sandstone bowl fragment, two igneous manos, one igneous tarring pebble, and two nondiagnostic biface fragments, made of island chert and basalt, respectively. The site has been interpreted as a temporary or seasonal camp used over several thousand years, based on the low diversity of faunal constituents and artifacts represented, as well as the limited depth and density of midden deposits.

Despite being exposed and windy, the location of SCRI-406 and similar Early period sites may have been attractive because of the presence of fresh water, chert outcrops, and oak stands in the immediate vicinity. Water is present in springs and seeps at the heads of several unnamed drainages on both sides of El Montañon, located between 10 m and 1 km from shell middens and quarries in this area. Other compelling reasons for occupying the top of El Montañon include visibility across the island and monitoring of land-based travel. Land-based travel from the East End to all other parts of the island requires traversing El Montañon, which can be easily monitored from SCRI-406. Therefore, if signaling of territories and/or resource use was important during the Early period, as argued by Kennett (1998:290–291) and Clifford (2001:101–103), then SCRI-406 was an ideal location to be visible to others as well as to regulate movement across El Montañon. Regardless of the particular factors influencing the location of SCRI-406, such sites support an interpretation of Early period inhabitants as seasonal foragers, moving between the coast and interior and relying on relatively abundant, low-cost resources, namely shellfish and plants.

Middle Period (2500–800 BP)

Middle period deposits at and near beaches suggest increased marine-oriented activities among East End inhabitants, which correlates well with island settlement patterns documented in the Coches Prietos watershed on the south side of the island (Peterson 1994) and elsewhere on Santa Cruz and Santa Rosa Islands (Kennett 1998). Seasonal residential bases were established at Scorpion Anchorage and Smugglers Cove, both of which are suitable areas for rocky-intertidal and sandy-beach shellfish gathering, nearshore and kelp bed fishing, and boat launching and landing. Kennett (1998:307) observes a shift to coastal occupation on both islands, with almost no residential bases present in the interior after 3000 BP. As population densities increased, people were "becoming more tethered to coastal locations" through technological innovations, such as the circular fishhook and plank canoe, that allowed for intensified fishing and exchange (Kennett 1998:307–308).

Based on seven radiocarbon dates, five sites have deposits that date to the Middle period, most of which are found in the Scorpion watershed both in the upper reaches of the canyon and at Scorpion Anchorage. The Scorpion watershed provides access to fresh water, as well as to a range of productive marine habitats including rocky headlands with abundant California mussel (*Mytilus californianus*), a sand and cobble beach, and kelp beds. Rocky headlands are present at both ends of the sand and cobble beach, and kelp is found close to shore, where sea mammals and birds are active hunters. Chert outcroppings, including the largest quarry on Santa Cruz Island (SCRI-610), are found along elevated landforms in the upper Scorpion watershed, with two quarries (SCRI-611 and -627) located near the anchorage. Besides providing access to water, chert, and food resources, Scorpion Anchorage is also convenient for boat launching because of its calm waters protected from the prevailing northwest winds.

Located on opposite sides of the beach at Scorpion Anchorage, SCRI-423 and SCRI-507 represent an emphasis on marine-oriented activities beginning in the Middle period. At SCRI-423, three calibrated radiocarbon dates between 2330 and 1300 cal BP (2 sigma values) were taken from marine shell in cultural deposits at depths of 210 cm, 150 cm, and 60 cm (Clifford 2001:135). Trapezoidal and TDR microblades, as well as glass beads and other historic artifacts, document occupation during subsequent periods (Clifford 2001:84). SCRI-507 dates to the Late or Historic period based on one calibrated radiocarbon date taken from marine shell at 10–20 cm in depth: 254 cal BP to recent (1 sigma value) (Kennett 1998:545). Based on the presence of these microblade forms at SCRI-423 and SCRI-507, other temporally diagnostic artifacts, radiocarbon dates, and ethnohistoric data, Kennett

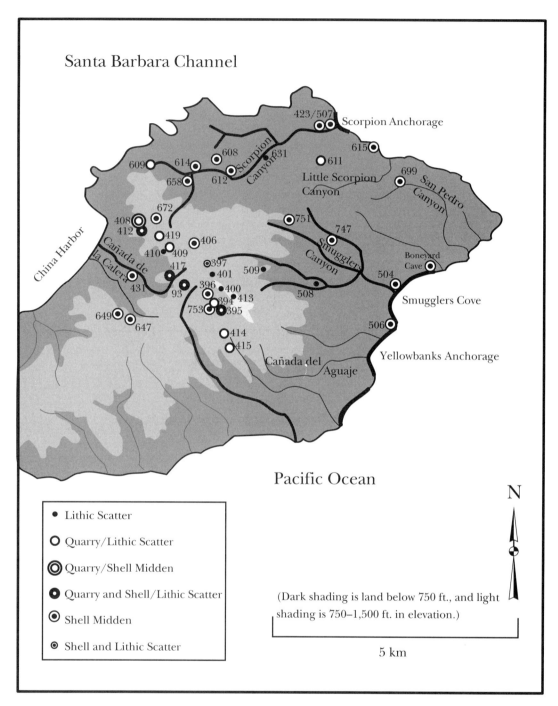

Figure 8.3. Regional distribution of late Middle and Transitional period sites. Map by author.

(1998:209–212) interprets these sites as part of the historic village of *Swaxil*, having its roots in the Middle period (see Johnson 1993; Kennett et al. 2000).

Another site that illustrates the coastal emphasis of the Middle period is SCRI-506, the location of the historic village of *Nanawani*

(Johnson 1993; Kennett 1998:211; Kennett et al. 2000), which is situated on and above a small rocky headland between Smugglers Cove and Yellowbanks Anchorage. The shell midden has been identified as a residential base dating to the late Middle and Late periods based on the presence of trapezoidal and TDR microblades and one calibrated radiocarbon date of 910–742 cal BP (1 sigma value) (Kennett 1998:474). Although the promontory is small and space is limited, the location is attractive with respect to the diverse marine habitats and fish and shellfish species present locally at sandy beaches, rocky intertidal areas, and kelp beds. The site location would have been most viable with the use of canoes to exploit the kelp beds and offshore waters, given the presence of good launching and landing areas to both sides. Furthermore, reliable fresh water is accessible in two productive watersheds: La Cañada del Aguaje to the south and Smugglers Canyon to the north. Both Scorpion Anchorage and Smugglers Cove would have been ideal locations to maximize access to diverse marine and terrestrial resources and support relatively sedentary populations.

Late Middle (1050–800 BP) and Transitional (800–650 BP) Periods

In addition to fishing intensification, the establishment of coastal residential bases has been interpreted as reflecting increased exchange between the islands and the mainland. Intensified trade interactions during the late Middle period are also manifested in the abundance of microblade manufacturing sites in the interior. Although there are only two radiocarbon dates that fall within this period (SCRI-506 and SCRI-647), the late Middle period is well represented based on the presence of 40 sites with evidence for trapezoidal microblade production (Figure 8.3). Of these 40 sites, 27 are found in the interior along El Montañon and in the upper reaches of major drainages including the Scorpion and Smugglers watersheds at or near chert quarries. There are also six coastal sites with trapezoidal microblades clustered around Scorpion Anchorage, nearby Little Scorpion Anchorage, and Smugglers Cove.

Based on the number and regional distribution of trapezoidal microblade manufacturing sites, several interpretations can be made with respect to the importance of specialist activities among East End inhabitants. First, the number of sites with trapezoidal microblades (40) compared to the total number of sites known on the East End suggests that microblade production was indeed a significant component of late Mid-

dle period activities. Second, given their presence in shell middens and lithic scatters throughout the interior, it appears that people continued to engage in mobile foraging strategies focusing on fresh water, chert, and other terrestrial resources. Third, as initially proposed by Arnold (1987), the dispersed nature and small size of sites with trapezoidal microblade production suggests that it was engaged in as a part-time, unregulated activity as opposed to being controlled by specialists.

Of the 27 late Middle period sites located in elevated areas on and around El Montañon, trapezoidal microblades have been identified at 13 quarries and at 14 other sites in close proximity to quarries. Ten of these sites have shell midden deposits: two middens at quarries (SCRI-93 and SCRI-408); three smaller, less dense middens at quarries (SCRI-395, -412, and -417); four middens nearby (SCRI-396, -406, -672, and -753); and one light scatter close to quarries (SCRI-397). The abundance of midden deposits on El Montañon implies that people were investing their time in traveling to quarries to extract chert and produce microblades, occupying both short-term and seasonal field camps. Kennett (1998) interprets camping at and near quarries as possible signaling of territory and resource ownership by interested parties, arguing that signaling is less expensive in terms of labor and possible harm than conflict and violence. However, another important variable to consider is that water is available seasonally in small springs and seeps at higher elevations. Based on personal observations, these sources are often more persistent than those at lower elevations. Therefore, I posit that these water sources would have been critical in drought conditions and would have influenced how people mapped onto the landscape as much as, if not more than, concerns for signaling and defense.

Trapezoidal microblades and associated microcores have been identified in 27 shell middens and scatters throughout the interior and along the coast: on El Montañon and above 800 feet along its slopes and adjacent ridges, around China Pines, and in Scorpion Canyon. With regard to coastal occupation there are two sites at the mouth of Scorpion Canyon (SCRI-423 and SCRI-507), one at Little Scorpion Anchorage

(SCRI-615), one at Smugglers Cove (SCRI-504), and one at Smugglers Point (SCRI-506). It appears that once coastal residential bases were established during the Middle period, they were occupied through historic times. In fact, SCRI-506 would have been one of the most viable locations to weather episodes of resource stress, given the range of resources available in relatively close proximity. However, in addition to coastal tethering, people were continuing to travel into the interior. There was increased emphasis on tapping the chert quarries rather than following the mixed subsistence-settlement strategies of the Early and Middle periods.

One such interior site is SCRI-753; this is a small rockshelter situated at an elevation of 1,275 feet and located about 100 meters downslope from a major chert quarry (SCRI-394) on the western side of El Montañon. There is a small but dense shell midden eroding down the steep slope below the rockshelter, with surface artifacts dominated by thousands of trapezoidal microblades and associated microcores. Based on the high density of trapezoidal microblades, the site has been assigned to the late Middle period. However, one calibrated radiocarbon sample from 10–15 cm in depth dates to 640–480 cal BP (2 sigma value), indicating occupation during the Late period. The site is interpreted as a temporary camp associated with chert extraction activities at SCRI-394, an extensive chert quarry and microblade manufacturing area, with thousands of trapezoidal microblades and cores (Arnold, unpublished site records). In addition to chert resources, ephemeral fresh water is available nearby in a seep adjacent to the quarry. Furthermore, given that it is a rockshelter, protection from the elements and from other people during chert extraction activities at the quarry may have been among the driving determinants in occupying SCRI-753.

In contrast to SCRI-753, SCRI-647 is a late Middle period residential base situated at 1,200 feet in the dense oak and pine woodland of the prominent China Pines to the west of El Montañon. Originally recorded in 2000 by Glassow et al. (unpublished site record), SCRI-647 was subjected to intensive mapping and surface collect-

ing, as well as limited subsurface testing in August 2001 as part of my dissertation research (Perry 2003). Taken from California mussel fragments at 29 to 39 cm in depth, one calibrated radiocarbon date of 970–690 cal BP (2 sigma value) along with evidence for trapezoidal microblade production places it within the late Middle period. The site has been interpreted as a seasonal residential base, given the distribution and density of cultural materials. Surface artifacts indirectly indicate plant collection and processing activities, including two sandstone and one igneous mortar fragments, two igneous manos, one serpentine digging stick weight fragment, and seven unidentifiable fire-affected groundstone fragments. Other surface artifacts are five igneous tarring pebbles, 20 island chert cores and microcores, and one thick triangular drill made of island chert, attesting to the range of activities conducted at the site.

Potential reasons for inhabiting SCRI-647 include the proximity of plant resources, seasonal fresh water in La Cañada de la Calera to the east, and chert quarries along the western flank of El Montañon, as well as excellent views of and access to El Montañon and China Harbor. In particular, the abundance of oak and pine interspersed with toyon (*Heteromeles arbutifolia*) trees in the area today is attractive as an indicator of past plant distribution. In addition to food, local tree species would have provided suitable materials for firewood and the manufacture of utilitarian items. The presence of five tarring pebbles stained with asphaltum among concentrated fire-affected volcanic rock at the southern end of the site is suggestive of basketry (water bottle) manufacturing or maintenance. Of all of the sites investigated, SCRI-647 and SCRI-506 are the most plausible candidates for occupation during the Transitional period, given the radiocarbon dates and types of artifacts identified, as well as the range of resources available near both locations.

Late Period (650–200 BP)

Leading up to the Late period, I identify some major trends with respect to increasing emphasis on marine resource exploitation, regional exchange, and craft specialization in the form of microblade production. Most significant, the number of sites where evidence for TDR microblade manufacturing is present (25) is smaller, and they are less dispersed than sites where trapezoidal microblades were produced (40). In contrast to the spatial distribution of trapezoidal microblade production, there is virtually no evidence for TDR microblades in quarries and lithic scatters on El Montañon and adjacent ridges (Figure 8.4). The few Late period sites situated in the interior are located along the Scorpion watershed, where there is access to large chert quarries, and prominent rockshelters afford protection from the elements.

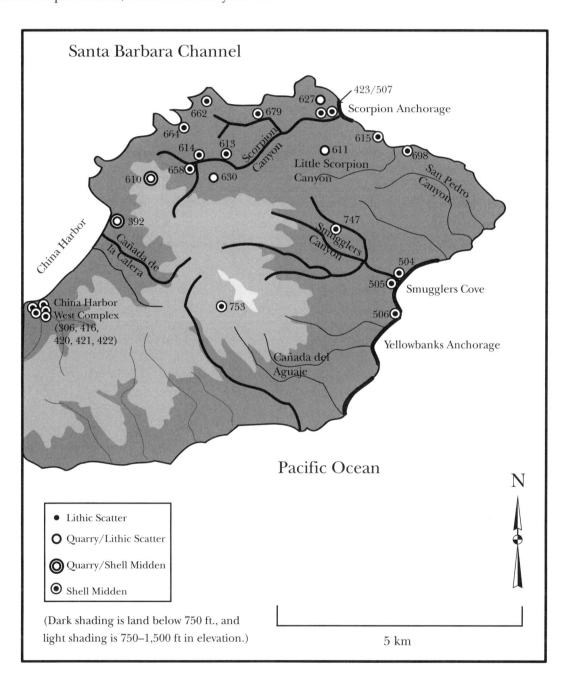

Figure 8.4. Regional distribution of Late period sites. Map by author.

Of the 25 sites dating to the Late period, the majority are dense shell middens concentrated in coastal areas at Scorpion Anchorage, Little Scorpion Anchorage, Smugglers Cove, and China Harbor. The data indicate that SCRI-423 and -507 at Scorpion Anchorage and SCRI-506 at Smugglers Cove were inhabited for several thousand years, although evidence for continuous occupation from the Middle period into the Historic period was not ascertainable. During the Late period, five sites (SCRI-306, -416, -420, -421, and -422) also were established at the western end of China Harbor, west of El Montañon (Arnold 1987). Microblade production was conducted at the China West complex from its inception, suggesting that interest in microblade specialization and exchange strongly influenced the selection of this particular locale (Arnold 1987:167–214). Therefore, as Arnold (1987) has argued, the transition from trapezoidal to TDR microblade production on the East End is manifest in the shift from dispersed, small-scale microblade-related activities at interior quarries to intensified manufacturing at coastal residential bases.

As at China Harbor, TDR microblades are found predominantly in or near coastal residential bases in statistically higher densities than their trapezoidal counterparts (Arnold 1987). Midden deposits with TDR microblades are also found at four rockshelters (SCRI-612, -614, -658, and -679) in the upper reaches of Scorpion Canyon (Clifford 2001; Kennett 1998). People's use of these rockshelters may relate to three main influencing factors: access to fresh water in the upper reaches of the canyon, access to abundant chert at the large quarries just south (SCRI-630) and west of Scorpion Canyon (SCRI-610), and protection from the elements and other people. Evidence for increased microblade specialization during the Late period includes fewer and more concentrated TDR microblade sites, higher production success rates, increased standardization, and the presence of TDR microblades primarily in coastal residential bases as opposed to interior camps.

DISCUSSION AND CONCLUSIONS

I conclude with several general interpretations regarding prehistoric settlement and subsistence patterns on the East End. During the Early period the East End was occupied by foraging groups that shifted between interior and coastal locales, depending on the seasonal availability of terrestrial plants and marine resources. Among the areas inhabited are El Montañon ridges and zones above 1,200 feet, which suggests that protection from the elements and convenient access to marine resources were not important considerations for Early period settlement. Instead, it appears that East End residents selected locations based on multiple terrestrial and marine variables, including water, island chert, plants, shellfish and other marine resources, and viewshed. The seasonal interior-coastal emphasis of this period contrasts with the specialized activities later in time, when exploitation of fish and chert were intensified and emphasized at the expense of other marine and terrestrial resources.

Middle period coastal habitation on the East End fits well within broader interpretations of intensified marine subsistence activities and increased cultural complexity among growing Chumash populations (Arnold 1987; Kennett 1998). During this time East End inhabitants appeared to shift their focus to marine resource–dominated activities, inhabiting coastal residential bases to intensively fish and interact in larger exchange networks to support increases in local population densities. The most intensively occupied sites, with respect to length of time and/or population, are found at Scorpion Anchorage, Little Scorpion Anchorage, and Smugglers Cove. Scorpion Anchorage and Smugglers Cove along with nearby Yellowbanks Anchorage have the broadest stretches of open coastline, which include sandy/cobble substrates, as well as access to rocky intertidal habitats, kelp forests, and pelagic fishing. Along with viable landing and launching areas for canoes, these areas would have been the most viable for sustaining sedentary populations based on intensive marine-oriented activities.

Furthermore, I argue that trapezoidal microblade production was conducted during the late Middle period as a part-time activity that required limited reorganization of the existing seasonal settlement-subsistence cycle but some degree of reprioritization of time and labor shifting from subsistence to socioeconomic-oriented activities. The abundance of sites with evidence for trapezoidal microblade manufacture and their dispersed distribution across the East End landscape implies that no specialization was occurring at that time. Instead, it seems that microblades were produced opportunistically along with other tools, integrated into seasonal rounds concentrating on interior resources.

If ownership and competition were indeed significant at this time, when environmental conditions were presumably deteriorating, then it is argued that territoriality and rights to particular resources such as quarries were signaled through habitation on-site or nearby rather than aggressive behavior such as violence. Nevertheless, any further interpretations of the Transitional period are difficult to make, given the overall lack of deposits dating to the late Middle and Transitional periods. The absence of data may be related to at least partial abandonment of the East End and most of the Channel Islands, as well as increased competition and circumscription among the remaining inhabitants because of resource stress (see Kennett 1998:318; Yatsko 2000). However, the problem is also related to limited archaeological visibility or the difficulty of identifying deposits dating to such a short interval.

By the Late period, people shifted from foraging to collecting strategies, perhaps because of increasing population densities and emphasis on maritime activities, including fishing and canoe-based transportation and exchange. Permanent residential bases with large populations were inhabited along the coast. For example, it has been estimated that 262 people inhabited *Swaxil* (SCRI-423/507) at Scorpion Anchorage in 1782 (Johnson 1982:111). Ongoing occupation at these locations was influenced by a combination of factors, with access to marine resources and maritime opportunities being among the most significant to Late period residents. As observed by Kennett (1998:322), "in this context, coastal

locations were at a premium and the costs of losing access to intertidal resources precluded the seasonal establishment of interior residences." Tethered to the coast, Late period inhabitants intensified microblade production through logistical forays into the interior to extract chert suitable to transport back to their residential bases in order to produce microblades at home rather than at the quarries themselves.

The spatial separation of chert extraction and microblade production represents a significant shift in resource prioritization during the Late period, which may be interpreted from several different perspectives. First, as people began to inhabit coastal bases for longer periods, extensive forays into the interior to collect and process resources would have become more costly in terms of time and labor expenditure. Instead, it would have been cheaper to quarry the appropriate-sized chunks of chert and transport them to their coastal base for the manufacture of microblades and other tools (Kennett 1998:343). Second, as competition intensified as a result of increased population densities, control over resources would have become more intensified as well. However, rather than investing energy into signaling use of and regulating access to chert quarries, East End inhabitants shifted their emphasis to specializing in the production of microblades and controlling their manufacture and distribution in the regional economy.

Third, it is also important to consider how this shift may represent some degree of regulation or control over microblade production. Specialization is manifested in where and how TDR microblades were manufactured and distributed in contrast to the dispersed activities of trapezoidal microblade production. With regard to production, TDR microblades were made in significantly higher quantities despite the higher raw material costs associated with manufacturing them, reflecting increasing amounts of labor invested in microblade production (Arnold 2001:17–18). In addition, there were increased standardization and success rates for TDR types, indicating increased efforts in tool design (Arnold et al. 2001:130). Furthermore, TDR microblades were produced exclusively on the East End at a limited number of coastal residential bases. Unlike during the late Middle period, when microblade activities were unregulated, it appears that East End inhabitants controlled TDR microblade production to some degree, at least with respect to preventing outsiders from taking advantage of their local specialist opportunities.

To answer the question originally posed in this chapter, microblade production did have an impact on East End settlement and subsistence strategies, although much more intensively during the Late period, when it was transformed from a dispersed, part-time activity into a formalized craft specialization. Arnold (2001) and others have documented bead-making industries of coastal residential bases on western Santa Cruz Island at that time and have argued for the emergence of craft specialists who invested their efforts in manufactured goods to be exchanged in Chumash trade networks. As population densities increased on the island and resources became more intensively exploited, island inhabitants turned to producing items for exchange in order to buffer resource stress through importing food resources from the mainland.

In this context East End participation in the Chumash economy during the Late period may be viewed as activated by motivated individuals who took advantage of increased dependence on exchange and maritime-oriented activities by manipulating local chert resources; who influenced and/or supported microblade specialists and others through intensified fishing; and who capitalized on ownership and use of canoes for fishing, transportation, and exchange. Late period inhabitants of the East End, with their nearby chert, fresh water, marine resources, and suitable launching and landing areas, had access to the raw materials and opportunities for control over resource production and distribution. In sum, all of the associated technological and organizational implications of microblade production, and the ability to exchange microblades for other resources across accessible land and maritime trade routes, ultimately provided East End inhabitants with one of the contexts in which wealth accumulation, social ranking, and complexity are believed to have emerged on the Channel Islands.

Acknowledgments. This chapter represents some of the results and interpretations of my dissertation research, which was funded and supported by Channel Islands National Park. I would like to thank the park and its employees wholeheartedly for assisting me throughout the fieldwork and for teaching me about island living, especially Ann Huston, Georganna Hawley, Sam Spaulding, Mike Morales, Mike Torkelson, Darcy McDonald, John Coggins, and many others. I would also like to thank the former park archaeologist, Don Morris, for originally providing me with the opportunity to conduct fieldwork on eastern Santa Cruz Island. Special appreciation is extended to my adviser, Mike Glassow, for encouraging and directing my graduate work on the Channel Islands and for being a seemingly infinite source of knowledge on Chumash prehistory. Thanks and gratitude are extended to all of the volunteers who assisted in the fieldwork: Kate Ballantyne, Corinna Bridges, Mike Caldwell, Nathan Craig, Dave Daniels, Alexa Delwiche, Skyler Denniston, Diana Dyste, Dave Hacker, Nina Harris, Cassandra Hensher, Jade Hoffman, John Jackson, Lauren Jelinek, Marley Kellar, Erin King, Karin Klemic, Philippe Lapin, Ian Lindsay, Talin Lindsay, Glennda Luhnow, Erica Maier, Dustin McKenzie, Rod McLean, Alex Morrison, Anna Noah, John Otte, Arianne Perez, Dann Perry, Jacob Perry, Laura Perry, Levi Perry, Margo Perry, Laurie Pfeiffer, Kate Rose, Claudia Rumold, John Sharp, Ves Snelson, Ian Stonerock, James Swan, and Chris Wright. I would also like to thank Jeanne Arnold, John Johnson, Terry Joslin, Doug Kennett, Peter Paige, Torrey Rick, and Andy Yatsko for their insights into various aspects of Channel Islands prehistory. In addition, I appreciate the assistance of Bonnie Yoshida, Melissa Chatfield, and Corina Kellner at the Central Coast Information Center. Finally, I would like to thank Jeanne Arnold, Gary Coupland, and two anonymous reviewers for their helpful editorial comments.

REFERENCES CITED

Arnold, J. E.
1987   *Craft Specialization in the Prehistoric Channel Islands, California*. University of California Press, Berkeley.
1991   Transformation of a Regional Economy: Sociopolitical Evolution and the Production of Valuables in Southern California. *Antiquity* 65:953–962.
1992a   Complex Hunter-Gatherer-Fishers of Prehistoric California: Chiefs, Specialists, and Maritime Adaptations. *American Antiquity* 57:60–84.
1992b   Cultural Disruption and the Political Economy in Channel Islands Prehistory. In *Essays on the Prehistory of Maritime California*, edited by T. L. Jones, pp. 67–83. Center for Archaeological Research Publication 10, University of California, Davis.
1995   Transportation Innovation and Social Complexity among Maritime Hunter-Gatherer Societies. *American Anthropologist* 97:733–747.
2001   The Chumash in World and Regional Perspectives. In *The Origins of a Pacific Coast Chiefdom: The Chumash of the Channel Islands*, edited by J. E. Arnold, pp. 1–19. University of Utah Press, Salt Lake City.

Arnold, J. E. (editor)
1996   *Emergent Complexity: The Evolution of Intermediate Societies*. International Monographs in Prehistory, Ann Arbor, Michigan.

Arnold, J. E., R. H. Colten, and S. Pletka
1997   Contexts of Cultural Change in Insular California. *American Antiquity* 62(2):300–318.

Arnold, J. E., A. M. Preziosi, and P. Shattuck
2001   Flaked Stone Craft Production and Exchange in Island Chumash Territory. In *The Origins of a Pacific Coast Chiefdom: The Chumash of the Channel Islands*, edited by J. E. Arnold, pp. 113–132. University of Utah Press, Salt Lake City.

Bettinger, R. L.
1991   *Hunter-Gatherers: Archaeological and Evolutionary Theory*. Plenum, New York.

Boone, J. L.
1992   Competition, Conflict, and the Development of Social Hierarchies. In *Evolutionary Ecology and Human Behavior*, edited by E. A. Smith and B. Winterhalder, pp. 301–337. Aldine de Gruyter, New York.

Clifford, R. A.
2001   Middle Holocene Hilltop and Ridgeline Settlement on the Northern Channel Islands of California: A Study of Evolutionary Stability. Unpublished Master's thesis, Department of Anthropology, California State University, Long Beach.

Feinman, G. M.
1995   The Emergence of Inequality: A Focus on Strategies and Processes. In *Foundations of Social Inequality*, edited by T. D. Price and G. M. Feinman, pp. 255–279. Plenum, New York.

Glassow, M. A.
1993   Changes in Subsistence on Marine Resources through 7,000 Years of Prehistory on Santa Cruz Island. In *Archaeology on the Northern Channel Islands of California: Studies of Subsistence, Economics, and Social Organization*, edited by M. A. Glassow, pp. 75–94. Archives of California Prehistory 34. Coyote Press, Salinas, California.
1996   The Significance to California Prehistory of the Earliest Mortars and Pestles. *Pacific Coast Archaeological Society Quarterly* 32(4):14–26.
1997   Middle Holocene Cultural Development in the Central Santa Barbara Channel Region. In *Archaeology of the California Coast during the Middle Holocene*, edited by J. M. Erlandson and M. A. Glassow, pp. 73–90. Institute of Archaeology, University of California, Los Angeles.
1999   Measurement of Population Growth and Decline during California Prehistory. *Journal of California and Great Basin Anthropology* 21(1):45–66.

Hayden, B.
1995   Pathways to Power: Principles for Creating Socioeconomic Inequalities. In *Foundations of Social Inequality*, edited by T. D. Price and G. M. Feinman, pp. 15–86. Plenum, New York.

Johnson, J. R.
1982   An Ethnohistoric Study of the Island Chumash. Unpublished Master's thesis, Department of Anthropology, University of California, Santa Barbara.

1993   Cruzeño Chumash Social Geography. In *Archaeology on the Northern Channel Islands of California: Studies of Subsistence, Economics, and Social Organization*, edited by M. A. Glassow, pp. 19–46. Archives of California Prehistory 34. Coyote Press, Salinas, California.

2000   Social Responses to Climate Change among the Chumash Indians of South-Central California. In *The Way the Wind Blows: Climate, History, and Human Action*, edited by R. J. McIntosh, J. A. Tainter, and S. K. McIntosh, pp. 301–327. Columbia University Press, New York.

Junak, S., T. Ayers, R. Scott, D. Wilken, and D. Young
1995   *A Flora of Santa Cruz Island.* Santa Barbara Botanic Garden, Santa Barbara, California.

Kantner, J.
1996   Political Competition among the Chaco Anasazi of the American Southwest. *Journal of Anthropological Archaeology* 15:41–105.

Kennett, D. J.
1998   Behavioral Ecology and the Evolution of Hunter-Gatherer Societies on the Northern Channel Islands. Unpublished Ph.D. dissertation, Department of Anthropology, University of California, Santa Barbara.

Kennett, D. J., J. R. Johnson, T. C. Rick, D. P. Morris, and J. Christy
2000   Historic Chumash Settlement on Eastern Santa Cruz Island, Southern California. *Journal of California and Great Basin Anthropology* 22:212–222.

Kennett, D. J., and J. P. Kennett
2000   Competitive and Cooperative Responses to Climatic Instability in Coastal Southern California. *American Antiquity* 65(2):379–395.

King, C. D.
1981   The Evolution of Chumash Society: A Comparative Study of Artifacts Used in Social System Maintenance in the Santa Barbara Channel Region before A.D. 1804. Unpublished Ph.D. dissertation, Department of Anthropology, University of California, Davis.

Lambert, P. M.
1993   Health in Prehistoric Populations of the Santa Barbara Channel Islands. *American Antiquity* 58:509–522.

1994   War and Peace on the Western Front: A Study of Violent Conflict and Its Correlates in Prehistoric Hunter-Gatherer Societies of Coastal Southern California. Unpublished Ph.D. dissertation, Department of Anthropology, University of California, Santa Barbara.

Lambert, P. M., and P. L. Walker
1991   Physical Anthropological Evidence for the Evolution of Social Complexity in Coastal Southern California. *Antiquity* 65:963–973.

Larson, D. O., J. R. Johnson, and J. Michaelsen
1994   Missionization among the Coastal Chumash of California: A Study of Risk Minimization Strategies. *American Anthropologist* 96:263–299.

Minc, L., and K. Smith
1989   The Spirit of Survival: Cultural Responses to Resource Variability in North Alaska. In *Bad Year Economics: Cultural Responses to Risk and Uncertainty,* edited by P. Halstead and J. O'Shea, pp. 8–39. Cambridge University Press, Cambridge, UK.

Perry, J. E.
2003   Changes in Prehistoric Land and Resource Use among Complex Hunter-Gatherer-Fishers on Eastern Santa Cruz Island. Unpublished Ph.D. dissertation, Department of Anthropology, University of California, Santa Barbara.

Peterson, R. R.
1994   Archaeological Settlement Dynamics on the South Side of Santa Cruz Island. In *The Fourth California Islands Symposium: Update on the Status of Resources,* edited by W. L. Halvorson and G. J. Maender, pp. 215–222. Santa Barbara Museum of Natural History, Santa Barbara, California.

Preziosi, A. M.
2001   Standardization and Specialization: The Island Chumash Microdrill Industry. In *The Origins of a Pacific Coast Chiefdom: The Chumash of the Channel Islands,* edited by J. E. Arnold, pp. 151–164. University of Utah Press, Salt Lake City.

Raab, L. M., and D. O. Larson
1997   Medieval Climatic Anomaly and Punctuated Cultural Evolution in Coastal Southern California. *American Antiquity* 62(2):319–336.
Timbrook, J.
1993   Island Chumash Ethnobotany. In *Archaeology on the Northern Channel Islands of California: Studies of Subsistence, Economics, and Social Organization*, edited by M. A. Glassow, pp. 47–62. Archives of California Prehistory 34. Coyote Press, Salinas, California.
Walker, P. L.
1996   Integrative Approaches to the Study of Ancient Health: An Example from the Santa Barbara Channel Area of Southern California. In *Notes on Populational Significance of Paleopathological Conditions: Health, Illness, and Death in the Past*, edited by A. Pérez-Pérez, pp. 97–105. Fundació Uriach, Barcelona.
Winterhalder, B., and E. A. Smith
1992   Evolutionary Ecology and the Social Sciences. In *Evolutionary Ecology and Human Behavior*, edited by E. A. Smith and B. Winterhalder, pp. 3–24. Aldine de Gruyter, New York.
Yatsko, A.
2000   Late Holocene Paleoclimatic Stress and Prehistoric Human Occupation on San Clemente Island. Unpublished Ph.D. dissertation, Department of Anthropology, University of California, Los Angeles.

9

Specialized Bead Making among Island Chumash Households

Community Labor Organization during the Historic Period

Anthony P. Graesch

The social, economic, and political fabric of hunter-gatherer societies is perhaps most tightly threaded around the organization and activities of individual households. The household is a remarkably stable social arena through which environmental risk is mediated and several of the most basic of human needs are satisfied: members gather and share food, divide and appropriate labor, and transmit both knowledge and wealth from one generation to the next. Despite cross-cultural variability in composition and rules of residential affiliation, households are bounded, corporate social groups to which everyday socially constituted activities, economic transactions, and political negotiations are anchored.

In this chapter I examine household behavior in later Chumash society, or specifically, the period of time spanning initial European colonization on California's Santa Barbara mainland in 1782 and the abandonment of northern Channel Island communities around 1819. At the time of European contact the Chumash of southern California were one of only a handful of complex hunter-gatherer societies in North America. Hereditary leadership, craft specialization, and remarkably complex regional exchange networks are just several of the defining cultural traits observed in the archaeological, ethnographic, and historic records. However, our understanding of Island Chumash society in later prehistory and the early Historic period has been reliant on both archaeological and textual data that speak

to *community*-level behavior. Conducted under the aegis of a broader, multiyear investigation on Santa Cruz Island (Arnold 1995a), this analysis addresses the internal organization of Island Chumash communities, focusing specifically on the socioeconomic contexts of household participation in specialized shellworking industries and the larger regional economy. Household data derived from analytically detailed, time-intensive archaeological investigations in Island Chumash houses are used to explore *interhousehold* variability in production activities, access to nonlocal trade items, and the social and political roles households and families played in the Historic-era political economy. These issues are of broader importance to the anthropological study of labor organization and processes of political evolution among intermediate societies.

A BACKGROUND TO THE HISTORIC PERIOD POLITICAL ECONOMY

Upon Spanish arrival in southern California during the 1770s and 1780s, much of the Chumash economy was fueled by the circulation of specialized shell valuables that were manufactured in communities on the northern Channel Islands and transported to mainland villages under the control of high-status individuals (or families) who owned redwood plank canoes. Specialized production of shell valuables emerged in the context of broader cultural changes on the northern Channel Islands during the Transitional period (AD 1150–1300). Environmental and political circumstances appear to have been catalysts for the emergence of an increasingly complex regional exchange network in which shell valuables were traded to the mainland in return for a wide variety of goods (Arnold 1992a, 1992b; Arnold and Munns 1994). Facilitating the transport of people and goods, plank canoe owners apparently adopted an increasingly important role in the economy and amassed wealth and power as regulators of cross-channel exchange throughout late prehistory. By virtue of controlling access to the means of craft distribution, canoe owners and their families were in a favorable position to manipulate the labor of nonelite households that manufactured shell valuables for trade (Arnold 1995b, 2000; Arnold and Munns 1994).

Transitional (AD 1150–1300) and Late period (AD 1300–1782) shellworking activities were most intensively focused on the production of beads made from the locally available gastropod *Olivella biplicata*. From the standpoint of labor investment and quantity of production, *Olivella* bead making remained one of the most important shellworking activities throughout the Late and Historic periods (Arnold and Graesch 2001). However, the introduction of European goods into the postcontact regional economy appears to have motivated substantial changes to specialized shellworking activities. The circulation of glass beads and iron needles, in particular, seems to have had the greatest effect on craft-manufacturing processes and the value of traditional shell beads (Graesch 2001; King 1990). Following European colonization of southern California, intensive shellworking activities were expanded to include the production of large numbers of beads and ornaments from *Haliotis rufescens* (red abalone) shells, and *Olivella* bead making shifted back to an emphasis on wall bead types (Arnold and Graesch 2001; King 1990). European goods appear to have also reinforced rather than disrupted the existing hierarchical relations apparent in Late period communities. Rare, valuable goods were used as markers of prestige and wealth both before and after contact, reinforcing status hierarchies in an already socially and economically stratified society. Postcontact circulation of European goods

and other exotic materials presented existing elites with the opportunity to acquire and manipulate goods potentially greater in value than those of local origin (Graesch 2001). It is in the context of these Historic period changes to specialized shellworking processes and the regional economy that I turn to an examination of socioeconomic behavior and labor organization at the level of the household.

THE ORGANIZATION OF ISLAND CHUMASH HOUSEHOLD LABOR

Much has been written on the incipient forms of labor organization that accompany the emergence of socioeconomic hierarchies and craft specialization (for instance, see Arnold 2000; Arnold and Munns 1994; Brumfiel and Earle 1987; Costin 1991; Earle 1987). Of salience to this investigation is the nature of the socioeconomic relationships that are formed between elites and nonelite craft specialists. Studies of complex societies have traditionally classified these relationships as examples of either *attached* or *independent* specialization (Brumfiel and Earle 1987). The extent to which the behavior and products of craftspersons are controlled by an elite class has by and large served as the defining characteristic of each form of labor relations: attached specialists produce for elite patrons who derive status and wealth from surplus craft goods, whereas independent specialists freely produce goods to satisfy open-ended demand. More recently, Arnold and Munns (1994) have questioned the universality of these categories by considering the conditions under which craft specialization emerges, the types of goods produced, and the spatial placement of both elites and nonelite specialists on the landscape. They have argued that traditional definitions of attached and independent labor relationships may be too rigid to apply to Island Chumash society, where the conditions under which socioeconomic relationships were formed between elites and specialists seemingly varied with the cultural and spatial contexts of economic change (Arnold and Munns 1994). Because Channel Islands elites controlled the means of distribution via their ownership of costly plank canoes, the management of craft production could have arisen without the need for elite supervision of specialist activities (Arnold and Munns 1994). In other words, specialist labor may have been controlled by elites only to the extent that elites controlled the means of craft product distribution to mainland consumers (Arnold 2000; Arnold and Munns 1994). Although elite control of craft distribution would have prevented nonelite specialists from being fully independent, it may have also freed both elites and nonelite specialists from the burdens of an attached relationship, such as the supervision of production activities. Socioeconomic relations between elite and nonelite households may be best characterized as having been *inter*dependent. In other words, while specialists *could* have been attached to elites in the traditional sense (that is, spatially proximate and producing for an elite audience), there is also a good chance that they were only dependent on elites to manage distribution (Arnold 2000; Arnold and Munns 1994). Moreover, although some of the specialist-produced beads and ornaments may have had a solely elite audience, the mass-produced currency beads were clearly not solely for elite consumption and were used by all in the society, a hallmark never associated with the products of attached specialists.

The nature of labor relations between elites and nonelite specialists has yet to be fully tested with archaeological data. The differences between attached and interdependent socioeconomic interactions are substantial and should have implications for the manner in which elite control of labor is manifested in the material culture of nonelite craft specialists, particularly at the level of the household. For instance, if nonelite bead-making specialists were closely attached to patron elites, then we should see evidence for rigid control over the production and distribution of craft products. In the Chumash case the organization of household labor with respect to production activities can be directly examined with the large specialized shellworking assemblages. Households producing shell valuables under the supervision of elite patrons should exhibit little variability with respect to production intensity and strategy. If nonelite specialist households were producing craft goods solely for elites, then it is not unreasonable

to expect that elites would want to maximize the efficiency of household labor expenditures. One rational approach to efficient production is to focus household labor on the manufacture of a specific type of shell good at a predetermined rate. In such a scenario, although different households may be instructed to produce different types of shell valuables, specialists within a household might be required to focus bead-making labor on only one product. Flexibility in production strategies and quantities would be discouraged.

Attached specialization, in the sense in which many archaeologists use the term, also has implications for the physical placement of elite and nonelite specialist households. Under circumstances in which elites needed to closely supervise specialist activities, we would expect to encounter at least one elite residence in every community of nonelite specialists. While the burdens of supervision could be costly, there was probably considerable incentive for elites to maximize production efficiency and discourage shirking behavior.

However, if nonelites were interdependent with elites but not attached spatially or in a patron-client relationship, then we might expect considerable variability with respect to the organization of household labor. Households that were dependent on elites for the movement of goods in and out of regional trade networks would still possess considerable autonomy in the organization of their domestic activities. We would expect to see considerable variability in shellworking strategies, including the intensity with which goods were produced and the kinds of valuables being manufactured. There is also little reason to expect an elite presence in every shellworking community if elites were not supervising specialist activities. By virtue of owning the only safe and reliable means of transportation (and distribution), elites were freed from the costly burdens of supervising craft production activities (Arnold and Munns 1994). Given that there is no archaeological or ethnographic evidence to suggest that elites had the power to physically coerce specialist labor, socioeconomic interactions between elite and nonelite specialists were likely cooperative: nonelite households could only access regional trade networks via boat owners, and boat owners could only stand to profit notably from exchange if nonelite households were willing to allocate household labor to the production of large quantities of shell valuables. Instead, we might expect elite households to be located in a few well-positioned communities, especially on the northeastern shores of Santa Cruz Island. These locations are the closest to the mainland and would afford frequent contact with established cross-channel trading activities. Elites who played a major role in the distribution and exchange of craft goods would certainly have been interested in minimizing transport costs and maximizing contact with mainland traders. But certainly other factors may have played roles in elite settlement, and, indeed, there is good ethnographic evidence for at least one elite community, *Liyam*, on the south-central shore of Santa Cruz Island (Johnson 1993, 2001).

We stand to learn a great deal about variability in the organization of labor and political economy among intermediate societies with the archaeological study of Historic-era Island Chumash households. In contrast to their mainland counterparts, the Island Chumash appear to have been less affected by early Spanish missionization efforts and were able to maintain many of their traditional lifeways for at least two generations following contact (Graesch 2001). This brief window in time is preserved in a near-pristine archaeological record on Santa Cruz Island and affords us the rare opportunity to examine variability in the role Chumash households played in the organization and operation of the postcontact political economy.

ISLAND CHUMASH HOUSES AND HOUSEHOLDS

Early observations and ethnographic notes by John P. Harrington suggest that Chumash houses were sturdy, semispherical, pole-and-thatch structures, encircling packed earth floors and small centrally placed hearths (Hudson and Blackburn 1983). Historic records culminating from a number of earlier European visits to the southern Californian coast generally support Harrington's descriptions, although many early European explorers and colonists may have exaggerated the size of Chumash houses, as well

as their total number of occupants. Past and present archaeological research indicates that circular house floors typically ranged from 4 to 12 m in diameter, with 6 to 8 m being the norm (Gamble 1991, 1995). Recent investigations on Santa Cruz Island revealed that the methods of floor construction varied among communities, and much of this variation is best explained with respect to the availability of certain soil types (see below). Most floors were likely covered with woven sea-grass (*Phyllospadix* sp.) mats, some of which are still visible in eroding coastal profiles. House interiors were often subdivided, with woven partitions hung from upper supporting poles, and doorways were typically positioned on the lee side of the structure (Hudson and Blackburn 1983).

Ethnographic data suggest that in contrast to the multiple-family households of the Northwest Coast, Chumash houses were occupied by a nuclear family or small extended family (Blackburn 1975). The cohabitation of a married couple, their children, perhaps an aging grandparent, and/or a child's spouse was probably not uncommon (Hudson and Blackburn 1983). A chief's house may have sheltered an additional wife and possibly more children, given the general practice of polygyny by high-ranking chiefs (Johnson 2001). However, variation in household composition has yet to be archaeologically tested. Changes in the prehistoric and/or postcontact economies that led to an expansion of the total range of subsistence and economic alternatives available to some domestic groups may have stimulated household growth. Late and Historic period households that controlled access to redwood plank canoes, for instance, may have been larger and more complex than other nonelite households by virtue of their privileged roles in the political economy.

Situated directly atop deep, stratified midden deposits, Historic period coastal communities on Santa Cruz Island typically consisted of 9 to 16 spatially clustered houses (known range, 4 to 20 houses; J. E. Arnold, personal communication 1999), some positioned no more than two meters apart. Considering the temperate climate of southern California, Chumash architecture was far from permanent, yet deep, well-defined house depressions, some approaching 1.5 m in depth, are still clearly visible on the landscape long after house abandonment and deterioration. Much of this is a result of refuse disposal behavior, as the Island Chumash would typically deposit food remains and other by-products generated from household activities directly around the walls of their domestic structures. The high visibility of house depressions affords us the opportunity to identify and sample domestic contexts without extensive exploratory excavation.

Formation Processes

The use of households as spatially discrete analytic units requires a clear understanding of the processes contributing to the formation of house depressions and associated artifact-bearing deposits (Hayden 1997; Schiffer 1987). Episodes of house construction, occupation, repair, abandonment, and postabandonment use will have different effects on the distribution of artifacts and features through space and time. For instance, the use of abandoned houses as trash dumps can result in concentrations of subsistence refuse, tools, and craft-related by-products in domestic contexts other than that from which they originated (Schiffer 1989). The potential for interpretive error can be reduced by studying how Island Chumash house deposits came to be formed. I have drawn on ethnographic observations, historic descriptions, and stratigraphic analyses to complete this task. In this analysis subsurface deposits are divided into three behaviorally significant strata: floors, floor accretion, and midden deposits.

Floors. House floors are packed-earth surfaces that were constructed from locally available soils and hardened by wetting and pounding with rocks (Hudson and Blackburn 1983). Most floors were built following the construction of a pole-and-thatch house frame, and house floors may have been rebuilt during episodes of house maintenance and structural repair (ibid.). Although the types of soil (clay and sand are common) used for floor construction vary with site location, all floor deposits tend to be highly consolidated and relatively barren with respect to household artifacts and refuse. Artifacts and subsistence refuse that are occasionally recovered in

floor deposits tend to be very small and/or highly fragmented. The excavations reported here did not fully penetrate any of the well-defined Historic period floors encountered, but augering at several houses and small-scale recovery of a floor segment at another Santa Cruz Island site indicate that floor deposits are typically no more than 4 to 5 cm thick (J. E. Arnold, personal communication 1999; see also Clemmer 1961 for similar observations at Morro Bay).

Floor accretion. Floor accretion deposits result from the accumulation of debris generated by daily household activities, wind, foot traffic, and slow organic deterioration of both thatch architecture and sea-grass mats. Despite efforts to keep house floors free of general clutter and refuse, residents appear to have regularly (and inadvertently) trampled debris on and into house floors. Over the course of house occupation, accumulated debris formed a discrete layer or layers of cultural remains that can be distinguished from constructed floor deposits. Deposits interpreted as floor accretion in Island Chumash houses are best characterized as moderately consolidated soil matrices containing low to moderate densities of highly fragmented subsistence remains and moderate to high densities of small craft-related artifacts, particularly shellworking goods (defined below).

Midden. Midden deposits are dense accumulations of refuse generated primarily from food-processing activities. Archaeologically these deposits are characterized by extraordinarily high densities of small, medium, and large fragments of unmodified shell and bone. Household artifacts, including shellworking by-products, fishhooks, chipped stone tools, and modified bone implements are also recovered in varying densities. Midden deposits tend to be loosely consolidated and contain very little soil. Because the Island Chumash were tossing much of their trash at the base of the exterior house walls, midden deposits typically circumscribe house floors and floor accretion. Small amounts of midden are occasionally observed directly under and above floor accretion deposits near house perimeters (see Figure 9.1). This stratigraphic arrangement may be the product of older thatch walls yielding

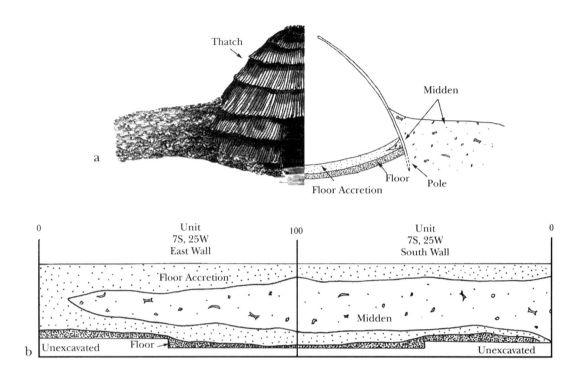

Figure 9.1. (a) Illustration and schematic profile of a Chumash house and associated floor and midden deposits, and (b) stratigraphic profile of a 1-x-1-m excavation unit placed at the edge of house 8 at SCRI-192. Illustration by author.

to the weight of external refuse heaps and allowing small amounts of midden to slide into the house interior (including before and during rebuilding of houses). It is also possible that the interior edges of Chumash houses may have differentially accumulated household-generated refuse and suffered less trampling because of the in-sloping walls, and such places may have been less accessible when house floors were cleaned.

DATA RECOVERY AND ANALYSIS

Data for this analysis are derived from recent archaeological investigations at four prominent Historic period villages on Santa Cruz Island (Figure 9.2). Investigations were directed by Jeanne E. Arnold (UCLA Department of Anthropology) and funded by the National Science Foundation (SBR 95-11576). Primary field and laboratory research was conducted between 1995 and 1998 with the assistance of trained UCLA undergraduate and graduate students as well as volunteers. Field methods included both

surface and subsurface investigation techniques, and I maintain an analytic distinction between data sets generated by these two separate collection strategies.

Surface data were collected from 2-x-1-m units systematically placed in the interior and/ or exterior of 31 house depressions distributed among three west-end Santa Cruz Island communities (Table 9.1). On removal of thick (1 to 2 cm) organic duff, ground surfaces within these units were gently scraped by trowel to a median depth of 0.5 cm. I use surface data to examine differences in household craft activities and access to nonlocal trade goods.

Subsurface data were recovered during the partial excavation of five Island Chumash houses (see Table 9.1) and are used to address temporal changes in Historic household production strategies. Although both interior and exterior house deposits were explored during house excavation, I discuss subsets of artifact assemblages recovered from 1-x-1-m excavation units placed in interior floor and floor accretion de-

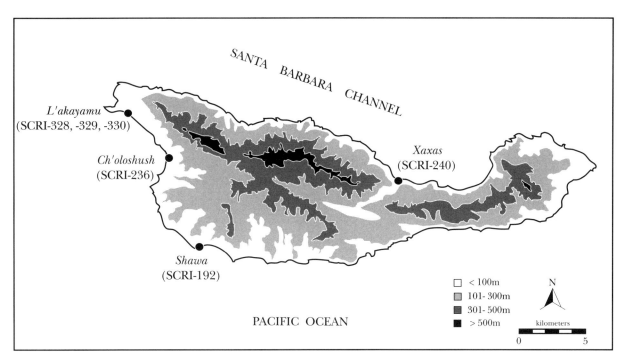

Figure 9.2. Historic period villages on Santa Cruz Island considered in this analysis. Map by author.

Table 9.1. Sources of Santa Cruz Island Data

Site	Village Name	House	
		Surface Units	Excavation Units
SCRI-192	*Shawa*	1, 2[a], 4[a], 5, 6[a], 7, 8	4, 8
SCRI-236	*Ch'oloshush*	1, 2, 4, 5, 7, 9, 11, 13	5, 9
SCRI-240	*Xaxas*	—	1
SCRI-328[b]	*L'akayamu*	1, 2, 3, 4, 5, 6, 7, 10, 11	—
SCRI-329[b]	*L'akayamu*	19[a]	—
SCRI-330[b]	*L'akayamu*	12[a], 13, 14, 15, 16[a], 18	—

[a] Houses at which only one surface unit (2 x 1 m) was established (see Graesch 2000).

[b] House numbers at SCRI-328, -329, and -330 were adjusted from those in Graesch (2000).

posits. All interior house deposits were excavated by trowel in 5-cm increments. Both surface and subsurface deposits were screened with 3-mm ($^{1}/_{8}$″) mesh and retained for full laboratory processing in the California Channel Islands Laboratory at UCLA.

Most or all of the houses considered in this analysis were seemingly occupied contemporaneously until or near the time of abandonment; thus, trash was not deposited in or next to other occupied houses. Furthermore, selected house depressions appear to have been only minimally affected by recent ranching activities and were not the focus of early twentieth century archaeological excavations. We have high confidence that craft-related artifacts and valuables are associated with the activities of the houses in or near which we find them.

Two ethnographic references to bead-making activities in much later Historic period communities on the mainland suggest that specialists of that era may have preferred to work in outdoor areas (Johnson 2001). Better lighting in outdoor work spaces might have facilitated intricate shellworking. However, our recent field investigations in and around Santa Cruz Island house depressions indicate that a considerable amount of bead making occurred both indoors and outdoors. In this analysis I assume that the shellworking artifacts found in and near individual house depressions (see below) are reasonably representative of the bead-making activities of the house's occupants.

Assemblages of craft-related artifacts considered in this analysis include the finished goods and manufacturing by-products associated with three major shellworking traditions. These include several categories of production-related artifacts manufactured from *Olivella biplicata* (purple olive), *Haliotis rufescens* (red abalone), and *Tivela stultorum* (Pismo clam) shells. Artifacts discussed include finished beads, beads-in-production, bead blanks, detritus, and chipped/modified shell fragments. In general, the bead-making process entailed the isolation of desirable shell fragments, perimeter chipping of these fragments to form a bead blank, and drilling followed by perimeter grinding. The use of excessive force during the drilling process sometimes caused bead blanks to split, and bead blanks (whole or broken) exhibiting fully or partially drilled holes but unfinished perimeters are classified as beads-in-production (abbreviated as "bip" in tables). Each stage of the production process required several different tools, including sandstone or wood bead-drilling anvils, bone and/or stone pressure flakers, chert micro-drills, and sandstone grinding slabs. Arnold and Graesch (2001) discuss in great detail each shellworking tradition; in the interest of space I do not review these here.

In the analysis that follows I use densities of both detritus and beads-in-production as separate indices of bead-production intensity. I assume that higher-intensity bead-making activities generated greater quantities of production by-products per volume excavated, including general detritus and beads-in-production. Because there are multiple ways to examine shell bead-production activities, an exclusive reliance on either of these artifact categories is problematic and introduces the potential for misinterpreta-

tion of variability in shellworking assemblages. Varying densities of *Olivella* or red abalone detritus, for example, could reflect variability in the extent to which each shell specimen is used during the bead-making process. More exhaustive use of shell material by some households may have resulted in lower quantities of detritus than generated by other households that produced more or less equivalent numbers of shell beads but processed individual shells less exhaustively. Similarly, interhousehold variability in densities of beads-in-production could reflect slight differences in bead-making proficiency (more-skilled specialists would be expected to make fewer mistakes than less-skilled specialists). Thus, a consideration of *both* artifact categories is a preferred way to examine variability in the intensity of shellworking activities. Although other bead-making artifact categories, such as bead blanks, are also informative with regard to production behavior, they are less useful as direct indices of production intensity. Bead blanks, for instance, can be manufactured in advance and cached for later use, whereas rejected beads-in-production are unambiguous indicators of a bead maker's attempt to produce a finished bead in a particular time and place.

However, *Tivela* beads-in-production (and finished beads) are exceptionally rare in these assemblages and cannot be used analytically in the same manner as *Olivella* and *Haliotis rufescens* beads-in-production. *Tivela* bead-making processes appear to have been different from the latter two shellworking industries in that proportionally more by-products were generated per individual bead produced. Thus, I use combined densities of *Tivela* flakes, detritus, and chipped/modified fragments (defined by Arnold and Graesch 2001:97–98) to evaluate variability in the intensity of bead-making activities that incorporated this particular shell.

Finally, variability in household wealth is examined with assemblages of prestige goods or objects that appear to have held high value by virtue of their exotic (nonlocal) origin or the considerable investments of time and energy required for their production or acquisition. In Historic-era assemblages these include nearly all goods of European origin, such as glass beads and other glass objects, metal tools, and ceramics. Other prestige goods include steatite vessels and tools, nonlocal lithic specimens, and rare shell beads, particularly *Mytilus californianus* (California mussel) tube beads and *Tivela stultorum* tube beads. Most prestige goods were available to island households only through cross-channel trade networks, but a few types, such as *Mytilus* and *Tivela* tube beads, were probably manufactured in island communities.

RESULTS

Shawa (SCRI-192)

The Morse Point site (SCRI-192), identified as the village of *Shawa*, was an important Late and Historic period village situated on the southwestern shore of Santa Cruz Island (Arnold 1990). The site features 10 well-defined house depressions arranged in a gentle arc on a low marine terrace (Figure 9.3). Eleven surface collection units were used to test the interior and exterior surface deposits associated with seven houses, and subsurface investigations were conducted in house 4

and house 8 (see Table 9.1). Excavation data used in this analysis were collected from deposits between 0 and 15 cm in depth in seven 1-x-1-m excavation units placed in house 4 and in five units established in house 8.

Surface assemblages. Correspondence analysis of surface-collected shellworking assemblages suggests that occupants of the majority of houses tested at *Shawa* were pursuing similar production strategies, allocating roughly equivalent amounts of time and labor to specialized bead-making activities (Figure 9.4). Surface assemblages recovered in and near houses 2, 4, 5, and 7 indicate a considerable degree of similarity with respect to *total* shellworking activities and an overall emphasis on *Olivella* wall bead making: these houses exhibit modest densities of *Olivella* detritus and relatively low densities of *Haliotis rufescens* and *Tivela stultorum* detritus and other bead-making artifacts. However, there is no evidence to suggest that specialists at these houses were coordinating their efforts, and

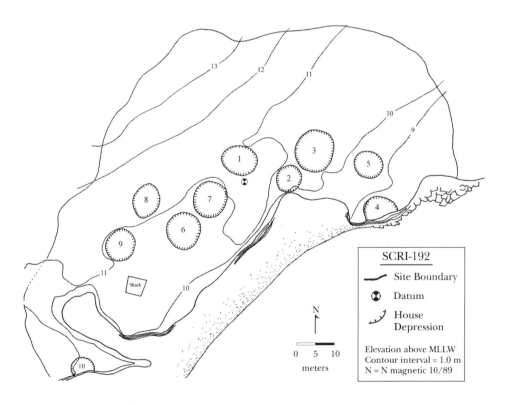

Figure 9.3. Map of *Shawa* (SCRI-192). After Arnold (2001:Figure 2.21).

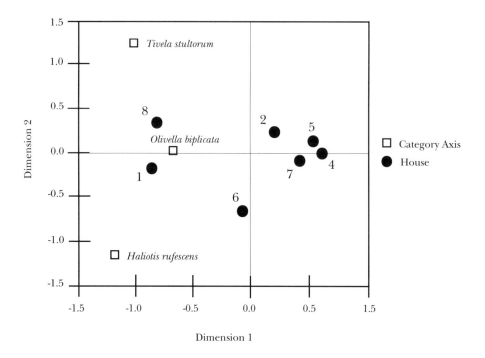

Figure 9.4. Correspondence plot of shellworking detritus densities by house at *Shawa* (SCRI-192).

Table 9.2. Surface Densities of *Olivella biplicata* Bead-Making Artifacts from Selected House Depressions at SCRI-192 (counts/m²)

House	*Olivella* Wall			*Olivella* Callus			*Olivella* Detritus
	bead	bip[a]	blank	bead	bip	blank	
1	12.3	43.3	18.3	2.5	3.5	21.5	4,245.0
2	4.5	6.0	5.5	1.5	1.5	9.0	1,600.0
4	8.0	11.5	6.5	3.0	1.0	17.0	1,350.0
5	6.8	7.0	8.0	3.3	0.5	11.0	2,306.3
6	12.5	74.5	21.0	1.0	1.5	22.5	3,400.0
7	6.5	32.5	11.3	1.5	3.5	17.5	2,918.8
8	24.5	49.3	23.3	3.5	3.0	39.5	5,762.5

[a]bip = bead-in-production

finer-scale variability in the intensity and type of shell bead production is apparent in the tabulated artifact densities (see Tables 9.2–9.4). For instance, house 7 exhibits comparatively higher densities of *Olivella* wall and callus beads-in-production and *Olivella* detritus than those observed in houses 2, 4, and 5. Similarly, house 2 exhibits significantly higher densities of *Tivela*

stultorum detritus and somewhat higher densities of by-products associated with *Haliotis rufescens* bead-making activities.

Dispersed to the left of the house cluster in Figure 9.4, houses 1, 6, and 8 can be contrasted as loci of high-intensity bead-production activities. The remarkably high densities of *Olivella* detritus and *Olivella* wall beads-in-production

Table 9.3. Surface Densities of *Haliotis rufescens* Bead-Making Artifacts from Selected House Depressions at SCRI-192 (counts/m^2)

House	*Haliotis rufescens*					
	bead	bip	blank	pre-blank	ch/mod[a]	detritus
1	0.3	20.5	28.3	1.0	—	101.5
2	0.5	3.5	2.0	0.3	—	23.5
4	—	2.0	6.0	0.5	0.3	11.0
5	0.3	0.8	3.5	—	—	5.0
6	—	12.0	19.0	0.5	—	79.5
7	0.3	8.3	10.3	0.5	—	20.8
8	1.3	13.3	45.0	5.8	0.5	59.3

[a]ch/mod = chipped/modified fragments (defined by Arnold and Graesch [2001:91] as *H. rufescens* pieces with part of the epidermis chipped away from the nacre)

Table 9.4. Surface Densities of *Tivela stultorum* Bead-Making Artifacts from Selected House Depressions at SCRI-192 (counts/m^2)

House	*Tivela stultorum*			
	bead	ch/mod[a]	flake	detritus
1	—	0.3	1.5	2.5
2	—	—	0.5	2.5
4	—	—	—	1.0
5	0.3	—	0.3	1.3
6	—	—	—	0.5
7	—	—	0.3	0.8
8	—	0.3	2.5	2.8

[a]ch/mod = chipped/modified fragments (defined by Arnold and Graesch [2001:98] as *Tivela* pieces with multiple overlapping flake scars)

recovered in and near these houses indicate significantly greater time and labor expenditures for the production of *Olivella* wall beads. House 8 is especially striking, exhibiting *Olivella* wall artifact densities that are between three and eight times greater than those recovered in houses 2, 4, and 5 (see Table 9.2). Interestingly, while detritus densities indicate that houses 1 and 6 were engaging in nearly as intensive *Olivella* wall bead making as house 8, densities of wall beads-in-production suggest that occupants of house 6 may have been generating as many, if not more, *Olivella* wall beads. Surface collections at house 6 yielded the highest densi-

ties of *Olivella* wall beads-in-production among all sampled houses at SCRI-192, as well as among all houses across the three Historic period communities examined in this analysis.

Specialists at houses 1, 6, and 8 were also producing roughly similar quantities of *Haliotis rufescens* beads. These three houses exhibit the highest densities of red abalone detritus, bead blanks, and beads-in-production among sampled houses at SCRI-192. Densities of red abalone beads-in-production and detritus at house 1, for example, are between 2 and 28 times greater than those observed in houses 2, 4, 5, and 7. However, surface assemblages of all sampled houses at SCRI-192 yielded very low densities of *Tivela stultorum* bead-making artifacts, suggesting only negligible labor and time investments when it came to working this particular shell (see Table 9.4).

The distribution of prestige goods recovered at SCRI-192 suggests that residents of houses 1, 6, 7, and 8 maintained access to regional trade networks (Table 9.5). Surface assemblages from house 8 yielded the overall highest density of valuables ($3.3/m^2$), all of which are glass beads and account for 48 percent of the entire assemblage of prestige items recovered at this site. House 8 assemblages are also striking in that they contain the highest frequency of rare glass beads, including three wire-wound specimens and a hand-drawn, polychrome variety. Slightly lower densities of prestige goods were recovered from house 1 ($2.0/m^2$), house 6 ($2.0/m^2$), and house 7 ($0.5/m^2$). Houses 1 and 6 yielded the greatest diversity of exotic items, including glass beads, nonlocal lithics, steatite, and a *Mytilus* tube bead.

Houses 1, 6, and 8 also yielded high densities of needle-drilled *Olivella* wall beads (see Table 9.5), perhaps reflecting differential access to iron needles. This is interesting, considering that members of all three of these households were engaging in some of the most intensive bead-making activities at this site, *and* these houses yielded the highest densities of prestige goods. These data suggest that there may be some relationship between production intensity and ac-

cess to prestige goods, although this relationship does not appear to be simple and/or easily assessed with these data subsets. For instance, while densities of iron needle-drilled beads are highest among houses practicing comparatively high-intensity bead-making activities, densities of needle-drilled beads do not neatly covary with densities of prestige goods (see Table 9.5). This issue is revisited in the discussion below.

Subsurface assemblages

House 4 at Shawa (SCRI-192). *Olivella* wall bead making dominated production activities at house 4 throughout the duration of Historic occupation. Mean densities of *Olivella* detritus and *Olivella* wall beads-in-production are nearly five times higher than densities of red abalone artifacts found in the same deposits. Densities of *Olivella biplicata* artifacts, however, vary with depth, and a general trend of declining production intensity over time is apparent in subsurface assemblages (Table 9.6). Changes in *Olivella* wall beads-in-production, bead blanks, and detritus are especially striking. For instance, densities of *Olivella* wall beads-in-production recovered in upper excavation levels ($873/m^3$ at 0–5 cm depth) are less than half of those recovered in deeper floor accretion deposits ($2,014.9/m^3$ at 10–15 cm depth). Similarly, upper levels exhibit 40 percent fewer pieces of *Olivella* detritus ($93,979.6/m^3$ at 0–5 cm) when compared to lower levels ($154,318.7/m^3$ at 10–15 cm).

Table 9.5. Surface Densities of Needle-Drilled Beads and Prestige Goods at SCRI-192 (counts/m^2)

House[a]	Needle-Drilled Beads	Prestige Goods	Description of Prestige Goods
2	4.0	—	
4	2.5	—	
5	0.5	—	
7	2.0	0.5	2 glass beads
1	6.0	2.0	5 glass beads; 1 *Mytilus* tube bead; 1 Franciscan chert flake
6	6.5	2.0	2 glass beads; 1 steatite fragment; 1 Vandenberg chert point
8	14.8	3.3	13 glass beads

[a]Houses are grouped according to clusters identified in Figure 9.4.

Table 9.6. Densities of *Olivella biplicata* Bead-Making Artifacts from House 4 Floor Deposits at SCRI-192 (counts/m³)

Depth (cm)	*Olivella* Wall			*Olivella* Callus			*Olivella* Detritus
	bead	bip	blank	bead	bip	blank	
00–05	423.4	873.0	689.1	93.4	64.2	294.9	93,979.6
05–10	461.5	1,235.9	794.9	138.5	87.2	405.1	105,600.0
10–15	545.0	2,014.9	1,023.9	115.6	107.3	619.3	154,318.7
Mean	476.6	1,374.6	836.0	115.8	86.3	439.8	117,966.1

Although *Olivella* callus bead making was a small component of the Historic shellworking activities, densities of callus artifacts also declined over time. Despite a reduction in total labor expended for the production of *Olivella* beads, ratios of finished *Olivella* beads to beads-in-production increased in later Historic period deposits. These data suggest that specialists at house 4 were either somewhat less aggressive about moving surplus finished beads into regional trade networks or were simply retaining many of their finished beads for their own use during the latter portion of their tenure at *Shawa*. Alternatively, regional demand for *Olivella* callus beads may have continued to decline following European contact, although data from other excavated houses (see below) suggest that this was not the case.

Historic-era changes in the densities of *Haliotis rufescens* artifacts, however, point to a slight intensification in red abalone bead-making activities (Table 9.7). Both red abalone bead-in-production and detritus densities show a 15–30 percent increase over time. Furthermore, ratios of finished beads to beads-in-production are lowest in deposits corresponding to the most intensive red abalone shellworking at this house. Collectively, these data suggest that residents of house 4 modified their labor allocation strategies in such a way that greater emphasis was placed on red abalone bead production and exchange.

Despite relatively higher densities of *Tivela* detritus in 0–5 cm deposits, the intensity of *Tivela* shellworking activities appears to have gradually declined over the course of Historic occupation (Table 9.8). When compared to deeper excavation levels, the sum of mean densities of *Tivela* detritus, flakes, and chipped fragments indicates a 10 percent reduction in total shellworking by-products at the surface of house 4 deposits. Given that specialists at house 4 were allocating very little by way of time and

Table 9.7. Densities of *Haliotis rufescens* Bead-Making Artifacts from House 4 Floor Deposits at SCRI-192 (counts/m³)

Depth (cm)	*Haliotis rufescens*					
	bead	bip	blank	pre-blank	ch/mod[a]	detritus
00–05	43.8	324.1	583.9	113.9	17.5	873.0
05–10	41.0	276.9	600.0	30.8	61.5	805.1
10–15	49.5	231.2	470.7	57.8	57.8	751.4
Mean	44.8	277.4	551.5	67.5	45.6	809.9

[a]ch/mod = chipped/modified fragments

Table 9.8. Densities of *Tivela stultorum* Bead-Making Artifacts from House 4 Floor Deposits at SCRI-192 (counts/m^3)

Depth (cm)	*Tivela stultorum*				
	bip	ch/mod[a]	flake	detritus	unmod
00–05	5.8	2.9	8.8	93.4	2.9
05–10	15.4	10.3	25.6	71.8	—
10–15	—	16.5	33.0	66.1	—
Mean	7.1	9.9	22.5	77.1	1.0

[a]ch/mod = chipped/modified fragments

energy to the production of *Tivela* goods, this subtle change in *Tivela* artifact densities may not be behaviorally significant.

Subsurface deposits also yielded a small assemblage of prestige goods, including glass beads, ground steatite fragments, and a steatite bead (Table 9.9). Most of these objects were recovered in upper levels of Historic period deposits (0–10 cm; $\mu = 15.0/m^3$), and densities of glass beads increased over time. Collectively, these data suggest that residents of house 4 were increasingly able to access regional trade networks over the course of Historic period occupation.

House 8 at Shawa (SCRI-192). Specialists at house 8 clearly dedicated considerable labor to the production of *Olivella* wall beads, and my analysis of shellworking assemblages suggests the presence of intensive *Olivella* bead making unparalleled at the four other excavated houses. Mean densities of *Olivella* wall beads-in-production (831.1/m^3) and pieces of *Olivella* detritus (228,626.0/m^3) recovered in subsurface deposits at house 8 are on the order of 2 to 13 times higher than those recovered elsewhere at SCRI-

192 and -236 (Table 9.10). However, densities of *Olivella* wall bead-making artifacts fluctuate with depth, suggesting that production intensity varied through time.

Throughout Historic occupation of house 8, specialists accorded *Olivella* callus bead making much less importance than *Olivella* wall bead-making activities. Mean densities of *Olivella* callus beads-in-production (90.5/m^3) are a mere fraction of wall bead-in-production densities ($\mu = 3,616.4/m^3$). However, densities of callus beads-in-production also fluctuate with depth (see Table 9.10), mirroring patterns observed above. It is unclear why residents of house 8 oscillated between somewhat less intensive and more intensive *Olivella* bead-making activities. *Olivella* bead production was less intensive just prior to house abandonment than earlier in the Historic period. However, despite the fact that densities of *Olivella* callus finished beads declined over time, ratios of finished callus beads to beads-in-production are 1:1 or greater throughout. These data suggest that house 8 residents retained some of their finished callus products.

Table 9.9. Densities of Prestige Goods from House 4 Floor Deposits at SCRI-192 (counts/m^3)

Depth (cm)	Glass Bead	Steatite Bead	Steatite Frag.	Ground Steatite
00–05	17.5	2.9	—	5.8
05–10	10.3	—	—	—
10–15	—	—	8.3	—
Mean	9.3	1.0	2.8	1.9

House 8 specialists also allocated considerable labor to the production of red abalone beads. Mean *Haliotis rufescens* bead-in-production (1,989.2/m³) and detritus (9,306.2/m³) densities are between 1.2 and 11 times higher than densities for similar artifact categories from excavated houses at SCRI-192 and -236 (Table 9.11). House 9 at SCRI-236 (discussed below) is the only locus from which we have *subsurface* data that point to comparable red abalone shellworking intensity. Densities of red abalone bead-making artifacts also decline in later Historic period deposits at house 8. Artifact densities in the shallowest excavation levels (0–5 cm) are on average half of those recovered in deeper (10–15 cm) levels.

Although the intensity of *Olivella* and red abalone bead-making activities at house 8 may have gradually declined over the course of Historic occupation, specialists appear to have allocated slightly more labor to *Tivela stultorum* shellworking activities during the latter years of occupation than they had earlier. Combined densities of *Tivela* detritus, flakes, and chipped

fragments increased from 72.2/m³ in earlier deposits to 103.1/m³ in later deposits (Table 9.12). House 8 also yielded many examples of finished and unfinished *Tivela* goods in the deeper excavation levels (5–10 and 10–15 cm), and despite the fact that production intensity increased over time, no finished *Tivela* artifacts were recovered in the shallower deposits (0–5 cm). These data are consistent with other trends observed regarding shellworking intensification. Evidence for increasing production intensity is usually accompanied by decreasing densities of finished goods, indicating an emphasis on production for exchange. Regardless, finished and unfinished *Tivela* artifacts are rare compared to the by-products of other shellworking industries, such as *Olivella* and red abalone beads, beads-in-production, and bead blanks. *Tivela* tube and disk beads were highly valued at contact (Arnold and Graesch 2001; King 1990), and Green (1999) presents evidence for Historic-era valuation of unfinished products, such as *Tivela* bead blanks, as well.

Finally, subsurface data from house 8 also mark an increase in the acquisition of prestige

Table 9.10. Densities of *Olivella biplicata* Bead-Making Artifacts from House 8 Floor Deposits at SCRI-192 (counts/m³)

| Depth (cm) | *Olivella* Wall | | | *Olivella* Callus | | | *Olivella* Detritus |
	bead	bip	blank	bead	bip	blank	
00–05	853.6	3,303.1	1,715.5	82.5	82.5	573.2	280,206.2
05–10	578.7	2,740.4	1,344.7	102.1	72.3	502.1	190,910.6
10–15	1,061.1	4,805.6	2,300.0	116.7	116.7	455.6	214,761.1
Mean	831.1	3,616.4	1,786.7	100.4	90.5	510.3	228,626.0

Table 9.11. Densities of *Haliotis rusfescens* Bead-Making Artifacts from House 8 Floor Deposits at SCRI-192 (counts/m³)

| Depth (cm) | *Haliotis rufescens* | | | | | | |
	bead	bip	blank	pre-blank	ch/mod[a]	detritus	whole
00–05	24.7	1,476.3	4,057.7	626.8	53.6	7,352.6	4.1
05–10	46.8	1,446.8	4,612.8	774.5	72.3	7,166.0	—
10–15	83.3	3,044.4	7,311.1	1,222.2	94.4	13,400.0	—
Mean	51.6	1,989.2	5,327.2	874.5	73.5	9,306.2	1.4

[a]ch/mod = chipped modified fragments

Table 9.12. Densities of *Tivela stultorum* Bead-Making Artifacts from House 8 Floor Deposits at SCRI-192 (counts/m^3)

Depth (cm)	*Tivela stultorum*						
	bead	bip	blank	ch/mod[a]	flake	detritus	unmod
00–05	—	—	—	—	16.5	86.6	—
05–10	4.3	4.3	4.3	8.5	21.3	63.8	4.3
10–15	5.6	—	—	11.1	11.1	50.0	5.6
Mean	3.3	1.4	1.4	6.5	16.3	66.8	3.3

[a]ch/mod = chipped modified fragments

Table 9.13. Densities of Prestige Goods from House 8 Floor Deposits at SCRI-192 (counts/m^3)

Depth (cm)	Glass Bead	Steatite Comal	Ground Steatite
00–05	41.2	4.1	4.1
05–10	21.3	—	4.3
10–15	11.1	—	5.6
Mean	24.5	1.4	4.6

items during the Historic period (Table 9.13). For example, densities of glass beads increase from 11.1/m^3 ($n = 2$) at 10–15 cm depth to an impressive 41.2/m^3 ($n = 10$) at 0–5 cm depth ($\mu = 24.5/$m^3, $n = 17$). The abundance of steatite artifacts ($n = 4$), including comales and undiagnostic vessel fragments, also increases through time. Complementing patterns detected in surface collection data, mean densities of prestige goods (30.5/m^3) recovered from subsurface deposits at house 8 are between 2 and 13 times greater than densities of such goods recovered in the other three excavated west-end houses. Moreover, excavations at house 8 recovered four of the seven (57 percent) rarer glass bead types found during subsurface investigations in the four west-end houses, and these four rare beads come from just 24 percent of the total volume of excavated interior house deposits considered in this analysis. These include two polychrome drawn varieties as well as two wire-wound specimens. Together, these data indicate that residents of house 8 had unusual access to rarer goods.

Ch'oloshush (SCRI-236)
Situated on the edge of a high marine terrace near the Cañada de Cervada stream, the west-

shore archaeological site SCRI-236, identified as the Historic village of *Ch'oloshush* (Johnson 1999), features a total of 15 house depressions (Figure 9.5). Surface data used in this analysis were recovered from eight of these depressions, whereas subsurface data are derived from seven 1-x-1-m excavation units placed in house 5 and eight units placed in house 9 (see Table 9.1).

Surface assemblages. Interhousehold variability in shellworking activities at SCRI-236 can be characterized somewhat differently from patterns observed at SCRI-192. Here, correspondence analysis reveals two clusters of houses (Figure 9.6), suggesting at least two general production strategies by which site occupants chose to organize household labor. A single outlier attests to yet a third strategy implemented by at least one of the Historic households.

Differences in household production strategies at *Ch'oloshush* are best understood in terms of shellworking intensity rather than focus. The presence of extraordinarily high surface densities of *Tivela stultorum* artifacts suggests that residents of this community were allocating significant labor to the production of *Tivela* beads and ornaments (see Tables 9.14–9.16). Mean surface

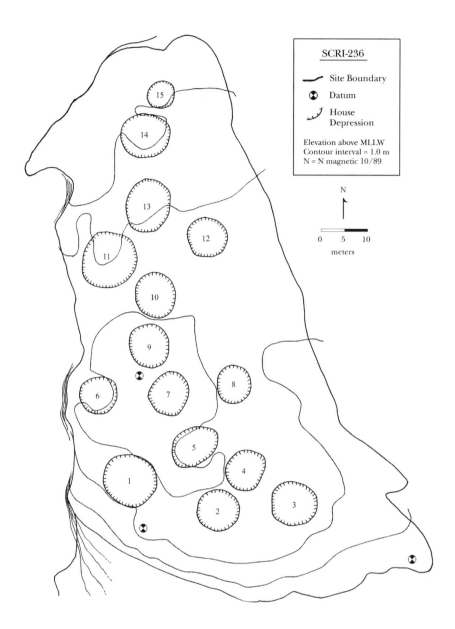

Figure 9.5. Map of *Ch'oloshush* (SCRI-236). Map by J. E. Arnold and A. P. Graesch.

densities of *Tivela* detritus recovered from *Ch'oloshush* (22.4/m²) are, respectively, 7 and 42 times higher than those observed at *Shawa* (3.2/m²) and *L'akayamu* (0.5/m²). Compared to specialists' activities at other island villages, households at *Ch'oloshush* were manufacturing far fewer *Olivella* wall and red abalone beads.

Variability in the extent to which *Ch'oloshush* households were involved in shell bead and ornament production is striking. Unique to SCRI-

236 are three households that made surprisingly small labor allocations to bead-production tasks. Clustering to the far left of the correspondence plot in Figure 9.6, houses 1, 11, and 13 exhibit comparatively low surface densities of shell artifacts. While finer-scale variability in production activities can be teased out of these three assemblages, surface artifact densities are undeniably the lowest observed among sampled houses across the three villages. This is particularly

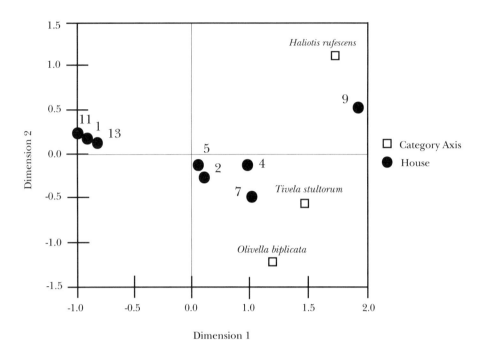

Figure 9.6. Correspondence plot of shellworking detritus densities by house at *Ch'oloshush* (SCRI-236).

Table 9.14. Surface Densities of *Olivella biplicata* Bead-Making Artifacts from Selected House Depressions at SCRI-236 (counts/m²)

House	*Olivella* Wall			*Olivella* Callus			*Olivella* Detritus
	bead	bip	blank	bead	bip	blank	
1	1.0	1.0	0.3	1.5	—	1.0	102.8
2	6.8	3.0	3.5	—	1.0	6.0	1,212.5
4	6.0	3.5	4.5	2.5	1.0	3.3	1,475.0
5	2.5	2.3	2.8	1.0	2.0	5.0	1,070.8
7	4.8	1.5	4.3	1.8	0.8	4.5	1,275.0
9	2.0	3.5	7.3	1.3	2.3	5.8	1,018.8
11	—	0.3	—	—	—	—	25.3
13	0.8	1.5	1.5	0.3	0.3	1.3	212.0

interesting in light of the fact that these are some of the largest house depressions among west-end Santa Cruz Island communities (see Figure 9.5), although it is unclear why occupants of these structures were only minimally partici-pating in shellworking activities. The extent to which these assemblages might mark special-purpose structures or perhaps unique social con-figurations is considered in the discussion be-low.

Table 9.15. Surface Densities of *Haliotis rufescens* Bead-Making Artifacts from Selected House Depressions at SCRI-236 (counts/m^2)

House	bead	bip	blank	pre-blank	ch/mod[a]	detritus
			Haliotis rufescens			
1	—	1.0	0.5	0.5	—	1.3
2	—	3.3	7.5	1.3	—	26.0
4	0.3	6.0	21.5	4.3	—	44.3
5	0.3	2.0	8.5	3.3	0.5	26.5
7	0.3	3.3	9.8	0.8	0.3	28.5
9	—	23.5	90.8	2.5	0.3	100.0
11	—	—	0.5	—	—	0.3
13	—	1.0	1.5	1.0	0.3	3.0

[a]ch/mod = chipped/modified fragments

Table 9.16. Surface Densities of *Tivela stultorum* Bead-Making Artifacts from Selected House Depressions at SCRI-236 (counts/m^2)

House	blank	ch/mod[a]	flake	detritus
		Tivela stultorum		
1	—	—	0.3	4.3
2	—	—	6.5	21.8
4	—	—	4.3	24.3
5	—	0.3	2.3	22.0
7	0.3	0.3	2.0	54.5
9	—	5.0	2.0	49.3
11	—	—	—	0.3
13	—	0.8	—	3.0

[a]ch/mod = chipped/modified fragments

In contrast, houses 2, 4, 5, and 7 yielded substantially higher densities of shellworking artifacts. Clustered near the center of the correspondence plot in Figure 9.6, these houses can be distinguished from their neighbors in that their occupants were investing modest amounts of time and energy in the production of both *Olivella biplicata* and *Haliotis rufescens* shell beads. Some of these houses, however, stand out as slightly more dedicated producers of one

bead type or another. Residents of house 7, for example, engaged in comparatively higher intensity *Tivela* bead- and ornament-making activities. In fact, surface collections at house 7 recovered the highest densities of *Tivela* shellworking by-products (56.8/m^2) for any individual house sampled during these investigations.

The outlier in Figure 9.6 indicates the unique production strategy represented by surface assemblages recovered at house 9. Although *Olivella* beads were not a major production focus for residents of this structure, a substantial amount of time and labor was dedicated to producing red abalone and (to a lesser extent) *Tivela* beads. The intensity of red abalone bead making at house 9 was unparalleled by other households at *Ch'oloshush* and *Shawa*. Densities of red abalone bead blanks, beads-in-production, and detritus are between 2 and 12 times greater than those observed in houses 2, 4, 5, and 7 and are still higher than densities of the same from house 1 at SCRI-192. Surface densities of *Tivela* shellworking by-products are second only to those accounted for in house 7.

Among other interesting aspects of shell-working activities at *Ch'oloshush*, houses 2, 4, 5, and 7 all exhibit high ratios of finished *Olivella* wall beads to beads-in-production. At house 7, for example, three or more finished beads were recovered for every bead-in-production found in surface assemblages. These data can be interpreted in several different ways. On the one hand, residents may have been retaining the bulk of *Olivella* wall beads they produced. On the other, members of these four households may have acquired finished beads that were produced elsewhere and obtained in trade. Alternatively, these data may suggest that specialists at house 7 were making relatively fewer production mistakes during the bead-making process. Densities of *Olivella* wall artifacts, however, are

somewhat too low to infer that craft specialists at SCRI-236 were more skilled than specialists producing substantially greater quantities of finished goods and by-products at other communities.

An analysis of bead attributes reveals that very few *Olivella* wall beads from household contexts exhibit needle-drilled signatures (Table 9.17). Surface investigations in houses 2, 4, and 9 yielded the highest densities (1.5–1.8/m^2) of needle-drilled beads, although these are considerably lower than surface densities of the same observed at *Shawa*. Given that *Shawa* households were allocating proportionally greater amounts of time and energy to the production of *Olivella* wall beads, this is not a surprising discovery. However, when surface densities of *Olivella* detritus and wall beads-in-production are considered, it is apparent that residents of houses 2, 4, and 9 were clearly engaging in the most intensive *Olivella* wall bead-making activities at *Ch'oloshush* and would be expected to have acquired and used iron needles more frequently.

Finally, nonlocal trade items were recovered in four of the eight houses sampled at SCRI-236. The total assemblage is constituted by three glass beads, all of which were recovered in house 5, and four exotic flakes distributed among three other houses (see Table 9.17). Two of these flakes were found in surface assemblages from house 11. This is interesting, given

Table 9.17. Surface Densities of Needle-Drilled Beads and Prestige Goods at SCRI-236 (counts/m^2)

House[a]	Needle-Drilled Beads	Prestige Goods	Description of Prestige Goods
1	—	—	
11	—	0.5	1 obsidian flake; 1 Franciscan chert flake
13	—	—	
2	1.8	0.3	1 Franciscan chert flake
4	1.8	—	
5	0.5	0.8	3 glass beads
7	0.3	—	
9	1.5	0.3	1 Franciscan chert flake

[a]Houses are grouped according to clusters identified in Figure 9.6.

that shellworking assemblages from this house suggest only minimal participation in the regional economy. Although flakes of exotic raw material may not be comparable to glass beads in terms of value, they nonetheless signify a household's ability to acquire goods (e.g., exotic projectile points) that could only be obtained through cross-channel exchange. These flakes are small and are likely by-products of tool finishing or maintenance, indicating that residents possessed larger tools made from the same exotic materials.

Subsurface assemblages

House 5 at Ch'oloshush (SCRI-236). Temporal changes in shell bead-making strategies at house 5 can be characterized much differently from those observed in shellworking assemblages at

houses 4 and 8 (SCRI-192). Here, specialists appear to have intensified labor investments in all three of the major shellworking industries over the course of Historic period residency. However, unlike the former two houses, specialists at house 5 dedicated most of their craft-related time and energy to the production of red abalone and *Tivela stultorum* shell beads and ornaments. Mean densities of red abalone beads-in-production (386.1/m^3) and bead blanks (1,090.8/m^3) are between 30 percent and 75 percent higher than the mean densities calculated for *Olivella* wall beads-in-production (267.6/m^3) and bead blanks (250.1/m^3) (see Tables 9.18 and 9.19). Although it is difficult to compare absolute levels of *Olivella* and *Tivela* shellworking intensity, the overwhelming abundance of *Tivela* shellworking by-products at house 5 indicates that proportionally greater amounts of labor

Table 9.18. Densities of *Olivella biplicata* Bead-Making Artifacts from House 5 Floor Deposits at SCRI-236 (counts/m^3)

Depth (cm)	*Olivella* Wall			*Olivella* Callus			*Olivella* Detritus
	bead	bip	blank	bead	bip	blank	
00–05	266.1	292.4	295.3	17.5	26.3	149.1	40,266.1
05–10	141.5	360.0	320.0	21.5	18.5	172.3	36,049.2
10–15	127.0	266.7	241.3	22.2	6.3	117.5	24,476.2
15–20	129.0	197.8	210.8	25.8	8.6	73.1	29,471.0
20–25	120.0	221.1	183.2	19.0	12.6	75.8	20,189.5
Mean	156.7	267.6	250.1	21.2	14.5	117.6	30,090.4

Table 9.19. Densities of *Haliotis rufescens* Bead-Making Artifacts from House 5 Floor Deposits at SCRI-236 (counts/m^3)

Depth (cm)	*Haliotis rufescens*					
	bead	bip	blank	pre-blank	ch/mod[a]	detritus
00–05	5.8	602.3	1,760.2	233.9	29.2	3,213.5
05–10	6.2	467.7	1,092.3	316.9	21.5	1,972.3
10–15	12.7	330.2	904.8	273.0	25.4	1,882.5
15–20	8.6	283.9	1,083.9	309.7	47.3	1,548.4
20–25	—	246.4	612.8	107.4	—	1,017.1
Mean	6.7	386.1	1,090.8	248.2	24.7	1,926.7

[a]ch/mod = chipped/modified fragments

were invested in this particular craft industry than at other houses and sites, and possibly more labor was expended on *Tivela* shellworking activities than on *Olivella* bead making (Table 9.20).

In fact, upper excavation levels at house 5 yielded the highest densities of *Tivela* detritus (2,348/m^3) and flakes (348/m^3) recovered from any of the excavated Historic-era houses. Historic period changes in the amount of labor allocated to *Tivela* shellworking at house 5 are also notable. Assemblages recovered in some of the deeper excavation levels (20–25 cm) suggest that residents were not focusing the bulk of their labor investments on any single shellworking tradition during earlier occupation of house 5. Production efforts appear to have consistently and rapidly intensified over the course of Historic occupation, with a notable intensification in *Tivela* and *Haliotis rufescens* bead-making activities just prior to house abandonment.

Although *Olivella* bead making was much less a production focus at house 5, similar patterns of intensification can be observed in *Olivella* shellworking assemblages (see Table 9.18). Members of this household appear to have intensified *Olivella* callus rather than *Olivella* wall bead-making activities in the later Historic period. Densities of callus beads-in-production became steadily higher through time, and densities of finished callus beads declined. A change in the opposite direction is apparent in densities of *Olivella* wall beads and beads-in-production. The ratio of the former to the latter is 0.9:1 in 0–5 cm deposits. These data suggest that *Olivella* callus beads were increasingly manufactured for trade, whereas many of the finished *Olivella* wall beads may have been retained for local use. Residents of house 5 appear to have increasingly allocated proportionally greater amounts of labor to the production of more labor-intensive shell valuables.

Table 9.20. Densities of *Tivela stultorum* Bead-Making Artifacts from House 5 Floor Deposits at SCRI-236 (counts/m^3)

Depth (cm)	*Tivela stultorum*						
	bip	blank	ch/mod[a]	flake	detritus	modified	unmod
00–05	2.9	2.9	23.4	348.0	2,348.0	2.9	—
05–10	—	9.2	6.2	184.6	1,440.0	—	—
10–15	6.3	—	54.0	161.9	1,279.4	—	3.2
15–20	4.3	8.6	90.3	73.1	1,157.0	—	—
20–25	—	—	12.6	132.7	701.2	—	—
Mean	2.7	4.2	37.3	180.1	1,385.1	0.6	0.6

[a]ch/mod = chipped/modified fragments

Table 9.21. Densities of Prestige Goods from House 5 Floor Deposits at SCRI-236 (counts/m^3)

Depth (cm)	Glass Bead	Steatite Fragments
00–05	17.5	—
05–10	9.2	6.2
10–15	3.2	—
15–20	12.9	—
20–25	—	—
Mean	8.6	1.2

With regard to prestige goods, 13 glass beads and two steatite fragments were recovered in subsurface deposits at house 5 (Table 9.21). The mean density of prestige goods (9.8/m^3) is notably lower than at house 4 at SCRI-192 (15.0/m^3) and at house 8 at SCRI-192 (30.5/m^3). As was the case at both houses at *Shawa*, the majority of the glass beads in house 5 were recovered in the upper level (0–5 cm) of floor accretion deposits. These data suggest that residents of house 5 were acquiring increasing numbers of prestige goods over the course of Historic period occupation at *Ch'oloshush*, although not many overall.

House 9 at Ch'oloshush (SCRI-236). Floor accretion deposits are considerably shallower at house 9. Occupants of this structure likely constructed a new floor closer to the time of site abandonment than their neighbors residing in the houses discussed above. Packed-clay floor surfaces were encountered at the 3–10 cm depth throughout excavated portions of the house. Consequently, notable temporal changes in shellworking activities at house 9 cannot be de-

tected (see Tables 9.22–9.24). Just prior to abandonment, however, occupants of house 9 were making considerable labor investments in the production of red abalone and *Tivela* shell beads. For instance, mean densities of *Haliotis rufescens* detritus (8,272/m^3) and beads-in-production (1,609.4/m^3) recovered in the two excavated levels at house 9 (Table 9.23) are more than three times higher than mean densities of red abalone beads (2,592.9/m^3) and beads-in-production (535/m^3) recovered in the upper two levels of floor accretion at house 5. When all of house 5 deposits are considered, mean artifact densities at house 9 are as much as four times greater.

Excavations at house 9 also yielded the highest mean densities of *Tivela* detritus (2,099.3/m^3) and *Tivela* flakes (389.1/m^3) among *all* excavated houses (Table 9.24), although densities of combined *Tivela* shellworking by-products recovered in upper excavation levels at house 5 are the highest overall *Tivela* densities observed in any one 5-cm level. The highest densities of finished *Tivela* beads (18.6/m^3) and bead blanks (20.8/m^3) were also recovered in house 9.

Table 9.22. Densities of *Olivella biplicata* Bead-Making Artifacts from House 9 Floor Deposits at SCRI-236 (counts/m^3)

Depth (cm)	*Olivella* Wall			*Olivella* Callus			*Olivella* Detritus
	bead	bip	blank	bead	bip	blank	
00–05	132.8	375.5	435.0	45.8	91.6	247.3	49,230.8
05–10	93.1	353.8	744.9	111.7	111.7	335.2	56,908.8
Mean	112.9	364.6	589.9	78.8	101.7	291.2	53,069.8

Table 9.23. Densities of *Haliotis rufescens* Bead-Making Artifacts from House 9 Floor Deposits at SCRI-236 (counts/m^3)

Depth (cm)	*Haliotis rufescens*					
	bead	bip	blank	pre-blank	ch/mod[a]	detritus
00–05	9.2	1,561.4	2,033.0	361.7	13.7	8,704.2
05–10	—	1,657.4	3,500.9	223.5	149.0	7,839.9
Mean	4.6	1,609.4	2,766.9	292.6	81.4	8,272.0

[a]ch/mod = chipped/modified fragments

Table 9.24. Densities of *Tivela stultorum* Bead-Making Artifacts from House 9 Floor Deposits at SCRI-236 (counts/m³)

Depth (cm)	*Tivela stultorum*				
	bead	blank	ch/mod[a]	flake	detritus
00–05	—	13.8	54.9	238.1	1,982.6
05–10	37.2	18.6	—	540.0	2,216.0
Mean	18.6	16.2	27.5	389.1	2,099.3

[a]ch/mod = chipped/modified fragments

As was the case in house 5, *Olivella* bead making was clearly not the focus of labor expenditures at house 9 in the Historic period. Although densities of *Olivella* detritus and *Olivella* wall beads-in-production indicate that some household members were investing at least small amounts of time and energy in *Olivella* bead-making activities (see Table 9.22), the greatest labor expenditures were made in the red abalone and *Tivela* shellworking traditions. Higher ratios of finished to unfinished *Olivella* wall beads and evidence for increasing *Olivella* callus bead making later in time mirror trends observed in house 5.

Calculated densities of prestige goods from interior deposits at house 9 (2.3/m³) are the lowest observed among all five excavated houses. This assemblage is constituted by a single glass bead recovered in the upper (0–5 cm) floor accretion deposits. As observed with surface assemblage data, there were far more prestige goods at house 5 than at house 9. It would appear that occupants of house 9 were receiving relatively few goods through regional trade networks, although increasing quantities of finished shell beads in shallower deposits suggest that the degree to which this household participated in the regional economy may have changed over the course of Historic occupation.

L'akayamu (SCRI-328, -329, -330)

The Historic village of *L'akayamu* was located on a long marine terrace near Forney's Cove (Johnson 1999). This deeply stratified shell midden is trifurcated by a freshwater stream and is designated by site numbers SCRI-328, -329, and -330 (Figures 9.7 and 9.8). Collectively, the sites

exhibit a total of 20 well-defined house depressions. Sixteen of these house depressions were sampled with the systematic placement of 29 surface collection units (see Table 9.1). Previous small-scale excavations at this Historic period village (by S. Horne and others) have targeted the margins of several house depressions, as well as general midden deposits (see Arnold 2001; Baldwin 1996; Glassow 1977).

Surface assemblages. Correspondence analysis of shellworking activities at *L'akayamu* suggests that most sampled households were pursuing similar production strategies (Figure 9.9). Specialist labor was predominantly focused on the production of red abalone and *Olivella* wall beads, and artifact assemblages from houses 1–7, 11, 14, 16, 18, and 19 are seemingly representative of the production norms at this village.

Tables 25–27 present surface densities of shellworking goods and by-products recovered from the 16 sampled houses at SCRI-328, -329, and -330. Most bead-making households were seemingly investing moderate amounts of time and energy in red abalone bead-making activities (μ = 5.1 beads-in-production/m²) and greater amounts of labor in *Olivella* wall bead production (μ = 6.4 beads-in-production/m²). The intensity of *Olivella* wall bead-making activities at this community, however, did not rival that of *Shawa* (μ = 14.3 beads-in-production/m²). On the other hand, when outliers are excluded from consideration, households at *L'akayamu* were on average producing much greater quantities of red abalone beads compared to their counterparts at *Shawa* (3.6 beads in production)

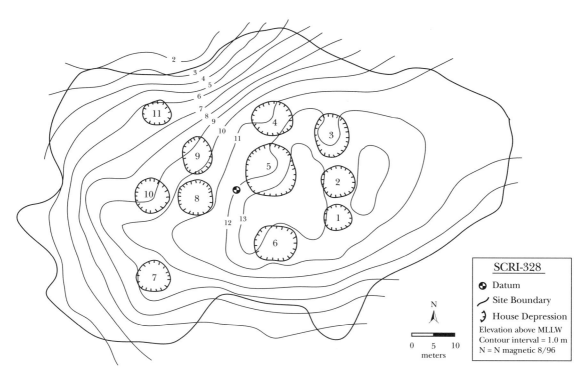

Figure 9.7. Map of SCRI-328, the eastern component of the Historic village of *L'akayamu*. Map by author.

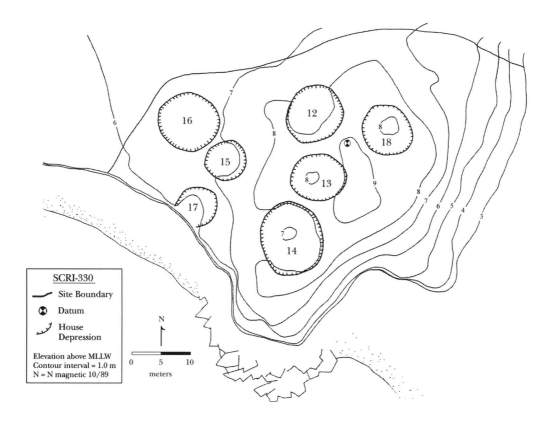

Figure 9.8. Map of SCRI-330, the western component of the Historic village of *L'akayamu* (after Arnold 2001:Figure 2.24). House numbers were adjusted from those in the 2001 map of SCRI-330 for purposes of this analysis.

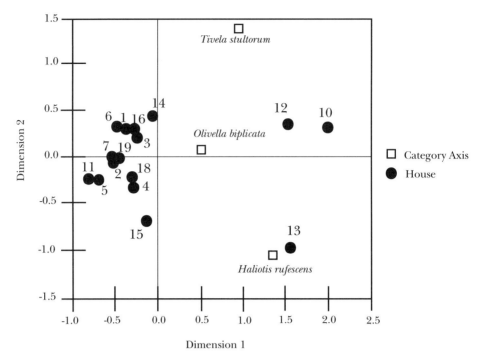

Figure 9.9. Correspondence plot of shellworking detritus densities by house at *L'akayamu* (SCRI-328, -329, and -330).

Table 9.25. Surface Densities of *Olivella biplicata* Bead-Making Artifacts from Selected House Depressions at SCRI-328, -329, and -330 (counts/m^2)

	Olivella Wall			*Olivella* Callus			*Olivella* Detritus
House	bead	bip	blank	bead	bip	blank	
1	4.3	2.5	5.8	3.8	2.3	5.5	1,450.0
2	2.5	4.0	5.5	3.0	2.8	5.8	1,673.8
3	4.5	7.3	10.8	1.0	3.3	12.3	1,686.3
4	3.3	10.5	7.8	1.0	0.5	11.0	1,000.0
5	4.5	3.0	10.8	4.5	2.8	5.8	1,587.5
6	2.8	1.3	4.0	2.3	1.0	2.0	1,050.0
7	1.8	3.8	4.3	0.5	1.5	12.8	1,196.3
10	10.5	19.3	11.8	1.3	2.8	7.3	3,450.0
11	3.5	6.0	5.5	1.3	—	2.0	881.3
12	6.5	29.0	26.0	3.5	5.5	41.0	5,000.0
13	7.5	21.5	15.5	1.5	4.3	26.8	3,035.0
14	1.0	10.3	5.5	1.0	1.0	10.0	1,175.0
15	3.3	4.5	7.0	0.5	1.5	7.8	1,202.5
16	5.0	14.0	12.0	0.5	3.0	33.0	2,322.0
18	3.3	7.8	6.8	2.0	4.5	20.0	3,317.5
19	7.5	6.5	4.0	3.5	3.0	11.5	1,726.0

Table 9.26. Surface Densities of *Haliotis rufescens* Bead-Making Artifacts from Selected House Depressions at SCRI-328, -329, and -330 (counts/m^2)

House	bead	bip	blank	pre-blank	ch/mod[a]	detritus
			Haliotis rufescens			
1	—	1.8	20.8	2.0	—	29.0
2	—	3.5	17.5	3.3	1.0	45.8
3	0.5	1.3	15.5	1.8	1.0	58.0
4	1.0	10.3	33.5	2.5	1.0	118.8
5	—	1.5	12.0	1.0	3.0	28.8
6	—	—	7.3	—	—	17.3
7	0.3	2.5	18.5	1.0	1.3	52.3
10	0.5	41.8	106.3	8.5	3.3	484.0
11	—	4.5	12.5	0.3	—	17.0
12	0.5	50.5	86.0	1.3	1.5	367.0
13	0.8	96.0	151.5	11.0	1.3	575.3
14	—	9.0	28.8	0.8	—	71.3
15	0.5	36.5	56.8	6.0	—	210.3
16	—	1.5	15.0	0.5	—	40.0
18	0.3	18.3	29.3	1.0	0.3	77.8
19	0.5	6.5	17.5	—	0.3	53.0

[a]ch/mod = chipped/modified fragments

and *Ch'oloshush* (3.7 beads-in-production), and this is the only site in this group to have demonstrated a production focus on red abalone beads almost equivalent to its focus on *Olivella* beads.

Extraordinarily high surface densities of red abalone bead-making by-products were recovered in houses 10, 12, 13, and 15 at *L'akayamu*. Densities of *Haliotis rufescens* detritus at house 10 (484/m^2), house 12 (367/m^2), house 13 (575.3/m^2), and house 15 (210.3/m^2) are between 3 and 12 times higher than the average density of detritus recovered among the 12 other *L'akayamu* houses clustered to the upper and middle left of Figure 9.9. Surface densities of red abalone bead blanks and beads-in-production are also notably higher (see Table 9.26), and occupants of *each* of these four houses appear to have been allocating more labor to the production of *Haliotis rufescens* beads than all of the sampled households at

Shawa (SCRI-192) *combined*. In aggregate these data point to a level of red abalone bead making that may be unparalleled in other Historic period Santa Cruz Island communities.

Surface assemblages from some *L'akayamu* houses contain high ratios of *Olivella* finished beads to beads-in-production and only modest surface densities of *Olivella* detritus. Houses 1, 5, 6, and 19, for instance, appear to have either differentially retained or received greater quantities of finished *Olivella* wall and callus beads, while producing considerably fewer *Olivella* beads than many of their neighbors. High ratios of finished beads to beads-in-production also occur among houses exhibiting low densities of *Olivella* detritus at SCRI-236 (see above). The practice of retaining greater quantities of finished beads may be one of the key differences in economic behavior distinguishing low- and high-intensity production specialists.

Table 9.27. Surface Densities of *Tivela stultorum* Bead-Making Artifacts from Selected House Depressions at SCRI-328, -329, and -330 (counts/m²)

House	bead	bip	blank	ch/mod[a]	flake	detritus
1	—	—	—	—	0.3	0.8
2	—	0.3	0.5	—	0.5	—
3	—	0.3	—	—	0.5	0.5
4	—	—	—	—	0.3	—
5	—	—	—	—	—	—
6	—	—	—	—	0.3	0.8
7	—	—	—	0.3	—	0.3
10	0.3	—	—	—	0.3	2.8
11	—	—	—	—	—	—
12	—	—	—	0.5	1.5	0.5
13	—	—	—	—	1.0	—
14	—	—	—	—	0.3	1.3
15	—	—	—	—	—	—
16	—	—	—	—	—	1.0
18	—	—	0.3	—	—	0.3
19	—	—	—	—	—	0.5

[a]ch/mod = chipped/modified fragments

Bead-making specialists at houses 10, 12, and 13 were also producing substantially more *Olivella* wall beads than their neighbors residing at *L'akayamu*. Surface densities of *Olivella* detritus and wall beads-in-production are on average between 2.5 and 3.6 times higher at these three houses (see Table 9.25). Densities of *Olivella* detritus in some cases even exceed those observed at houses 1, 6, and 8 at SCRI-192, although the same cannot be said of *Olivella* wall beads-in-production and finished beads. These data may indicate that certain households at *L'akayamu* manufactured *Olivella* wall beads at a level of intensity similar to that observed at *Shawa*, yet they made fewer production mistakes and retained fewer finished beads. Alternatively, these data may point to community differences in resource use and production techniques. For instance, a more exhaustive use of *Olivella* shells would yield higher ratios of beads-in-production to detritus, such as those observed at houses 1, 6, and 8 at SCRI-192. Households at *Shawa* may have been engaging in higher-intensity *Olivella* bead-making activities *and* maximizing the number of beads made from individual *Olivella* shells.

A more intensive analysis of *Olivella* detritus from both sites provides some insights into how *Olivella* shells were being used and lends support to the latter interpretation. Because of their near equivalent weight, *Olivella* detritus samples recovered from house 1 at SCRI-192 and house 18 at SCRI-330 were selected for comparison. All detritus fragments were size sorted with 3 mm (¹/₈″) and 6 mm (¹/₄″) wire mesh and then weighed. Shell fragments in the 6-mm class were further subdivided by specific shell component and then weighed again (Table 9.28). The results of this analysis suggest that specialists at house 1 (SCRI-192) were discarding fewer large shell fragments than specialists at house 18 (SCRI-330). For instance, greater than 50 percent of the total *Olivella* detritus weight is constituted by fragments in the 6-mm class at house 18, whereas fragments of similar sizes account for only 30.6 percent of the total weight at house 1. House 18 also yielded higher percentages (65 percent) of unused wall components by weight than did house 1 (36.7 percent). The bulk of *Olivella* detritus weight in the 6-mm class at house 1 is accounted for by columella fragments (48.2 percent), or those pieces that would have had little utility in Historic period bead-making industries. Combined, these data strongly suggest more intensive use of *Olivella* shell raw material at SCRI-192.

Turning now to prestige goods, surface collections at *L'akayamu* revealed a total of 23 specimens distributed among 12 of the 16 houses (Table 9.29). Densities of prestige goods range

Table 9.28. *Olivella biplicata* Detritus Weight by Size Class and Part of Shell

Site	House	Total Weight (g)	Size Class				Shell Part ($^1/_4$″ [6 mm] sample)					
			$^1/_4$″ (6 mm) mesh weight (g)	%	$^1/_8$″ (3 mm) mesh weight (g)	%	columella weight (g)	%	wall weight (g)	%	whole weight (g)	%
192	1	1,423.8	435.6	30.6	988.2	69.4	210.1	48.2	159.9	36.7	58.4	13.4
330	18	1,485.3	761.9	51.3	723.4	48.7	161.9	21.3	495.3	65.0	94.2	12.4

Note: Samples were collected in 2-x-1-m surface units.

Table 9.29. Surface Densities of Needle-Drilled Beads and Prestige Goods at SCRI-328, -329, and -330 (counts/m^2)

House[a]	Needle-Drilled Beads	Prestige Goods	Description of Prestige Goods
1	1.3	0.3	1 exotic chert flake
2	1.5	0.5	2 Franciscan chert flakes
3	1.0	1.0	1 glass bead; 2 Franciscan chert flakes; 1 exotic chert biface
4	1.3	0.5	1 glass bead; 1 steatite fragment
5	0.5	0.3	1 glass bead
6	0.5	0.5	2 glass beads
7	0.3	0.3	1 Vandenberg chert point
11	0.3	—	
14	0.5	—	
16	3.0	—	
18	1.3	0.3	1 Franciscan chert flake
19	4.0	—	
10	3.5	0.5	1 glass bead; 1 exotic chert flake
12	5.5	1.5	3 glass beads
13	4.8	0.8	3 glass beads
15	2.0	0.3	1 glass bead

[a]Houses are grouped according to clusters identified in Figure 9.9.

from as low as 0.3/m² (many houses) to as high as 1.5/m² (house 12). Surface assemblages from most houses contained at least one glass bead, and several yielded a combination of glass beads and exotic lithics, including flakes and/or bifaces. Although none of the houses at *L'akayamu* exhibit surface densities of prestige goods as high as those observed at *Shawa*, proportionally more houses at *L'akayamu* yielded one or more exotic item.

Xaxas (SCRI-240)

The sample of Historic period houses is further augmented by subsurface data from *Xaxas* (SCRI-240), a north-shore community that has been identified archaeologically and historically as a center of exchange as well as the residence of at least one high-status family (Arnold 1994; Johnson 1993, 2001). No house depressions appear on the surface of this village. Previous investigations at this site have documented a buried redwood pole structure associated with deposits characterized by high densities of prestige goods and high ratios of finished to unfinished shell beads (Arnold 1994, 2001; Arnold and Graesch 2001; Graesch 2001). Compared to other archaeological contexts on Santa Cruz Island, these deposits are unique and may represent the activities of an elite household. Artifacts from the Historic floor and living surface deposits (40–50 cm depths), recovered from six 1-x-1-m excavation units, are incorporated into this analysis (see Graesch 2000). Deposits 10–20 cm above the floor and floor accretion layers appear to be associated with the abandonment of this structure (J. Arnold, personal communication 1999).

Subsurface assemblages. Subsurface investigations in the redwood pole structure at *Xaxas*, or house 1, have recovered one of the most interesting shellworking assemblages on Santa Cruz Island. Here, from the Historic floor and floor accretion levels, there is evidence of light to moderately intensive shellworking activities yet high densities of finished shell beads. Mean densities of *Olivella* wall beads-in-production are more than 10 times lower at house 1 (348/m³) than at house 8 at SCRI-192 (3,616.4/m³; see Table 9.30), but mean densities of finished *Olivella* wall beads are considerably higher (1,010/m³ at house 1 and 831.1/m³ at house 8). Similarly, analysis of *Haliotis rufescens* and *Tivela stultorum* artifacts indicates that household members were allocating very little labor to either of these shellworking industries. Mean densities of *Haliotis rufescens* beads-in-production (66/m³) and detritus (234/m³) are the lowest observed among all excavated Historic period houses addressed in this analysis (Table 9.31), and mean densities of *Tivela* flakes (36/m³) and detritus (60/m³) are comparable to the low numbers observed in houses 4 and 8 at *Shawa* (see Table 9.32). However, with respect to these two shellworking industries, the ratios of finished to unfinished goods are substantially higher at *Xaxas*, house 1. For instance, excavations in house 1 recovered more red abalone finished beads per bead-in-production than at any other Historic-era house. The same relationship can be drawn with *Tivela stultorum* artifacts when comparing combined densities of beads and blanks to combined densities of flakes and detritus (see also Arnold and Graesch 2001).

Table 9.30. Densities of *Olivella biplicata* Bead-Making Artifacts from House 1 Floor Deposits at SCRI-240 (counts/m³)

Depth (cm)	*Olivella* Wall			*Olivella* Callus			*Olivella* Detritus
	bead	bip	blank	bead	bip	blank	
40–45	1,296	460	388	384	144	812	80,416
45–50	724	236	328	484	212	668	82,808
Mean	1,010	348	358	434	178	740	81,612

Table 9.31. Densities of *Haliotis rufescens* Bead-Making Artifacts from House 1 Floor Deposits at SCRI-240 (counts/m³)

Depth (cm)	*Haliotis rufescens*					
	bead	bip	blank	pre-blank	ch/mod[a]	detritus
40–45	44	88	48	24	8	276
45–50	28	44	96	24	4	192
Mean	36	66	72	24	6	234

[a]ch/mod = chipped/modified fragments

Table 9.32. Densities of *Tivela stultorum* Bead-Making Artifacts from House 1 Floor Deposits at SCRI-240 (counts/m³)

Depth (cm)	*Tivela stultorum*					
	bead	blank	ch/mod[a]	flake	detritus	unmod
40–45	4	—	4	60	64	8
45–50	4	16	—	12	56	—
Mean	4	8	2	36	60	4

[a]ch/mod = chipped/modified fragments

Of the five excavated Historic period houses, specialists at *Xaxas* house 1 were allocating the most labor to the production of *Olivella* callus cupped and lipped beads. Mean densities of *Olivella* callus beads-in-production (178/m³) are as much as 12.3 times higher than those observed at the other four houses. Similarly, mean densities of callus bead blanks (740/m³) are about 6.3 times higher. These data suggest that specialists at house 1 were perhaps more interested in manufacturing callus beads, which commanded greater value in the regional economy (see also Arnold and Graesch 2001; King 1990).

Temporal changes are difficult to address with these data. On average, shellworking artifacts are more common in shallower levels, perhaps suggesting an overall intensification of shellworking activities later in time. However, the stratigraphic distinction between floor and floor accretion is ambiguous in house 1. Because this floor was made from a thin layer of sand, the transition between the floor surface and overlying accretion deposits is difficult to discern. Most of the floor surface in the excavation

units analyzed here was encountered between 45- and 50-cm depths. Thus, it is reasonable to expect cultural deposits immediately above the floor (40–45 cm) to be floor accretion, in which we would also expect to encounter higher artifact densities.

Perhaps the most striking characteristic of house 1 deposits is the sheer number of prestige goods. More than 60 specimens were recovered in just 0.5 m³ of floor and floor accretion deposits, yielding a mean density of 122 prestige goods per cubic meter. Compared to the other four excavated houses in this analysis, mean densities of prestige goods are up to 53 times higher at house 1. The bulk of this assemblage is constituted by European glass beads (*n* = 37). Densities of glass beads are as high as 108/m³ at depths of 40 to 45 cm (Table 9.33), and the mean density of glass beads (78/m³) is more than three times greater than that calculated for house 8 (24.5/m³) at *Shawa*. Yet despite an overall greater abundance of glass beads at house 1, fewer rare varieties were recovered (6/m³) when compared to excavations at house 8 (10.6/m³).

Table 9.33. Densities of Prestige Goods from House 1 Floor Deposits at SCRI-240 (counts/m^3)

Depth (cm)	Glass Bead	Glass Frag.	Metal Nail	Metal Frag.	Steatite Frag.
40–45	108	32	4	36	4
45–50	48	4	4	—	4
Mean	78	18	4	18	4

House 1 deposits, however, did yield a much greater diversity of prestige goods. Other wealth items recovered from house 1 include nine fragments of English black glass, two hand-wrought iron nails, nine unidentified iron fragments, and two fragments of steatite.

Collectively, excavation data from *Xaxas* house 1 indicate that members of this household were expending the least amount of time and energy of the five households on shellworking activities. All four of the excavated west-end households were allocating substantially greater amounts of labor to production. However, residents of house 1 were allocating the most labor to the specialized production of *Olivella* callus beads. These beads commanded greater value than most other shell beads circulating in the regional economy. Residents of the *Xaxas* house were also accumulating substantial quantities of finished shell beads, probably from several sources. Mean densities and ratios of finished *Olivella* beads are exceptionally high in subsurface deposits at house 1. Excavations in floor and floor accretion deposits also yielded the highest densities and greatest diversity of prestige goods. These data signify a unique connection to the regional exchange networks, and members of this household appear to have played a significantly different role in the political economy when compared to the other excavated houses.

DISCUSSION

The combined analysis of surface and subsurface data suggest that *all* Historic period households were allocating at least small amounts of labor to the production of shell beads. These data provide some insights into how the household economy was integrated with the larger re-

gional economy. As discussed above, incentives for these time and energy expenditures were probably linked to a household's desire to acquire certain nonlocal (or European) goods and food items available primarily through regional trade networks. Terrestrial plant resources, such as acorns, acorn flour, chia, and various tubers were probably overexploited on the islands and desired as essential complements to a predominantly marine-oriented diet of shellfish, fish, and marine mammals. Nonlocal goods (e.g., steatite vessels, exotic lithics, European tools) and goods that were made more easily on the mainland as a result of variability in plant distributions (e.g., large baskets, fish nets) were also likely coveted by island households. Households may have been able to improve their diet, their inventory of gear, and their overall quality of life by allocating labor to the production of shell beads and ornaments for exchange. The products of specialist labor probably also satisfied labor obligations incurred from services provided by plank canoe owners, including the transportation of goods and brokering of exchange but also the movement of people to and from social gatherings and ritual celebrations (Arnold 1995b; Arnold and Graesch 2001). Elites may have also solicited shell goods from nonelite households as a prerequisite for participating in specific ceremonies and feasting events.

There appears to have been considerable latitude in the economic strategies designed and implemented by individual households during the Historic period. First, household production strategies varied with respect to total labor contributions and the focus of production activities. Simply put, households were engaging in shellworking tasks at significantly different levels of intensity *and* emphasizing the production of different types of shell valuables. Numerical analysis of surface assemblages at the three west-end Historic-era communities demonstrates the degree of this flexibility on two scales. At a gross level of analysis, correspondence plots (see Figures 9.4, 9.6, and 9.9) reveal major differences in production strategies among *groups* of households within individual communities. However, small-scale variability in shellworking emphasis and intensity is also apparent. Despite general clustering, no two households were exactly alike with respect to the type and intensity of specialized production activities. Moreover, no single household was producing just *one* type of bead. While most households appear to have allocated proportionally greater amounts of labor to one industry or another, nearly all were producing two to three different types of beads.

Aside from confirming patterns observed in surface assemblages, subsurface data indicate that there was no regularity in the manner in which household production strategies changed over the course of the Historic period. While any one household may have increasingly allocated more time and energy to a specific shellworking industry, another may have exercised just the opposite strategy. For example, Historic period residents of house 4 at *Shawa* appear to have intensified red abalone bead production through time, whereas residents of house 8 made fewer red abalone beads later in time. Variability in the intensity and focus of household production strategies across space and through time suggests that households retained considerable autonomy in allocating labor to various craft activities. This interpretation is consistent with archaeological expectations for an interdependent but not attached relationship between elite and nonelite households.

Although individual households at all four Historic-era communities in this analysis were producing multiple types of shell beads, there is evidence of distinctive community-level shellworking emphases. Each of the three west-end villages analyzed here allocated greater amounts of labor than others to a specific shellworking industry. Moreover, none of the Historic-era villages specialized in the same shellworking tradition. For example, *Olivella* wall bead making clearly dominated the production activities of *Shawa*'s shellworking spe-

cialists. On average, all seven *Shawa* houses yielded much higher surface densities of *Olivella* wall beads-in-production and detritus than were observed in houses in the other two west-end Historic communities. Craft specialists at *L'akayamu*, however, produced comparatively greater quantities of red abalone beads than their neighbors at *Shawa* and *Ch'oloshush*. Surface densities of red abalone beads-in-production at *L'akayamu* suggest that *Haliotis rufescens* bead making dominated shellworking activities at this site. Households at *Ch'oloshush* appear to have allocated comparatively greater amounts of labor to the production of *Tivela* shell goods. Mean surface densities of *Tivela* shellworking by-products at *Ch'oloshush* are over ten times greater than those calculated for *L'akayamu* and *Shawa* combined. Low surface densities of both *Olivella* and red abalone beads-in-production and detritus suggest that *Tivela* shellworking activities were the focus of specialized labor expenditures at this community.

Village proximity to shell resources was probably an important factor in the evolution of some of these shellworking specializations. For instance, *Tivela* shells are most abundant in western Santa Cruz Island beach habitats adjacent to the Historic village of *Ch'oloshush*. It makes sense that households at *Ch'oloshush* would specialize in the production of goods, such as *Tivela* beads and ornaments, made from a raw material to which they had superior access. *Haliotis rufescens* populations are widely distributed in deeper, rocky-bottom, cold-water habitats, primarily off the southwestern and northwestern coasts of Santa Cruz Island, and *Olivella biplicata* shells can be found in deep sandy beaches near headlands around the island's perimeter. Whereas craft specialists at *Shawa* and *L'akayamu* thus did not have exclusive access to these shell resources by any means, residents of *Shawa* had reasonably good access to *Olivella* shells, perhaps better than the other sites in this analysis, and residents of *L'akayamu* likely had well above average access to red abalone off the cold, rocky northwestern shores. Such comparative advantages in village location with respect to shell resources meant that communities could develop emphases in the production of certain bead types. By focusing household labor on shellworking traditions different from those of neighboring villages, Historic-era communities may have been able to secure viable niches in the regional economy.

The results of the combined analysis of surface and subsurface assemblages suggest that none of the sampled houses from the three west-end Santa Cruz Island communities can be unambiguously identified as the residence of an elite family. On the other hand, assemblages of shellworking artifacts and prestige goods from house 1 at *Xaxas* stand out when compared to household assemblages from the west-end communities. Much higher densities of prestige goods and finished shell beads suggest a level and range of economic activities consistent with archaeological expectations for Chumash elite residences.

These findings have important implications for models of Chumash labor organization. It would appear that Chumash elites and nonelite specialists were not always spatially juxtaposed. Although this analysis does not consider other assemblages that may also be sensitive to variability in household status (e.g., subsistence data), my results suggest that elites could have been located in relatively few Santa Cruz Island villages, including *Xaxas* on the northern shore.

However, both surface and subsurface data clearly indicate that selected houses at *Shawa* exhibit higher densities of prestige goods than at any other sampled west-end sites. It would appear that some households at this community had comparatively greater access to goods and valuables obtained only through regional trade networks. This is interesting, given that we would predict that selected households that were engaged in roughly equally intensive shellworking activities at *Ch'oloshush* and *L'akayamu* would exhibit more or less equal densities of prestige goods. Why, then, are such marked differences in household prestige objects observed among these three west-end Historic communities?

There may be a relationship between production intensity and the relative status or prosperity of a household. In other words, households investing greater amounts of time and energy in the production of shell valuables may have been able to acquire a steady return on their labor investments. When assemblages from all 31 west-end houses are considered, clustered by site, there is a strong relationship ($r = 0.8$, $p = 0.001$) between shellworking intensity and densities of prestige goods (Figure 9.10). However, this relationship is only significant when evidence for *Olivella* wall bead-making activities is used as a measure of production intensity. When evidence for either *Haliotis rufescens* or *Tivela stultorum* bead production is considered separately, there is no strong relationship between these particular bead-making activities and densities of prestige items ($r = .25$ and $r = .131$, respectively).

These findings suggest that different shellworking activities (focusing on different types) may have had an effect on the quantities or types of prestige goods received by shellworking specialists. However, there is no particularly good reason to believe that *Olivella* wall beads commanded a higher absolute value in the regional economy, although, along with callus beads, they may have served in part as a currency in the Historic period (Arnold and Graesch 2001; Hudson and Blackburn 1987). In addition, if *Olivella* beads conferred a great economic advantage, it makes little sense that some household production strategies were constructed in a way that deemphasized *Olivella* bead-making activities. (For instance, excavations in house 4 at *Shawa* revealed that densities of *Olivella* beads-in-production declined over the course of Historic period occupation.) Moreover, the relationship between production intensity and abundance of prestige goods is heavily influenced by three somewhat anomalous cases at SCRI-192 (see Figure 9.10, top). When data for *Shawa* houses 1, 6, and 8 are removed from the regression analysis, there is no strong relationship between household production intensity and wealth ($r = 0.4$). Based on these findings, it would appear that neither the intensity with which households were engaging in the production of shell beads, nor the types of beads that were being produced, can be used as a singular measure of overall household status. If a household's prestige goods can be used to gauge its role in the political economy and, in turn, its socioeconomic status, then these data suggest that household status was to some degree independent of shellworking activities. This may not

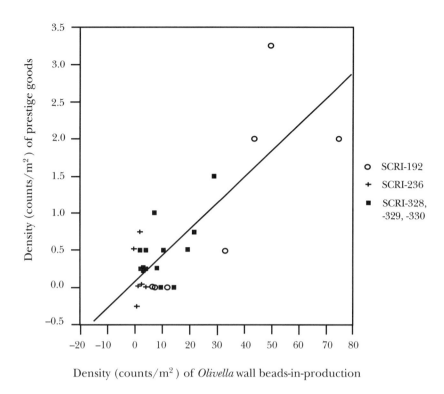

Figure 9.10. Relationship between surface densities of *Olivella* wall beads-in-production and surface densities of prestige goods.

be particularly surprising given that existing hierarchical status structures were rooted in earlier prehistoric developments in the political economy. However, while the social division between elite and nonelite ranks may not have been transcended by craft production activities, nonelite specialists still may have been able to advance their socioeconomic standing within their own rank by working harder. Nonelite households that produced greater quantities of shell goods were likely able to acquire greater quantities of valued food and goods available through regional trade networks. Hard workers may have also been differentially rewarded by elites who regularly brokered exchange between mainland and island communities.

It is possible that some of the interhouse and intersite variation in prestige goods observed among Historic period villages is primarily accounted for by the existing distribution of individuals and/or families of varying status at the

end of the Late period. Although none of the 31 surface-sampled houses at the west-end sites yielded artifact assemblages that unambiguously fit our profile of an elite residence, several independent lines of evidence, including data from recent household excavations, suggest that high-status persons maintaining access to plank canoe technology were present at *Shawa* in the Late and Historic periods. Earlier excavation (1988–1989) of midden deposits at *Shawa* yielded artifact assemblages that may be markers of on-site plank canoe manufacturing activities (Arnold 1995b). These assemblages include chert macrodrills, tarring pebbles, and numerous redwood fragments. The construction of redwood plank canoes, or *tomols*, required a significant investment of labor and resources. Highly skilled specialists belonging to a craft guild known as the Brotherhood of the Tomol labored for nearly six months on the construction of a single vessel (Arnold 1995b). Such costly labor expenditures were historically financed by chiefs and other high-status individuals.

Late period midden deposits at *Shawa* also exhibit unusually high densities of swordfish remains (Pletka 1996, 2001). Swordfish typically inhabit pelagic environments accessible only by sturdy, dependable watercraft, such as the Chumash tomol, and their capture required considerable fishing and boat-handling expertise. A deep submarine canyon near *Shawa*, a favored habitat of swordfish, may have enhanced their availability at this site (Pletka 2001). Such fishes were symbolically important and highly prized by the Island Chumash in the Late and Historic periods (Arnold 1995b; Bernard 2001, this volume; Pletka 2001). The only other excavated site on Santa Cruz Island that exhibits such high densities of swordfish remains is *Xaxas* (SCRI-240). Here, swordfish elements are encountered throughout house 1, in association with numerous imported objects. The abundance of such a highly valued food item, obtainable only through access to costly plank canoe technology, and associated in large quantities with other high-status contexts, may suggest the presence of high-status persons at *Shawa*. Furthermore, the analysis of vertebrate faunal remains recovered from *Shawa* houses suggests that residents of house 8 had greater access to swordfish and other fishes acquired with harpoons from tomols than did the occupants of house 4 (Noah 2003).

However, this explanation begs the question of why elites would choose SCRI-192 as a home. Located on the southwestern coast of Santa Cruz Island, *Shawa* is positioned at one of the farthest points from regular cross-channel trade routes. If leaders and plank canoe owners were interested in maximizing contact with mainland traders, and thus maintaining regular exchange relationships with important coastal mainland communities, *Shawa* would probably have been less than ideal for establishing a permanent residence. However, *Shawa* may have been an attractive location to live for other important reasons. The village was located on a gentle sloping marine terrace that affords a 180-degree view of a long coastline. On average it is less foggy and windy than many other coastal terraces on the island. Most important, this site is

also close to extremely rich marine resources, including shellfish, marine mammals to the east, and an abundance of nearshore kelp forest, deep water, and pelagic fishes.

Thus, although elites may have been attracted to *Shawa* for various reasons, the economic limitations imposed by their location may have selectively favored different economic pursuits or roles in the political economy. One such role might have been that of high-ranking negotiators between Santa Cruz Island elites and nonelite specialist communities. The houses of high-ranking families at *Shawa* may have acted as staging areas for finished goods that were to be transported to elite distribution centers on the northeastern part of Santa Cruz Island. Considering that elites were probably fairly active in operating and maintaining cross-channel exchange networks, an intermediary who oversaw the transport of goods to and from distribution centers may have been essential. Such a position may have been occupied by lower-level elites. The presence of such persons would confirm the variability in elite status positions observed in the ethnographic literature (Blackburn 1975:12–13) and may account for the relative abundance of prestige goods at a few houses at *Shawa*.

Conclusion

The internal organization of Island Chumash communities was anything but simple. Household data presented in this analysis are consistent with archaeological expectations for an interdependent form of labor relations between elites and nonelite specialists. However, the socioeconomic context of these labor relations was far more complex than previously understood. Analysis of specialized shellworking assemblages and nonlocal trade goods suggests that elite and nonelite households played varying roles in the organization and operation of the Historic period political economy.

Data from the three west-end villages indicate that nonelites participated in the regional economy at varying levels of intensity. Some households allocated very little labor to specialized craft activities, whereas others made substantially greater labor contributions. Moreover, households that were willing to work harder may have been able to advance their socioeconomic standing among their nonelite cohort of households. Elite roles in the political economy also varied. High-standing hereditary elites, such as chiefs, were likely instrumental in the movement of goods in regional trade networks. Some such individuals appear to have lived at *Xaxas*. Other lower-ranking elites, such as tomol owners who were not chiefs (Arnold 1995b), may have facilitated the operation of the regional economy by acting as intermediaries between nonelite specialist households and higher-ranking chiefs. Households of this type may have lived at *Shawa*, perhaps at house 8.

These findings are important in that they provide insights into elite and nonelite lifeways that are otherwise lacking in the ethnographic record. Moreover, they demonstrate that anthropological investigations into the organization of labor among stratified societies can benefit greatly from the analysis of household activities.

Acknowledgments. Santa Cruz Island data discussed in this paper were derived from several years of fieldwork and laboratory processing generously supported by a National Science Foundation Grant (SBR 95-11576) awarded to Jeanne Arnold. I thank Jeanne Arnold, Julie Bernard, Terisa Green, Richard Lesure, Anna Noah, Scott Pletka, Dwight Read, and two anonymous reviewers for many useful comments and suggestions that aided and improved this analysis. I accept sole responsibility for all errors and omissions.

REFERENCES CITED

Arnold, J. E.
1990   An Archaeological Perspective on the Historic Settlement Pattern on Santa Cruz Island. *Journal of California and Great Basin Anthropology* 12:112–127.
1992a   Complex Hunter-Gatherer-Fishers of Prehistoric California: Chiefs, Specialists, and Maritime Adaptations of the Channel Islands. *American Antiquity* 57:60–84.
1992b   Cultural Disruption and the Political Economy in Channel Islands Prehistory. In *Essays on the Prehistory of Maritime California*, edited by T. L. Jones, pp.129–144. Center for Archaeological Research Publication 10, University of California, Davis.
1994   Studies in Prehistoric Sociopolitical Complexity in the Northern Channel Islands and Preliminary Findings from Prisoners Harbor. In *The Fourth California Islands Symposium: Update on the Status of Resources*, edited by W. L. Halvorson and G. J. Maender, pp. 193–200. Santa Barbara Museum of Natural History, Santa Barbara, California.
1995a   Inter-Household Variability in Status, Wealth, and Production in the Later Prehistory of the Channel Islands. Proposal submitted to the National Science Foundation. In possession of the author.
1995b   Transportation Innovation and Social Complexity among Maritime Hunter-Gatherer Societies. *American Anthropologist* 97(4):733–747.
2000   The Origins of Hierarchy and the Nature of Hierarchical Structures in Prehistoric California. In *Hierarchies in Action: Cui Bono?* edited by M. W. Diehl, pp. 221–240. Center for Archaeological Investigations, Occasional Paper 27. Southern Illinois University, Carbondale.
2001   The Channel Islands Project: History, Objectives, and Methods. In *The Origins of a Pacific Coast Chiefdom: The Chumash of the Channel Islands*, edited by J. E. Arnold, pp. 21–52. University of Utah Press, Salt Lake City.
Arnold, J. E., and A. P. Graesch
2001   The Evolution of Specialized Shellworking among the Island Chumash. In *The Origins of a Pacific Coast Chiefdom: The Chumash of the Channel Islands*, edited by J. E. Arnold, pp. 71–112. University of Utah Press, Salt Lake City.
Arnold, J. E., and A. Munns
1994   Independent or Attached Specialization: The Organization of Shell Bead Production in California. *Journal of Field Archaeology* 21:473–489.
Baldwin, K. P.
1996   A History of Channel Islands Archaeology. Unpublished Master's thesis, Department of Anthropology, California State University, Northridge.

Bernard, J. L.
2001   The Origins of Open-Ocean and Large Spe-
        cies Fishing in the Chumash Region of
        Southern California. Unpublished Mas-
        ter's thesis, Department of Anthropology,
        University of California, Los Angeles.

Blackburn, T. C.
1975   *December's Child: A Book of Chumash Oral
        Narratives.* University of California Press,
        Berkeley.

Brumfiel, E. M., and T. K. Earle
1987   Specialization, Exchange, and Complex So-
        cieties: An Introduction. In *Specialization,
        Exchange, and Complex Societies,* edited by E.
        M. Brumfiel and T. K. Earle, pp. 1–9. Cam-
        bridge University Press, Cambridge, UK.

Clemmer, J. S.
1961   Archaeological Notes on a Chumash House
        Floor at Morro Bay. A Central California
        Archaeological Foundation Report for Pa-
        cific Gas & Electric.

Costin, C. L.
1991   Craft Specialization: Issues in Defining,
        Documenting, and Explaining the Organi-
        zation of Production. In *Archaeological
        Method and Theory,* Vol. 3, edited by M. B.
        Schiffer, pp. 1–56. University of Arizona
        Press, Tucson.

Earle, T. K.
1987   Specialization and the Production of
        Wealth: Hawaiian Chiefdoms and the Inka
        Empire. In *Specialization, Exchange, and
        Complex Societies,* edited by E. M. Brumfiel
        and T. K. Earle, pp. 64–75. Cambridge Uni-
        versity Press, Cambridge, UK.

Gamble, L.
1991   Organization of Activities at the Historic
        Settlement of Helo': A Chumash Political,
        Economic, and Religious Center. Unpub-
        lished Ph.D. dissertation, Department of
        Anthropology, University of California,
        Santa Barbara.
1995   Chumash Architecture: Sweatlodges and
        Houses. *Journal of California and Great Basin
        Anthropology* 17(1):54–92.

Glassow, M. A.
1977   *An Archaeological Overview of the Northern
        Channel Islands, California, Including Santa
        Barbara Island.* Western Archaeological Cen-
        ter, National Park Service, Tucson.

Graesch, A. P.
2000   Chumash Houses, Households, and Econ-
        omy: Post-Contact Production and Ex-
        change on Santa Cruz Island. Unpublished
        Master's thesis, Department of Anthropol-
        ogy, University of California, Los Angeles.
2001   Culture Contact on the Channel Islands:
        Historic-Era Production and Exchange Sys-
        tems. In *The Origins of a Pacific Coast Chief-
        dom: The Chumash of the Channel Islands,*
        edited by J. E. Arnold, pp. 261–285. Univer-
        sity of Utah Press, Salt Lake City.

Green, T. M.
1999   Spanish Missions and Native Religion:
        Contact, Conflict, and Convergence. Un-
        published Ph.D. dissertation, Archaeology
        Program, University of California, Los An-
        geles.

Hayden, B.
1997   *The Pithouses of Keatley Creek: Complex
        Hunter-Gatherers of the Northwest Plateau.*
        Harcourt Brace, Fort Worth, Texas.

Hudson, T., and T. C. Blackburn
1987   *The Material Culture of the Chumash Interac-
        tion Sphere.* Vol. V: *Manufacturing Processes,
        Metrology, and Trade.* Ballena Press Anthro-
        pological Papers No. 31. Ballena Press/
        Santa Barbara Museum of Natural History
        Cooperative Publication, Menlo Park and
        Santa Barbara, California.

Johnson, J. R.
1993   Cruzeño Chumash Social Geography. In
        *Archaeology on the Northern Channel Islands
        of California: Studies of Subsistence, Econom-
        ics, and Social Organization,* edited by M. A.
        Glassow, pp. 19–46. Archives of California
        Prehistory 34. Coyote Press, Salinas, Cali-
        fornia.
1999   The Chumash Sociopolitical Groups on the
        Channel Islands. In *Cultural Affiliation and
        Lineal Descent of Chumash Peoples in the
        Channel Islands and the Santa Monica Moun-
        tains,* edited by S. McLendon and J. R.
        Johnson, pp. 51–66. Report prepared for the
        National Park Service, Washington, DC.
2001   Ethnohistoric Reflections of Cruzeño Chu-
        mash Society. In *The Origins of a Pacific Coast
        Chiefdom: The Chumash of the Channel Islands,*
        edited by J. E. Arnold, pp. 53–70. University
        of Utah Press, Salt Lake City.

King, C. D.

1990   *Evolution of Chumash Society: A Comparative Study of Artifacts Used for Social System Maintenance in the Santa Barbara Channel Region before A.D. 1804.* Garland, New York.

Noah, A. C.

2003   Status and Fish Consumption: Inter-Household Variability in a Simple Chiefdom Society on the California Coast. In *Presencia de la Arqueoictiología en México*, edited by A. F. Guzmán, Ó. J. Polaco, and F. J. Aguilar, pp. 125–134. Libro de Memorias de la 12ª Reunión del Grupo de Trabajo en Restos de Peces del Consejo Internacional para la Arqueozoología. Instituto Nacional de Antropología e Historia e Museo de Paleontología de Guadalajara "Federico A. Solórzano Barreto," México.

Pletka, S. M.

1996   Chumash Fishers and the Emergence of Complex Social Organization on Santa Cruz Island in their Economic and Ecological Context. Unpublished Master's thesis, Department of Anthropology, University of California, Los Angeles.

2001   The Economics of Island Chumash Fishing Practices. In *The Origins of a Pacific Coast Chiefdom: The Chumash of the Channel Islands*, edited by J. E. Arnold, pp. 221–244. University of Utah Press, Salt Lake City.

Schiffer, M. B.

1987   *Formation Processes of the Archaeological Record.* University of Utah Press, Salt Lake City.

1989   Formation Processes of Broken K Pueblo: Some Hypotheses. In *Quantifying Diversity in Archaeology*, edited by R. D. Leonard and G. T. Jones, pp. 37–58. Cambridge University Press, Cambridge, UK.

10

Complex Hunter-Gatherers of the Southern California Coast

A View from One Thousand Miles North

Gary Coupland

Those of us studying prehistoric complex hunter-gatherers form a small but important group. We are few because the count of ethnographic and archaeological examples of complex hunter-gatherers from around the world remains rather small. But that number is growing. At one time anthropologists recognized only the First Nations of the Northwest Coast as complex hunter-gatherers, and, accordingly, they were treated as an anomaly. And we are important because as the number of complex hunter-gatherer cases grows, the anomalous status of the Northwest Coast peoples becomes more difficult to maintain, and our research poses an ever-stronger challenge to the long-cherished evolutionary model that links complexity to farming. In decoupling complex societies from plant and animal domestication, we begin to see not only hunter-gatherers in a different light but agriculturalists too, for as Barbara Bender (1985), Brian Hayden (1990, 1994), and others have recently argued, it may have been social complexity, developing in the late stages of hunting and gathering in some parts of the world, that led to the first daring steps in farming rather than the other way around. In sum, complex hunter-gatherers, whether or not they go on to become farmers, challenge one long-standing point of view, but they simultaneously reinforce another that most of us feel comfortable with: that there are multiple pathways to complexity.

Agriculture does pose a problem to the study of complex hunter-gatherers in one sense

though. Where moderately complex hunter-gatherers have gone on to take up farming—as, for example, in the Neolithic of the Near East (Belfer-Cohen 1991; Henry 1985, 1989; Wright 1978) and northern Europe (Price 1985; Rowley-Conwy 1983; Woodman 1985), the Late Woodland period in the American Midwest (Bender 1985; Brown 1985), the Preceramic of coastal Peru (Feldman 1987; Moseley 1975), and the Later Jomon in Japan (Nishida 1983; Watanabe 1983)—we have lost the all-important ethnographic record of hunter-gatherer complexity (although the Ainu are sometimes cited as an analogue for Jomon hunter-gatherer complexity [e.g., Watanabe 1968, 1970]). And where complex hunter-gatherers do not exist as the ethnographic end point, it has proven very difficult to make the case in prehistory. Why, it seems fair to ask, do so many archaeologists readily, often uncritically, accept reconstructions of complexity where there is wheat, corn, or rice but not where there are salmon, acorns, or gazelles?

Happily, those of us working on the west coast of North America are not faced with the problem of the forager-to-farmer transition, nor do we face much opposition to our arguments for hunter-gatherer complexity in this region. From Alaska to southern California there is clear evidence of cultural complexity with nary an ethnographic farmer in sight. This rich ethnographic record, partly a product of late European contact on the west coast, makes it absolutely clear that hunter-gatherer complexity

173

was the end point of the historical trajectory and informs us about what cultural configurations must have been like during the late period of prehistory. The tasks before us are to document this complexity in all its regional variability in the archaeological record and to try to account for its origins and development. The contributors to this volume have these tasks clearly in mind.

A REVIEW OF THIS VOLUME

Although Arnold and Graesch lament the fact that John Peabody Harrington did not bring the Chumash to the ethnographic forefront early in the twentieth century in the manner that Franz Boas and his colleagues did for the First Nations of the Northwest Coast, the work that has been done in southern California in the past few decades by ethnographers and archaeologists—in particular, the work of Jeanne Arnold and her students (e.g., Arnold 2001)—has done much to resolve this situation. The Chumash now provide one of the best and best-documented cases of complex hunter-gatherers in the archaeological literature. A large group of scholars with occasionally opposing points of view (a healthy situation) is now involved in the research (Arnold 1992, 1993, 1997; Arnold and Tissot 1993; Arnold et al. 1997; Raab and Bradford 1997; Raab et al. 1995); several recently published articles and books have brought the Chumash case to the attention of a wider audience (Arnold 1987, 1992, 1995; Arnold, ed. 2001; Arnold and Munns 1994; Erlandson et al. 1992; Erlandson and Jones 2002; Gamble et al. 2001; Glassow 1996; Raab and Larson 1997); and, perhaps most important, models of hunter-gatherer complexity that should have widespread applicability are being developed and tested (Arnold 1993, 1996; Johnson 2000; Kennett and Kennett 2000; Lambert and Walker 1991). Where anthropologists once looked only to the Northwest Coast for their models of hunter-gatherer complexity, our attention is increasingly being drawn to the southern California coast and the Chumash example.

And the Chumash case has a lot to offer. In their introductory chapter Arnold and Graesch refer to the Island Chumash, post-AD 1150, as a "simple chiefdom," and they are careful to use this term in its political sense, to mean an integrated regional unit incorporating several formerly autonomous villages. It is important, especially when looking at complexity in intermediate societies—and all examples of complex hunter-gatherers fall into this category—that the distinction between "social complexity" and "political complexity" be recognized. The Northwest Coast, for example, was socially complex, in the sense that there was great inequality among individuals and families, but not politically complex (cf. Martindale 1999, 2003), in the sense of having regional integration, as Leland Donald has argued on several occasions (Donald 1985, 2003; Mitchell 1983). Northwest Coast villages, even households, were largely autonomous. If the late prehistoric Chumash were indeed politically complex, several interesting and important questions arise. What was the basic Chumash political unit? Can it be discerned archaeologically? Did the Channel Islands as a group constitute a separate polity, or was each island an autonomous unit, much like Hawaii at the time of European contact? How was Chumash political organization affected by relations between mainlanders and islanders? Each of these questions may herald exciting future research.

Arnold and Graesch go on to review some of the key features of Chumash complexity that have emerged in recent years: specialized (but not necessarily full-time) craft production, advanced boat building, and intensive trade and subsistence production—all features examined in greater detail in later chapters. They conclude their introduction with a brief look at the current emphasis of the Santa Cruz Island Project, household archaeology (e.g., Graesch 2000), intended, in their terms, to reveal "the inner workings of a simple chiefdom." This focus on households promises to provide important information about the relations of production that existed among drill makers, bead makers, and *tomol*-owning elites. Arnold and Graesch use the term *interdependence* to characterize these relations, arguing that there is currently no evidence of rigid elite control of specialized bead production (Arnold and Munns 1994). Yet island elites presumably controlled trade of finished beads to the mainland. This idea of interdependent relations of production is intriguing and should be developed further. It suggests an alternative form of specialized production that lies somewhere between independent and attached specialization (Brumfiel and Earle 1987). Indeed, interdependent specialization may be common in "simple chiefdoms," where tension exists between local autonomy and regional integration. Elites may exert influence over producers in neighboring communities, but they do not fully control production. In more complex chiefdoms characterized by attached specialization, regional integration is achieved because elites exert much more control over production. This model of interdependent specialization may have applicability beyond the Chumash region and should be examined carefully by Northwest Coast archaeologists.

Several chapters in this volume engage the issue of specialization in one way or another. Julie Bernard, Jennifer Perry, and Scott Pletka are mainly concerned with craft specialization and the implications this may have for resource and subsistence specialization. Bernard shows that the invention of the tomol at about AD 500 coincides with evidence for increasing acquisition of tuna and perhaps some other deepwater fish, but it is not until much later that we see a spike in swordfish remains. Bernard's feasting argument to explain the rise in swordfish is persuasive, especially in light of Arnold and Graesch's model of interdependence in the relations of production between craft specialists and elites. If elites were increasingly competing with each other for access to labor during the Transitional and Late periods, then offering rare and highly valued foods at feasts may have been a key strategy (Dietler and Hayden 2001; Hayden 2001). A possible parallel to this on the Northwest Coast may have been whaling and, to a lesser extent, hunting of other large sea mammals like sea lions.

Perry takes a diachronic look at changes in subsistence strategy, beginning with an interior focus in the Early period, shifting to increasing marine resource intensification in the Middle period, and thence to an increasing separation of subsistence activities and the political economy

in the Late period. This change through time fits well with what we know of evolving complexity and specialization in the region (including Bernard's deep-sea fishing model).

Pletka shows that the rate of change in microdrill manufacture, from forms that are trapezoidal in cross section to ones that are triangular, occurs in lockstep with the change from *Olivella* wall beads to callus beads. Pletka's chapter is a rare attempt to apply formal theory—in this case, evolutionary ecology—to the problem of craft specialization. Through simulation studies he is able to distinguish three mechanisms responsible for changes in artifact frequency: indirect bias, drift, and conformist transmission. Pletka argues that the archaeological evidence from SCRI-191 most closely resembles the changes simulated by indirect bias in a changing selective environment. What remains to be answered is why callus beads were more highly valued than wall beads—why would callus bead makers appear to be "better off"? Pletka's evolutionary approach usefully distinguishes patterns of selection-driven functional change from stylistic change, but more work needs to be done.

The research by Bernard, Perry, and Pletka highlights the importance of two questions that have already been raised in this chapter. What kind of political order is coordinating this increasing specialization? How will the evidence of specialization be revealed in the household data?

Several chapters in this volume shift the focus from Chumash craft specialization to ritual specialization, one of the more famous aspects of ethnographic Chumash culture. Ray Corbett and Sandra Hollimon are both concerned with aspects of ritual specialization in the evolution of Chumash complexity. Corbett, in showing that the earliest deer tibia whistles date to the late Middle period, makes a plausible case for increasing ceremonial integration and perhaps even ritual specialization at this time. To strengthen the case for elaboration of ceremony at the close of the Middle period, future work should examine more lines of evidence than this single artifact type. At the moment, Corbett's argument is best seen as a hypothesis in need of further testing. Interestingly, this evidence for ceremonial elaboration predates the Transitional period evidence for climate change (Arnold 1992; Jones et al. 1999; Raab and Larson 1997). From a functionalist point of view one might expect ceremonial integration to be a response to environmental perturbation. But in this case the evidence for ritual precedes certain documented environmental changes. This observation may have relevance to Arnold's model of "opportunistic elites" (Arnold 1996). When the time came, around AD 1150, emerging elites could take advantage of existing tomol production and the trend toward ceremonial elaboration. One question remains: what sparked this elaboration of ceremony and ritual late in the Middle period?

Sandra Hollimon argues that aspiring elites could strengthen their hold on power by aligning themselves with ritual specialists. In its most benign form this alignment simply gives the elite access to certain forms of power based in knowledge and ritual that they would not otherwise hold. But in its more extreme form such an alignment is really a form of coercion, in which ritual power could be used against those who question the authority of the elite. Dominique Legros (1985) has shown how coercion was the main source of power among Tutchone elites in southwestern Yukon.

Throughout the Pacific Rim chiefs and shamans certainly coexisted for hundreds if not thousands of years. Hollimon's chapter is one of the few studies that actually explores their relationship. Her work mines the Chumash ethnographic record more than any other in this volume and, not surprisingly, raises more questions for archaeologists than it answers. Like Corbett, Hollimon challenges orthodoxy by arguing that ritual elaboration and ceremonial integration may have been important sources of cultural change in Chumash society.

The chapters I have discussed so far have been concerned mainly with Santa Cruz Island from the Middle period onward. Torben Rick and Mike Glassow expand the niche, as it were. Rick reviews the prehistoric sequence of San Miguel Island and shows that although the overall trend is quite similar to Santa Cruz, there are

some notable differences, especially in the last 1,500 years. One of the most interesting differences from the Santa Cruz Island evidence is that microblade production was never intensive on San Miguel, but *Olivella* bead production was. Were San Miguel islanders importing drills? Arnold and Graesch note that among the Santa Cruz villages, we see lithic *or* shell specialization but not both. When we look at the San Miguel data, are we seeing a similar kind of pattern, except on a larger scale? And does the bowl production on San Miguel have any analogue on Santa Cruz? Are these interisland differences a result of locally available resources or emerging elites trying to find a way to compete (or both)?

Mike Glassow examines evidence from Santa Cruz Island, but from a much earlier period, and asks whether a degree of social complexity may have existed in the Chumash region some 6,000 years ago. The burial evidence from El Montón is intriguing in this regard but not overwhelming; no grave seems to have more beads than could be accounted for by one necklace. The Punta Arena evidence is more significant, however, because intensive dolphin hunting requires considerable coordination of labor (Porcasi and Fujita 2000). This, combined with the evidence for mainland trade, suggests some degree of complexity, but why during this period? And why does complexity seem to decline after 5300 BP? Glassow's chapter raises several important issues in the study of Channel Islands complexity and reminds us that complexity is not a one-way street; oscillations through time can and do happen.

A VIEW OF SOUTHERN CALIFORNIA COMPLEXITY FROM THE NORTHWEST COAST

Collectively, the chapters in this volume make several important contributions to the study of cultural complexity on the southern California coast. We see some familiar themes in many of these essays, such as craft specialization and the importance of ritual and ceremony in the evolution of complexity, but it is important to contextualize these themes in terms of the southern California coast example. Indeed, what I find most striking, having studied complex hunter-gatherers on the Northwest Coast, are the different paths to complexity taken in these two regions. In the remainder of this chapter I will highlight some of those differences in an effort to show that variability, worthy of future research, exists among complex hunter-gatherers.

One important difference between the two regions is the emphasis placed on craft specialization—much greater, I believe, on the southern California coast. From a Northwest Coast perspective the sheer numbers of microdrills and shell beads and bead detritus found in Island Chumash sites are truly remarkable. This is not to suggest, of course, that craft specialization was unknown on the Northwest Coast. Some of the great indigenous artwork of the world comes from this region. And arguably, since the medium for much of Northwest Coast specialized craft production was wood, which does not preserve as well archaeologically as stone or shell, the difference in emphasis on craft specialization between the two regions may be more apparent than real. But this argument should not be taken too far. Much of the wood carving for which Northwest Coast First Nations are justly famous appears to date to the early and mid-nineteenth century, the period just after European contact, when new sources of wealth fueled a florescence in Northwest Coast artwork. It is not at all clear that wood carving was nearly as developed during the prehistoric period, and although craft specialization in earlier times is seen in other media—for example, stone bowls and bead production—it is clear that this production was quite limited in comparison to the shell-bead-making industry of the southern California coast.

The two regions also differ in terms of the organization of craft production. Not only was there a greater emphasis on craft specialization in the Chumash area, but craft production was more complexly organized in this region and more directly linked to the acquisition of power by elites. Most telling in this regard is Arnold and Graesch's observation in chapter 1 that island villages tended to specialize in drill manufacturing or bead manufacturing but rarely both. Thus, bead production was broken down into specific tasks or activities, and specialists were engaged in one or another of the activities but not in the production process from beginning to end. The tasks were performed sequentially by different specialists or groups of specialists. This segmented organization of production may have been a strategy used by elites to maintain control over the entire production process. Craft specialization on the Northwest Coast was organized much more simply. As far as we know, Northwest Coast specialists were engaged in all stages of production. A wood carver, for example, would have secured his own raw material, made his own woodworking tools, and done his own carving, although he may have been aided by assistants at any stage of production. Although on occasion prominent chiefs may have served as patrons to some carvers, this simple organization of production would have given the Northwest Coast craft specialist much more control over his or her own labor, making it far more difficult for elites to gain power through control of craft specialization.

The differences between the two regions in craft specialization may be related to another important difference: the ways that goods were exchanged. On the southern California coast the dramatic increase in bead production on the Channel Islands beginning about AD 1150 coincides with a period of drought and fluctuations in the abundance of key marine resources due to changing sea surface temperatures. Faced with the possibility of food shortages, islanders increased the production of wealth items that were exchanged for foodstuffs and other materials from the mainland. Several sources make it clear that shell beads functioned more or less as a form of currency in the Chumash region. There exists no analogue to this on the Northwest Coast, although during the nineteenth century commodities such as "coppers" (breast plates) and even slaves may have had very specific exchange values (Donald 1997). Craft specialists on the Channel Islands were mainly engaged in the production of wealth (shell beads), whereas much (but not all) craft production on the Northwest Coast was in the form of social symbols such as masks and clan crests that reflected certain rights and prerogatives of the owner and his family. Wealth items could be widely exchanged but symbols of family rights and prerogatives could not.

On the southern California coast wealth was manufactured and used to "purchase" food. On the Northwest Coast wealth was used to "purchase" prestige (Suttles 1968). Indeed, the Chumash exchange system that began to take shape after the Middle period might well be characterized as "wealth-for-food exchange," precisely the reverse of the well-known "food-for-wealth" exchange practiced by the Coast Salish of the Northwest Coast (Suttles 1960).

The two regions were also different in terms of the relationship between craft specialization and food production. Among the Chumash there was a sharp division between wealth producers or craft specialists (islanders) and surplus food producers (mainlanders). This is not to say, of course, that islanders did not engage in food production after AD 1150 or that craft production was unknown on the mainland. But craft specialization must have occupied many more hours of labor on the islands during this period and must have been far more important to the subsistence economy than it was on the mainland. Again, there is no analogue to this situation on the Northwest Coast, where food surplus producers were also, invariably, producers of wealth. A large Northwest Coast household could actively engage in food production, including production of surpluses, and craft/wealth production at the same time. Households were the main producing units on the Northwest Coast, and the key to diversifying production in this region was expanding the size of the household. The ideal on the Northwest Coast was household independence; the household "did it all." Island Chumash households, and even villages, were far more specialized, at least with respect to craft production, engaging in some but not all aspects of key production processes. This may partly explain the smaller size of Chumash houses and households in comparison to the Northwest Coast.

Island Chumash craft specialization must have reduced the economic independence of the producing units (households?) because microdrill makers were not producing the "end product" (shell beads were the end product), and bead makers were dependent on a steady supply of microdrills. This interdependence among

specialists may partly explain another important difference between the Chumash and the cultures of the Northwest Coast, seen in terms of level of political integration. The Northwest Coast cultures are often described as having had a high level of social inequality, with three class divisions including slaves, but a low level of political integration. Villages remained autonomous, and even within villages a chief could only command the labor of the members of his household (De Laguna 1983; Drucker 1983; Mitchell 1983). As I noted above, Northwest Coast households were largely independent and self-sufficient. Since there was no stable producing unit beyond the level of the household, production and political organization were decentralized. For the Island Chumash Arnold makes a compelling argument for at least moderate political integration beginning about AD 1150. After this time households and villages were no longer autonomous, at least not completely so. The interdependence of the highly specialized Island Chumash craft-producing units suggests some centralized control over craft production. Indeed, as I have suggested above, creating interdependence among craft specialists may have been an elite strategy for building power.

Thus far I have focused on differences in craft specialization between the southern California coast region and the Northwest Coast and on how these differences may have led to differing levels of political integration. Another major difference between the two regions existed in subsistence resources. Although both regions were rich in food resources, including marine species, at least during periods of climatic stability, the Northwest Coast resource structure was dominated by the presence of one major subsistence resource, Pacific salmon. Intensive fishing and storage of salmon was the critical step that enabled the surplus production that underlay the ranked social systems of the Northwest Coast. In other words, Northwest Coast cultural complexity was largely built on an economic base of large-scale salmon production (Matson and Coupland 1995). Other food resources were certainly important in Northwest Coast economies (Monks 1987), but none were capable of providing such steady, reliable, and abundant surpluses. Archaeological evidence indicates that salmon fishing was being intensified on the Northwest Coast prior to 3000 BP (Matson and Coupland 1995).

In the Chumash region a variety of marine and terrestrial (on the mainland) resources supported the complex social system, and although acorns may have been the most important of these resources, at least on the mainland, there was no single resource, like salmon on the Northwest Coast, that underlay the entire system. As a result, Chumash cultural complexity was based more on resource diversity than on intensive production of any single resource.

The differences in the subsistence economies of the two regions had important implications for ownership of resources and resource locations. Ownership of corporeal and noncorporeal resources was a critical aspect of the Northwest Coast prestige system. Households that owned productive resource locations were generally highly ranked, whereas households that owned less productive resource locations were usually lower ranked. Donald and Mitchell (1975) have shown that this correlation between resource abundance and social precedence applied at the local group level as well. The concept of resource ownership is poorly developed or nonexistent in most hunter-gatherer societies (Lee 1990). This may be so for a variety of reasons, but one of the most important reasons is that most nondomesticated resources are not well suited to ownership. Either they are not sufficiently reliable or predictable in their distribution or they do not occur in enough abundance on an annual basis to make ownership worthwhile. Pacific salmon are a rare exception to this rule. As Matson (1983) has argued, Pacific salmon are worth the effort of ownership because they combine several key attributes for which other resources have been domesticated. Pacific salmon occur in tremendous abundance. This abundance is reliable on a year-to-year basis and is predictable in terms of access locations. Moreover, although they are seasonal, salmon can be preserved and stored for delayed consumption. Finally, and perhaps most important to the question of ownership, salmon are a localized resource. Using traditional technologies, humans

can take salmon only at discrete locations, usually in fresh water. Prominent rocks and back eddies along the edges of rivers and river narrows and canyons were the preferred fishing locations. A good freshwater fishing location was usually owned by a household group, use of that location by anyone outside the owning household required permission, and permission usually incurred some form of debt. Matson argues that ownership strategies on the Northwest Coast probably evolved in conjunction with salmon intensification and subsequently spread to control of other resources. By the time of European contact virtually all resources or resource locations on the Northwest Coast were subject to ownership. Perhaps the most telling example of how important the concept of ownership became on the Northwest Coast is the fact that ownership of a human being—slavery—had evolved prior to European contact (Donald 1997:201–213).

A good analogue to salmon is acorns. Acorns in southern California were abundant, predictable, localized, and storable, and, as mentioned above, acorn-producing oak groves were owned by the Chumash. The concept of ownership was extended by the Chumash to some other resources, such as shellfish beds, but not to all resources. A good contrast to salmon is swordfish on the southern California coast (Bernard, this volume). A pelagic fish that required fishing from boats in open water, swordfish were certainly not a localized resource. The same was true of tuna. Because these fish are widely dispersed in open water, it would be all but impossible to claim ownership of a resource location. On the other hand, a good analogue to the swordfish on the Northwest Coast would be whales, in the sense that both resources are associated with prestige, and both can only be hunted in open water. But here the similarity ends. The right to fish for swordfish was not "owned" in any sense among the Chumash, but the right to hunt whales was very definitely owned on the Northwest Coast. For example, among the Nuu-chah-nulth (Nootka) of the west coast of Vancouver Island, whale hunting was strictly a chiefly prerogative. It seems that the concept of ownership of the right to acquire key animals was not as well developed among the Chumash and was not as critical to the acquisition of prestige and power as on the Northwest Coast.

CONCLUSION

The Chumash of the southern California coast present a good case for hunter-gatherer complexity, as the chapters in this volume clearly show. From a Northwest Coast archaeologist's perspective there are some basic similarities in cultural complexity from southeastern Alaska to southern California, such as pronounced social inequality, high population density, relative sedentism, and, of course, use of marine resources. But underlying the similarities are some striking differences. The intensification of craft production on the southern California coast, resulting ultimately in a form of shell bead currency, is unparalleled on the Northwest Coast. In particular, the highly specialized nature of shell bead production, with some groups manufacturing microdrills and other groups using the drills to produce beads, created a situation in which emerging elites could gain power by centralizing the overall production process. Indeed, as I have mentioned, the high degree of specialization in bead production may have been an elite strategy for gaining power, as there seems to be no good reason why microdrill makers could not also have been bead makers. In any event it seems that craft specialization was a far more important force in producing complexity on the southern California coast than it was on the Northwest Coast. Turning to the Northwest Coast, intensification of a single, critical subsistence resource and ownership of resource locations may have been much more important to the development of complexity than on the southern California coast.

This brief comparison between the Northwest Coast and the Chumash of the southern California coast suggests that different paths to complexity were taken by the hunter-gatherers in these regions. This should come as no surprise. A great deal of research in recent decades has emphasized the high degree of diversity that exists among hunter-gatherers in general, so it is not surprising to find diversity among complex

hunter-gatherers as well. Future research may well expand on this theme.

REFERENCES CITED

Arnold, J. E.
1987   *Craft Specialization in the Prehistoric Channel Islands, California.* University of California Press, Berkeley.
1992   Complex Hunter-Gatherer-Fishers of Prehistoric California: Chiefs, Specialists, and Maritime Adaptations of the Channel Islands. *American Antiquity* 57:60–84.
1993   Labor and the Rise of Complex Hunter-Gatherers. *Journal of Anthropological Archaeology* 12:75–119.
1995   Transportation Innovation and Social Complexity among Maritime Hunter-Gatherer Societies. *American Anthropologist* 97:733–747.
1996   The Archaeology of Complex Hunter-Gatherers. *Journal of Archaeological Method and Theory* 3:77–126.
1997   Bigger Boats, Crowded Creekbanks: Environmental Stresses in Perspective. *American Antiquity* 62:337–339.
Arnold, J. E. (editor)
2001   *The Origins of a Pacific Coast Chiefdom: The Chumash of the Channel Islands.* University of Utah Press, Salt Lake City.
Arnold, J. E., R. H. Colten, and S. Pletka
1997   Contexts of Cultural Change in Insular California. *American Antiquity* 62:300–318.
Arnold, J. E., and A. Munns
1994   Independent or Attached Specialization: The Organization of Shell Bead Production in California. *Journal of Field Archaeology* 21:473–489.
Arnold, J. E., and B. Tissot
1993   Measurement of Significant Marine Temperature Variation Using Black Abalone Shells from Middens. *Quaternary Research* 39:390–394.
Belfer-Cohen, A.
1991   The Natufian in the Levant. *Annual Review of Anthropology* 20:167–186.
Bender, B.
1985   Prehistoric Developments in the American Midcontinent and in Brittany, Northwest

France. In *Prehistoric Hunter-Gatherers: The Emergence of Cultural Complexity*, edited by T. D. Price and J. A. Brown, pp. 21–58. Academic Press, Orlando, Florida.

Brown, J. A
1985 Long-Term Trends to Sedentism and the Emergence of Complexity in the American Midwest. In *Prehistoric Hunter-Gatherers: The Emergence of Cultural Complexity*, edited by T. D. Price and J. A. Brown, pp. 201–231. Academic Press, Orlando, Florida.

Brumfiel, E., and T. K. Earle
1987 Specialization, Exchange, and Complex Societies: An Introduction. In *Specialization, Exchange, and Complex Societies*, edited by E. L. Brumfiel and T. K. Earle, pp. 1–9. Cambridge University Press, Cambridge, UK.

De Laguna, F.
1983 Aboriginal Tlingit Sociopolitical Organization. In *The Development of Political Organization in Native North America*, edited by E. Tooker, pp. 71–85. American Ethnological Society, Washington, DC.

Dietler, M., and B. Hayden
2001 Digesting the Feast: Good to Eat, Good to Drink, Good to Think: An Introduction. In *Feasts: Archaeological and Ethnographic Perspectives on Food, Politics, and Power*, edited by M. Dietler and B. Hayden, pp. 1–22. Smithsonian Institution Press, Washington, DC.

Donald, L.
1985 On the Possibility of Social Class in Societies Based on Extractive Subsistence. In *Status, Structure, and Stratification: Current Archaeological Reconstructions*, edited by M. Thompson, M. T. Garcia, and F. Kense, pp. 237–244. University of Calgary Archaeological Association, Calgary, Alberta.
1997 *Aboriginal Slavery on the Northwest Coast of North America*. University of California Press, Berkeley.
2003 The Northwest Coast as a Study Area: Natural, Prehistoric, and Ethnographic Issues. In *Emerging from the Mist: Studies in Northwest Coast Culture History*, edited by R. G. Matson, G. Coupland, and Q. Mackie, pp. 289–327. University of British Columbia Press, Vancouver.

Donald, L., and D. H. Mitchell
1975 Some Correlates of Local Group Rank among the Southern Kwakiutl. *Ethnology* 14:325–346.

Drucker, P.
1983 Ecology and Political Organization on the Northwest Coast of North America. In *The Development of Political Organization in Native North America*, edited by E. Tooker, pp. 86–96. American Ethnological Society, Washington, DC.

Erlandson, J. M., M. A. Glassow, C. Rozaire, and D. Morris
1992 4,000 Years of Human Occupation on Santa Barbara Island, California. *Journal of California and Great Basin Anthropology* 14:85–93.

Erlandson, J. M., and T. L. Jones (editors)
2002 *Catalysts to Complexity: Late Holocene Societies of the California Coast*. Cotsen Institute of Archaeology, University of California, Los Angeles.

Feldman, R.
1987 Architectural Evidence for the Development of Nonegalitarian Social Systems in Coastal Peru. In *The Origins and Development of the Andean State*, edited by J. Haas, S. Pozorski, and T. Pozorski, pp. 9–14. Cambridge University Press, Cambridge, UK.

Gamble L., P. L. Walker, and G. Russell
2001 An Integrative Approach to Mortuary Analysis: Social and Symbolic Dimensions of Chumash Burial Practices. *American Antiquity* 66:185–212.

Glassow, M. A.
1996 *Purisimeño Chumash Prehistory: Maritime Adaptations along the Southern California Coast*. Harcourt Brace, Fort Worth, Texas.

Graesch, A. P.
2000 Chumash Houses, Households, and Economy: Post-Contact Production and Exchange on Santa Cruz Island. Unpublished Master's thesis, Department of Anthropology, University of California, Los Angeles.

Hayden, B.
1990 Nimrods, Piscators, Pluckers, and Planters: The Emergence of Food Production. *Journal of Anthropological Archaeology* 9:31–69.

1994   Competition, Labor, and Complex Hunter-
        Gatherers. In *Key Issues in Hunter-Gatherer
        Research*, edited by E. S. Burch Jr. and L. J.
        Ellana, pp. 223–239. Berg, Oxford.

2001   Fabulous Feasts: A Prolegomenon to the
        Importance of Feasting. In *Feasts: Archaeo-
        logical and Ethnographic Perspectives on Food,
        Politics, and Power*, edited by M. Dietler and
        B. Hayden, pp. 23–64. Smithsonian Institu-
        tion Press, Washington, DC.

Henry, D. O.
1985   Preagricultural Sedentism: The Natufian
        Example. In *Prehistoric Hunter-Gatherers:
        The Emergence of Cultural Complexity*, edited
        by T. D. Price and J. A. Brown, pp. 365–384.
        Academic Press, Orlando, Florida.

1989   *From Foraging to Agriculture: The Levant at
        the End of the Ice Age*. University of Pennsyl-
        vania Press, Philadelphia.

Johnson, J. R.
2000   Social Responses to Climate Change among
        the Chumash Indians of South-Central Cal-
        ifornia. In *The Way the Wind Blows: Climate,
        History, and Human Action*, edited by R. J.
        McIntosh, J. A. Tainter, and S. K. McIntosh,
        pp. 301–327. Columbia University Press,
        New York.

Jones, T. L., G. M. Brown, L. M. Raab, J. L.
        McVickar, W. G. Spaulding, D. J. Kennett,
        A. York, and P. L. Walker
1999   Environmental Imperatives Reconsidered:
        Demographic Crises in Western North
        America during the Medieval Climatic
        Anomaly. *Current Anthropology* 40:137–170.

Kennett, D. J., and J. P. Kennett
2000   Competitive and Cooperative Responses to
        Climatic Instability in Coastal Southern
        California. *American Antiquity* 65:379–395.

Lambert, P., and P. L. Walker
1991   Physical Anthropological Evidence for the
        Evolution of Social Complexity in Coastal
        Southern California. *Antiquity* 65:963–973.

Lee, R. B.
1990   Primitive Communism and the Origin of
        Social Inequality. In *The Evolution of Political
        Systems: Sociopolitics in Small-Scale Sedentary
        Societies*, edited by S. Upham, pp. 225–246.
        Cambridge University Press, Cambridge,
        UK.

Legros, D.
1985   Wealth, Poverty, and Slavery among the
        19th Century Tutchone Athapaskans. *Re-
        search in Economic Anthropology* 7: 37–64.

Martindale, A.
1999   The River of Mist: Cultural Change in the
        Tsimshian Past. Unpublished Ph.D. disser-
        tation, Department of Anthropology, Uni-
        versity of Toronto.

2003   A Hunter-Gatherer Paramount Chiefdom:
        Tsimshian Developments through the Con-
        tact Period. In *Emerging from the Mist: Stud-
        ies in Northwest Coast Culture History*, edited
        by R. G. Matson, G. Coupland, and Q.
        Mackie, pp. 12–50. University of British Co-
        lumbia Press, Vancouver.

Matson, R. G.
1983   Intensification and the Development of
        Cultural Complexity: The Northwest ver-
        sus the Northeast Coast. In *The Evolution of
        Maritime Cultures on the Northeast and North-
        west Coasts of America*, edited by R. Nash,
        pp. 125–148. Simon Fraser University, De-
        partment of Archaeology, Publication No.
        11, Burnaby, British Columbia.

Matson, R. G., and G. Coupland
1995   *The Prehistory of the Northwest Coast*. Aca-
        demic Press, San Diego.

Mitchell, D.
1983   Tribes and Chiefdoms on the Northwest
        Coast: The Tsimshian Case. In *The Evolution
        of Maritime Cultures on the Northeast and
        Northwest Coasts of America*, edited by R.
        Nash, pp. 57–64. Simon Fraser University,
        Department of Archaeology, Publication
        No. 11, Burnaby, British Columbia.

Monks, G.
1987   Prey as Bait: The Deep Bay Example. *Cana-
        dian Journal of Archaeology* 11:119–142.

Moseley, M.
1975   *The Maritime Foundations of Andean Civiliza-
        tion*. Cummings, Menlo Park, California.

Nishida, M.
1983   The Emergence of Food Production in
        Neolithic Japan. *Journal of Anthropological
        Archaeology* 2:305–322.

Porcasi, J. F., and H. Fujita
2000   The Dolphin Hunters: A Specialized Prehis-
        toric Maritime Adaptation in the Southern

California Channel Islands and Baja California. *American Antiquity* 65:543–566.

Price, T. D.
1985 Affluent Foragers of Mesolithic Southern Scandinavia. In *Prehistoric Hunter-Gatherers: The Emergence of Cultural Complexity*, edited by T. D. Price and J. A. Brown, pp. 341–363. Academic Press, Orlando, Florida.

Raab, L. M., and K. Bradford
1997 Making Nature Answer to Interpretivism: Response to J. E. Arnold, R. H. Colten, and S. Pletka. *American Antiquity* 62:340–341.

Raab, L. M., K. Bradford, J. F. Porcasi, and W. J. Howard
1995 Return to Little Harbor, Santa Catalina Island, California: A Critique of the Marine Paleotemperature Model. *American Antiquity* 60:287–308.

Raab, L. M., and D. O. Larson
1997 Medieval Climatic Anomaly and Punctuated Cultural Evolution in Coastal Southern California. *American Antiquity* 62:319–336.

Rowley-Conwy, P.
1983 Sedentary Hunters: The Ertebølle Example. In *Hunter-Gatherer Economy in Prehistory: A European Perspective*, edited by G. Bailey, pp. 111–126. Cambridge University Press, Cambridge, UK.

Suttles, W.
1960 Affinal Ties, Subsistence, and Prestige among the Coast Salish. *American Anthropologist* 62:296–305.

1968 Coping with Abundance: Subsistence on the Northwest Coast. In *Man the Hunter*, edited by R. B. Lee and I. DeVore, pp. 56–68. Aldine, Chicago.

Watanabe, H.
1968 Subsistence and Ecology of Northern Food Gatherers with Special Reference to the Ainu. In *Man the Hunter*, edited by R. B. Lee and I. DeVore, pp. 69–77. Aldine, Chicago.
1970 Ecology of the Prehistoric Jomon People: Possible Use of Their Stone Axes as Seen from Food Processing Habits of Northern Hunter-Gatherers—A Preliminary Report. *Journal of the Anthropological Society of Nippon* 78:208–212.
1983 Occupational Differentiation and Social Stratification: The Case of Northern Pacific Maritime Food-Gatherers. *Current Anthropology* 24:217–219.

Woodman, P. C.
1985 Mobility in the Mesolithic of Northwestern Europe: An Alternative Explanation. In *Prehistoric Hunter-Gatherers: The Emergence of Cultural Complexity*, edited by T. D. Price and J. A. Brown, pp. 325–339. Academic Press, Orlando, Florida.

Wright, G.
1978 Social Differentiation in the Early Natufian. In *Social Archaeology: Beyond Subsistence and Dating*, edited by C. Redman, M. J. Berman, E. V. Curtin, W. T. Langhorne, N. M. Versaggi, and J. C. Wanser, pp. 201–223. Academic Press, New York.

Index

Page numbers followed by *f* indicate pages with figures; *t* indicates tables; page numbers in italics indicate photographs.